Abiding in Nondual Awareness

exploring the further implications
of living nonduality

Robert Wolfe

Karina Library Press
2013

Abiding in Nondual Awareness: exploring the further implications of living nonduality

ISBN-13: 978-1-937902-17-9

Library of Congress Control Number: 2013948701

2013

Karina Library Press
PO Box 35
Ojai, California 93024
www.karinalibrary.com

Michael Lommel, Publisher

Manuscript preparation by Rafael Stoneman, with the assistance of Natalie Gray.

"Time is Comparison" appears in Elementary Cloudwatching

Cover: Digital adaptation of a painting by the author.

Table of Contents

"So we come back to the question of whether it is possible in daily life to live in a state which, for the moment, let us call enlightenment."

– Krishnamurti

Introduction

After my first book, *Living Nonduality*, was published in 2009, I received dozens of e-mails, in addition to some letters, from people all over the U.S. and also from abroad. In many instances, particular questions or quandaries concerning the subject of enlightenment were expressed. My publisher set up a blog page on my website (livingnonduality.org) and the more succinct queries were often responded to there. In other instances, I sent my reply by mail.

So, the monographs printed in this volume are mainly a timely expansion on the material published four years ago; a few of the selections are those for which there wasn't room in my previous book; and a few others are akin to journal entries. All of them relate to various aspects of nondual realization.

These writings are not in a particular order. However, the more basic pointers were generally placed toward the front, and some of the more specific topics toward the back.

Ojai, 2013
RW

Everything is nothing

with a twist

– Kurt Vonnegut

Disturbing the Peace

The word *crucial* has the same Latin root (*crux*) as cross, such as in crossroad; it is defined as "of supreme importance; decisive; critical," (like the high point of an illness is critical).

Many people who've come to Self-realization have done so at a crucial developmental point in their life, catalyzed by a divorce, loss of job or savings, death of a child, and so on. The evaporation of presumed security has often been the stimulant for reappraisal of mundane existence.

At a point in my own life after a divorce, I contemplated my options: I could remarry; I could continue to be a homeowner; I could continue in my business career.

What factored into this contemplation was a recognition that I was living in a condition (or out of a condition) which I understood that the enlightened mystics called confusion. I knew that I had not penetrated through to the untroubled clarity that the mystics agreed was the substance of what they spoke of as enlightenment, or the clarity of Self-realization.

This dictum seemed to be central to what these mystics had been telling me: "Where there is confusion, all that you do will be out of confusion; where there is clarity, all that you do will be out of clarity." I concluded that I was definitely familiar with the confusion part. The crux of the matter appeared to me to be that I could either spend the rest of my days living out a life of confusion and conflict—in "ignorance," as Buddhists call it—or a life of operating out of established clarity from day to day.

I recognized that all I needed to do, to enact the former, was to continue doing what I was accustomed to do. But if I was to accommodate the latter, I needed to turn my attention to comprehending what was involved in living a life of enlightened clarity. I had, in earlier times, dallied with this matter of enlightenment; but being materially secure and (I supposed) self-secure, I had not engaged the enlightenment teachings with a view to change my life in any significant way.

In other words, what now rose to the top of my agenda was to unequivocally investigate Self-realization, wherever that lead. To remarry, to continue my career and thus my home ownership were somewhere further down on the list of what seemed to me to be crucial.

From my experience, when we live out of confusion, we live a dissatisfied (or at least unsatisfied) life. Due to this dissatisfaction, there has to be an incentive of some sort to continue it. My priorities were different now. I relinquished my career and home, and likely prospects for remarriage.

There is something about commitment, in burning your bridges behind you. Many of the enlightened teachers, at one point or another, did just that. For some, discovering ultimate truth was a critical matter, even a life-or-death pursuit.

A conflicted and confused Siddhartha sat down under a bo tree and said: I'm not going to move from here until I have unbounded clarity.

Determined to follow the light where it might lead, I envisioned that when my savings departed I might find myself homeless, hungry, cold, wet, sick—maybe all of this at once.

As it has turned out, some twenty-two years later, my worst fears have not materialized. I may have had to work at a few jobs I didn't like and to have lived in places I didn't prefer, but I have never even suffered (for whatever reason) a serious lack of funds.

There have been other unexpected developments and changes too: and not necessarily changes that I would have chosen for myself. But do I have any regrets? No. Am I grateful for what has so far unfolded in my life? Yes, very much so. It has been, for me, all that the teachers indicated it could be. (As a Zen master said on his enlightenment, "Buddha and the five hundred patriarchs have not deceived me!")

Were the "renunciations," that I made, necessary? The developments early on seemed to be merely preparations for the divestiture that would be inevitable in later stages. The enlightenment process leads to thorough non-attachment; it may as well *begin* with non-attachment.

So, if you are at this crossroad and you are pondering what to do, it is not my place to give you advice. All I can tell you is that material security is not, in the long run, the highest value; in fact, security is fickle and deceptive. There is only one condition in which we can be absolutely secure, and we're always given the hint that it has something to do with "death before you have died." The word *nirvana* actually means "to snuff out." Krishnamurti's parting advice to his public, after sixty years of harangue, was simply "give up your attachment—to everything."

What's the Bottom Line?

From the time we are infants, we are conditioned to perceive our reality in a dualistic context; to compare *this* thing in contrast to *that* thing. Each of these things, which we are taught to recognize, acquires its special identity by comparison with all other things: there is "me," for example, and all else that is not-me. Each of the separate forms, that we learn about, is limited to its particular definition (whether it is a material form, such as "my body" or an immaterial form such as "my interests"). And each of these limiting definitions has a relationship to all other definitions, in that each depends on the others for its separate identity.

Such relative distinctions have a value, in a world in which there are practical applications for discerning *up* from *down*, or *right* from *left*. But the dualistic perspective is not the only perspective available to us.

Of value to us in a broader, or more inclusive manner, is a perception of our reality which spiritual sages have (for 3,500 years of written history) referred to as nonduality. The point of these teachings is that each identifiable form, being limited, has a beginning and an ending: all *things* are impermanent.

The *condition* into which all things arise and subside is not itself impermanent or limited. Being without limitation, this overarching condition is without boundaries, borders or restrictions; it is without beginning or ending: infinite, in space; eternal, in time. Thus, without relationship to time or space, this ground of being is formless. Encompassing all which is in existence, there is not anything outside of it; not anything comparable to it; not anything by which its identity can be defined. Because of its "not-twoness," it is said to be the essence of nonduality.

In every spiritual and religious tradition is a common word for this ever-present actuality, the Absolute. For those elements of reality which are not everlasting and formless, the word *relative* is applied. The nondual teachings say that every one of the impermanent, limited forms arises and subsides within the infinite and eternal Absolute.

And, the nature of the formless and infinite Absolute being omnipresent, it penetrates, permeates and saturates all of relative existence. "All is One, One is all."

Hence, the Absolute and the relative are, in actuality, in no way apart. The relative is merely a manifest appearance of the all-pervading Absolute.

There are major aspects of this teaching which have a profound implication for how one's life is lived.

First of all, there is clarity that ultimate Reality (which has generally been regarded as the sacred, or divine) surrounds and *penetrates every form*; as the Vedas say, "nowhere is It not." Therefore, for each and every one of us—whether we profess to be aware of it, or not—its presence is thoroughly *inescapable*.

Secondly, the Absolute being the fundamental essence which all things are pervaded by in common, the ultimate identity (or true nature) of each thing *is* the Absolute. Any relative "self" identity is merely a temporarily manifest appearance; when this principle is realized, self-image *dissolves* into the formless Presence. As the Vedas say, Tat Tvam Asi: *That* thou art.

Thirdly, the condition from which all forms *appear* is from the timeless and unlimited formless presence. This Absolute condition was existent before your particular form arose and will continue to persist after your material form has dis-integrated. It is the source from which the cosmos arose. Your material form, or organism, is a product of this same source, or Intelligence. Your brain is a product of this source. Hence, your thoughts and actions owe their manifestation to this ultimate actuality. Thus, the teachings instruct, "*You* are not the Doer."

Finally, when one recognizes that "all that's being done, is That doing what it does," it becomes clear that (from the ultimate standpoint) all which is unfolding is an unprecedented, spontaneous development of the Omnipresent manifesting as, and through, every immediate occurrence. From the vantage point of the Absolute, it makes no difference what occurs, since there is no confinement to a finite consequence. Regardless how the individual organism may evaluate each occurrence, in the final analysis it makes no difference.

This nondual perspective of non-attachment is reminded to us each night, in our deepest sleep. We return to a condition of empty awareness in which the self-perception disappears, all relative interests disappear, the world disappears, the cosmos disappears. In that unperturbed awareness, there is an emptiness which is choiceless and in which nothing really matters.

For those who realize the implications of the nondual teachings, the fact that ultimately nothing really matters is carried over into one's waking awareness and daily life.

It is also clear that while we are embodied in this material form and continue to function in the relative world, the dualistic perspective (rather than the nondual awareness) is the state of mind which pertains for most persons—who are typically not prepared to hear that their "self" has no meaning in the ultimate sense.

It's probably not surprising that such teachings were once kept secret. However, they're not secret anymore, and can lead to a life-changing perspective, or Consciousness.

Ancient Wisdom

Sanskrit, as a coherent written language, dates back to about 2000 B.C. By about 1800 B.C., it was used to record/write the Vedas, the oldest known (and thus anonymous) spiritual manual(s); Veda means, approximately, "knowledge."

Around the first half of 700 A.D., Shankara (spelled variously Sankara, Shancara, etc.) "codified" the wisdom of the Vedas as "Vedanta" (meaning, roughly, the end of knowledge), the essence of which is, basically, "All is Brahman" (Brahman being the Hindu equivalent of Absolute).

Of the various forms of yoga, those adept in jnana (which emphasizes contemplation) have been particularly conversant with the thrust of Vedanta; and their simplified form of its teaching is called Advaita ("not two"). Perhaps the most renowned exemplar of Advaita Vedanta has been Ramana Maharshi. His teachings are of "classical" non-dualism.

"Times Change"

All things change. Another word for change is *evolve*. The spiritual teachings, I submit, have followed a development over the centuries and continue to do so.

From the time of the popularity of written language at least (perhaps around 3,500 years ago), there have been enlightened sages who have attempted to convey the substance of what came to be known as Self-realization, the perception of the nondual actuality.

Naturally, from the beginning it was difficult to find words for this. A reading of the Vedic literature, Upanishads and Gitas, demonstrates the rambling attempts.

11

And in ancient times, for whatever murky reasons, there was a tendency to make these teachings available only in secret.

There has also been a long period of time when a seeker was required to undergo a lengthy period of testing of his sincerity before even a dialogue with a master began.

As the teachings of nonduality—which seem to have their deepest roots in the East—migrated into Western cultures, there has also been a period of attention to "translation" of words and pointers into a culturally-different idiom.

In the process of expression over centuries (and across borders), the message has been continually refined and clarified.

What has been taught even in decades past may not necessarily be the most efficacious teaching for the generally well-informed seeker of today. The format in which these teachings are presented needs to change—and will change—as there is increasing receptivity by the populace.

An increasing number of the Self-realized today have not: slogged through the Vedic scriptures; undergone initiation into secret esoteric schools; performed years of manual labor for a master, to prove their commitment; sat months of silent meditation in a cold, damp cave; or solved even a single koan.

Many have simply heard the nondual teachings expounded by a seasoned exponent who is both direct and knows first-hand the Truth of which he or she speaks.

There will likely always be some seekers who will want to continue to follow older patterns of behavior in their "process." But it continues to be demonstrated that this is not necessary.

The Secret

We are keepers of a shared secret. The wasp is scarcely larger than a black ant, with long, slender wings. It has apparently stung a jumping spider, and is pulling this squat, angular body. It crosses the path and moves about a yard up the embankment, hind-part first but in a steady direction.

Its destination is a tiny hole in the ground, its burrow, no wider than a straw. A few inches directly in front of the burrow is a rock about the size of a ping-pong ball. Approaching it, the wasp releases the body, goes around to the burrow, and busily widens the entryway to accommodate the plump captive. Returning to the task of transport, the wasp walks around the body a few times in each direction, as if assaying which path past the rock would be most direct.

Grasping the body again with its foreparts and moving backward, it continues the haul, in what it has determined the appropriate direction: up, over the rock, and down the other side. It then pulls the spider down into the hole after it.

Having somehow squeezed around the torpid dinner guest, it emerges from the hole. Its day of hunting has not yet come to a close. Until its later return, it carefully covers all traces of entry to the hole. It jauntily flies away, and we remain the only two in the world who have access to this important secret.

Advaita Vocabulary

Thanks for your query.

With the introduction of Zen to the West, some half century ago, terms such as *satori* (spiritual awakening)—now found in your dictionary—are commonplace. Some of the Sanskrit words, from the Vedas, are now likewise finding their way into our culture. Of the six you asked about:

jnani: a person with "direct knowledge" of nonduality; enlightened. Jnana is enlightenment, or Self-realization, itself. An ajnani is a person who is said to be not Self-realized; said to be lacking in "knowledge" or "wisdom" (in Buddhism, "ignorant").

moksha (sometimes *mukti*): spiritual awakening; nondual "knowledge" or "wisdom."

rishi: sage; knowledgeable teacher.

sadhana: journey of the spiritual life; or, seeker's path.

sahaja samadhi: embodied enlightenment; natural, effortless, abiding oneness; Absolute awareness.

vasanas: conditioning; dualistic drives; habitual ideation; doership.

Advaita (nonduality) teachers tend to use these words because of the subtleties which make single-word translations difficult. Sanskrit is a nuanced language, suitable for describing spiritual precepts. Says the (late) translator Edward Conze:

Sutras are written in *Sanskrit*, a highly rational language, capable of great precision, and amenable to thorough grammatical analysis. Not all languages are equally suited to the adequate expression of abstract ideas. Little of these Sutras would, I fear, survive their translation in cockney or the patois of Liége. Literary English benefits to some extent from the influence of Latin—like Sanskrit a largely artificial language. It is nevertheless occasionally very useful to also consult the Sanskrit original. The meaning of Sanskrit words depends very largely on their verbal roots. When words with the same root are translated into English, the similarity of their derivation is sometimes unavoidably obscured, and the unity of the original argument destroyed.

SAGE ADVICE

The ground (fundament) of all religions and true spirituality is "non-duality," as the sages have referred to it throughout written history. As far back as the writings in Sanskrit, the essential truth has been known as Advaita, which means specifically "not two." When Jesus stresses that "I and the Father are one"; or when Krishnamurti says "The observer is the observed"; or Meister Eckhart says "Who sees not God everywhere, sees God nowhere"—all are emphasizing "not two."

The sages who have a profound, life-shattering experience, engulfing them in unitive consciousness, have emerged from the divisive confusion (which Buddhists call "ignorance") that is the normative lot of the bulk of mankind. No longer operating in the typical self-centered confusion that is pandemic, they cast a light of clarity which each of us may (should we choose) be illuminated by. In fact, if you will study the lives of such enlightened teachers as Buddha, Jesus, Ramana, Krishnamurti, etc., you will find that their time was dedicated 24/7 to serving others in the highest form possible: the severing of human suffering at its root, by urging each individual to take responsibility for *personally* ending selfish ego-centered divisiveness. Jesus, for example, could presumably have spent every waking hour of every day healing bodies or feeding the hordes; he responded, as a healer, to those who asked, but his passionate drive was to instruct (all those who would listen) that the treasure that can be *secured* "lies within you." As Jesus is quoted in (the so-called "fifth Gospel") the Gospel of Thomas, "seek the treasure that is unfailing, that is enduring." How is that found?: "those who enter the Domain... make the two into one..."

As long as confusion is one's present condition, all that one does is done in confusion—further adding to the confusion already prevalent in the world. When one has awakened to the clarity of unitive consciousness, all that one does is in clarity. (Jesus again: "If a blind person leads a blind person, both of them will fall into a hole.") "Self-realization," [awakening to unitive consciousness], says Ramana, "is the primary duty of mankind." This means removing the divisive mote from one's own eye before attempting to operate on another person. "The only help worth giving," said Nisargadatta, "is to free someone from the need for *further* help. Repeated help is no help at all. Do not talk of helping another until you can put him beyond all *need* of help." Only when your candle is aflame can you light another's.

WHAT NONDUAL MEANS

Alan:

You must be aware, with your long experience, that there are (for example) Buddhists who understand the true core of the teachings (assuming that Buddha wasn't the *only* one who understood his message), and there are a *vast* number who *call* themselves Buddhists but haven't quite yet gotten the full message.

And this applies to any, and all, spiritual categories: Tao included.

At the *deepest* root of all these categories is a genuine comprehension of *nonduality*. What *passes* for an "understanding" in these categories is *usually* a *dualistic* perspective.

When *yours* is actually the nondual perspective, you will recognize these dualistic (and thus false) teachings *instantly*.

You have looked at these matters for many years—and have not found satisfaction: you cannot say that you are aware of the complete truth of our ultimate reality. That is because yours (as that of most others) is still a confused, dualistic perspective.

Not everyone seems to be capable of breaking through this mind-set, even when the desire is presumed to be present. This may be your case, as well. But your pursuit of this desire is sincere, so I will respond, to that extent. What you do with that input is up to you.

What we're talking about here is the primary teachings concerning *nonduality*—which goes right to the root of all named spiritual traditions.

As a starting point: these teachings say that there is a "world" of *appearances*. But the *appearances* do not reveal the entire, true *actuality*.

The appearances are every thing which is *recognized*, or "seen," by the see-er. This *includes* the *see-er* himself, and everything "outside"—as well as "inside"—the seer. The seer considers himself to be in *relation* to all that is seen. Thus, this is said to be the "relative" viewpoint; and it is, obviously, dualistic (dual: two, but meaning here "two *or more*"); seer, 1; seen, 2. The "seen" includes what is seen in imagination: in other words, *all* things which you *relate* to, whether material *or* immaterial. If I presume that I have a relationship to a God, this is a dualistic viewpoint: I, 1; God, 2.

All appearances are subject to change. (To appear means "to come": and what comes, can go.) What is the *condition* in which all "the ten thousand things" (Buddhist term for all impermanent appearances) come and go? It would need to be, itself, permanent; ever-lasting and unchanging: it has been called the ground, or source, of "being" as we know it. Every tradition has referred to it as the Absolute, a word which *means* "not relative"—in *transcendence* of any thing which is relative. This is what the *idea* of "God" *points* to.

All relative things, *because* they come and go, are *limited*. The field, or condition, in which they come and go must be unlimited: infinite (in space), eternal (in time): Absolute. Anything which is relative (impermanent) is *not* "absolute," not infinite—except in the following sense.

Anything which is finite *must* be inclusive *within* the infinite. But the infinite—by definition having no borders (*end*-less)—could not be withheld by anything: its presence would be every *where*, in every *time*... which is what the word omni-present means.

Thus, the Absolute, being unlimited, *permeates*, saturates, *all* of space and all of time. The teachings say: "nowhere is it *not*."

All of the appearances are not only (with) *in* it, but are in no possible way "apart" from it. The teachings say: "It is the *essence* of all that *is*."

Therefore, it is *your* essence. Not only yours, but everyone's. And not something *separate*, like a "soul": there is not anything which *can* be separate—by its very nature—from the Absolute. You *are* That, because *all* things—at their basic existence—are That.

So, the non-dual realization is, as the teachings say, "All that *is*, is *That*." (Call it "God," if you want: but it is not a God that is *apart* from *you*; you and God are the same, singular actuality. As are *all* things.)

Consequently, there is nowhere you need to go and nothing you need to *do* in order to be "one" with God. To comprehend this is the *non-dual* realization, so-called enlightenment.

I could have written this out as a book: I have given it to you in four pages. You are not busy. Re-read it phrase by phrase. *Contemplate* the import of *each* phrase; don't proceed to the next until each phrase is clearly comprehended. This is not a "philosophy" to be debated: it is the truth of *your* existence right now. *Despite appearances*, the ultimate reality and "you" are in no way apart. "Oneness" does not mean that you (1) and God (2) are *joined*: it means that you and God are the *same* one thing. No division. Non dual. *Realize* what non dual *means*.

WAVE-FUNCTION COLLAPSE

Krishnamurti (as others before him) said "the observer is the observed." If so, a so-called "observer" could not interact with the so-called "observed" without both elements being affected. You watch a bird; wary of your attention, the bird takes flight; your activity has been aborted: all of this is one event, connecting as its elements the two creatures.

There has been a simultaneous effect on the *present* reality of the universe, in such an instance, mutually by the observer and the observed—as a singular action.

Scientists are now thoroughly aware that in the observation, or measurement, of any thing, reality is inadvertently affected. Because, for example, subatomic elements are indeterminate, by their nature, an ordinary element "exists" simultaneously as a particle and as a wave. If an observer has set out to measure, or examine, particles (an electron, for example) the electron will present as a particle; if the scientist has instead chosen to measure waves, the electron will be discernible as a wave just as readily. We could say, then, that whether an electron presents as a particle or a wave depends upon the observer's mind, or at least depends upon whatever happens to be his or her conscious choice.

Another way of saying this would be that the electron "collapses"— into *either* particle or wave form—in the consciousness of the observer. And so, consciousness—in this sense—can be said to "create" reality. It can be said, further, that the electron had no reality or "existence" until the event of the (as it's called) "wave-function collapse." At best, one would have to say that the electron was in a "super-position"—existing with equal reality as both a particle and a wave—prior to the collapse contingency.

The consciousness of the observer is involved in the outcome of the observation, in this situation; and the outcome of the observation, presumably, has an effect on the consciousness of the observer. It would be very difficult, under these circumstances, to maintain the idea of "separateness" of the observer and the observed. In fact, one might say that the reality of either the observer or the observed, in this instance, depended on one thing: consciousness. Or, if we were to posit that there was a reality for the electron and a reality for the observer, we would have to say that reality—in the form of observer and observed—was in interaction with itself.

Since this reality is not the sole property (or reality) of the observer, it is "universal" reality. And to the extent to which the observer's consciousness "creates" reality, it is a universal consciousness. It would be difficult for an observer to maintain that a consciousness which can affect universal reality is purely his—the observer's—private consciousness. This would seem to indicate that there is but one consciousness.

"I stamped on the wave—but it was only water."
(Buddhist wave-collapse, via Meng Shen)

NOT JUST A LEGEND

Imagine having good looks, an athletic figure, the best wardrobe in your community, sexual partners at your whim, palatial lodgings, attendants galore, the best of foods, the liveliest of entertainments—and no work to do; but knowing that you'll inherit your father's wealth, power and prestige. Imagine too that, despite all this, you are aware that none of these things ensure happiness. This, according to the accounts, was the situation of Siddhartha Gautama at the prime of his life.

The *motivating* story, throughout the ages, has been to go from rags to Siddhartha's riches. But Siddhartha, having all that, chose to go from riches to rags. In fact, less than rags: a few years after abandoning his princely life and his family (including wife and child), he was homeless, penniless, barely clothed and subsisting on tree leaves and river water.

Why the surrender of every comfort, security and pleasure that most everyone seeks? Because only one thing remained of importance to him: to discover the source of unending peace and contentment. The accounts tell us that he achieved this aim.

These accounts have been relayed to us over a period beginning about 500 B.C. We have no substantive way to verify how much of the biographical detail is accurate; nor even how much of the alleged teachings, ascribed to Siddhartha after his enlightenment, are truly his.

(Even less is known about the life of Jesus, and the accounts of his teachings are in greater doubt due to the number of inconsistencies and discrepancies in those that exist.)

Fortunately, Buddha is not the only such teacher who is regarded as having been enlightened. In our own time, there have been those whose life story is similarly remarkable, and whose biography and teachings are verified.

Ramana Maharshi, as a case in point (who died as recently as 1950), went from having next to nothing, to having nothing. He left his modest family home at around age 16, and chose to be homeless. He was often without even shelter, in the earlier years, before taking up lodging in a cave. When afoot, he begged for his food, and throughout his life he wore only the barest covering. He evidently never had a romantic relationship, nor did he ever travel more than a few miles from his abode near the foot of a mountain. Though an ashram was eventually formed around him, he never handled money.

The divan on which he slept and sat (while discoursing his enlightenment teachings) was in a room open to anyone, at all hours of the day. Two possessions are said to have been his, a walking stick and a water pot.

He, like Siddhartha, had surrendered every comfort, security and pleasure that most people desire. And he, too, achieved his aim of discovering the source of unending peace and contentment. And, he taught to others the means by which to do so, until he died fifty-five years after he left home. (Buddha taught for 45 years).

His teachings of nonduality are not dissimilar to those ascribed to the Buddha, but in his case we can verify the details of the accounts.

So, in terms of the sagacious teachings on the ultimate Reality, we are fortunate to not have to rely on the hearsay of millennia past.

Peace

Recorded history alone goes back something like eight thousand years. During that period of time—some three billion days—

there has evidently never been a day when there wasn't strife and turmoil in some part (if not all) of the world.

Societies, however large or small, are nothing more than a group of individuals. How is there ever to be "peace," harmony, within societies or among societies, while conflict rages within the individual?

Peace has the definition of "freedom from threat of war or disorder" or "freedom from quarrels and disturbance." And it also has this definition: "an undisturbed state of mind, absence of mental conflict: serenity."

Where do you have the most capacity to make a change: in the unabated world of conflict, or in your own internal conflict?

THE OFFER

All of us know what duality is: we have been conditioned to it from the earliest days of our life. Its most elemental proposition is that "I" exist, and all else in the universe is "not I," something "other." In its most expansive application, it compares anything we designate "this," with everything we conversely regard as "that." It provides us with the judgmental spectrum which posits "negative" at one pole, and "positive" at the other. It allows us to make perpetual distinctions, such as day and night, hot and cold, north and south, etc. But it also ingrains a habitual mindset, thought patterns, based inevitably on division. In other words, our dualistic viewpoint—which we take for granted—is at the root of our divisiveness, dissatisfaction, and conflicting values; in short, unhappiness.

For millennia, teachers of nonduality—in "enlightenment" traditions such as Buddhism, Tao, Vedanta—have assured us that it is possible to transcend the limitation of dualistic conceptions, and to thereby live in an awareness of harmony, contentment and equanimity. Non-dual, of course, means "not two"; so, nonduality is the condition of Oneness as a *living* experience; and its offer is the transcendence of our perceived unhappiness.

This or That

Our first form of identification is "I." And when the mind has thus succeeded in establishing identity, it proceeds to another identity: "you" (or "it"). *This*: and something which is not this, *that*.

And what is not this or that is *neither*. And that which is any of these possibilities is *either*. And so on; distinctions proliferate. As soon as we have *blue*, we have *light* blue and *dark* blue. Then we have *not blue*; we have *green*...and *light green*, and so on.

That "first thought" is the most deeply rooted, and thus the most tenacious. All of the structure of one's apparent life rests on the foundation of the self. When the structure crumbles, the foundation is the last to go. But should the foundation crumble first, the structure would immediately fall.

Responsibility

If there is any responsibility (whose meaning is "capacity to respond") which you could possibly be in relation to in this life, it is to correct your myopia. That being the apparent first item on the cosmic agenda, it is the first step and last. In all likelihood, it shall require every ounce of energy and attention which you can bring to it.

Until you know who you are, without a doubt, you cannot rest. Until you fully recognize *your true* identity, there is no meaningful *relationship* which you can maintain. You must realize this. Realize means "to make real"—as real as one's chronic selfishness is real.

THOUGHT IS DIVISIVE

Thought is division, separation, distinction; parsing, defining; all that thought knows is the process of isolation.

All activities are separated, by thought, into such categories as "seeing" or "not seeing." And when something is seen, there are the distinctions of "observing" that which is "observed" by the "observer." And so, for you to perceive reality, there is the concept of "you," there is the concept of "perceiving" and there is a concept of "reality."

Initially, when you grasp the understanding that the universe is one of inclusion and not exclusion—that there is not anything which is isolated or separate from anything else in actuality—it is still "you" who is "grasping" this "understanding."

We could say that, were the observer not existing where you are, there would be only That Which Is Everything, and which does not isolate itself in *any* way (the "observer" *here*, the "hill" over *there*); no residue. Therefore, It *is* where you are, It *is* where the hill is, and It is anything and *everything* which could possibly exist "between."

When you put your "self" back in the picture, to understand it, there will again be "you" "understanding" "it."

You needn't be confused by some of the terminology, in the writings concerning Advaita. All of the "many names for God" are—despite their origin in different cultures—pointing ultimately to the same One, the same Absolute, the infinite and eternal omnipresence that is considered to be the ground of all being.

Ramana, for example, uses the word Self (with a capital S) to denote the Absolute. The reason for this is because he is trying to emphasize that the "you"—the "self" with the small s—is, in essence, the very same Self.

Some writers, in Vedanta, use the word Brahman rather than Self, but again both words equate with the Absolute.

Then again, the word Consciousness—as in "cosmic Consciousness"—is also sometimes used; usually capitalized, to make clear that the allusion is not to the limited sense of consciousness (as "awareness") that the self supposes that it possesses "individually."

And then there's what Ramana calls the "false I"—the sense that the subjective "person" embodies some sort of separate entity—which predicates the "I-versus-you" dichotomy. Thus when he speaks of the "true I" of course, he means your essential nature as an aspect of the Absolute—in which the I/you perspective disappears.

Adding to the confusion, Ramana sometimes also uses the word Heart—not meaning the organ you call the heart, but rather the "center" or essence of your being (in the dictionary distinction: "the central, vital or main part; core"). He sometimes calls this "the cave of the Heart." In all cases, he means to designate the Absolute.

And, like others, he occasionally speaks of the "light," a word which for centuries has been an equivalent for Absolute presence.

So, the point is that as you encounter these myriad, generalized descriptive terms simply read them as merely alternate names for the Absolute. There need be no confusion whatever if you bear this consistently in mind.

Also: do not ever lose sight of the fact that an intellectual (or scholarly) understanding of what is written will not, of itself, result in enlightenment.

What *will* result in enlightenment is when the seeker herself dissolves into the Absolute omnipresence. In other words, as long as there is a "self" which is in search of the Absolute, duality will persist. What is infinitely and eternally omnipresent need not be searched for: it, pervading all things, cannot even be *avoided*; it is present *as* all that *is* present, saturating even the seeker herself—thus *non*-dual.

That is *why* Ramana makes the point, the self *is* the Self: there is but one actuality.

You appear to be grasping this point, when you write: "It seems to me that there is no difference between the Self and Consciousness—like, you cannot separate the sun from light, water from wetness, etc."

Put another way, "cosmic" Consciousness and "your" very own moment-to-moment consciousness are not separate. In Buddhism, they use the word Mind (capital M) for Absolute "consciousness" to make the point (like Ramana's Self/self) that this universal Mind is the same as "your" sense of being imbued with a mind (small m). It's just that your *idea* of mind is limited, rather than (as with the enlightened) unlimited. Remove the limits you construe for the self, and you discover that there can *only* be the Self.

Admit One

If I were to focus on just one element of the nondual teachings, it would be this fundamental issue: wherever division exists, conflict will be a product. Conversely, wherever you can identify a conflict, divisiveness will be involved.

This applies not only to what we can witness externally in the world, it applies equally in regard to our inner turmoil and confusion, even to the choices we ponder.

The nondual teachings instruct us that if conflict is to end—inner or outer—divisiveness must come to an end. Put another way, as long as we remain in (separative) confusion, everything which we attempt to do will be a product of that confusion. But once (awakened) clarity is present, all that we do will be a product of that clarity. So it is important, in the balance of our life, for Self-realization to be at the top of the agenda.

A second fundamental element, of the teachings, is this: the Truth that you'll discover is the same Truth that is present this very moment. There is not anything in the *future* that will bring you closer to the prospect of this Truth than you are right *now*. You need not transit in time, in order to end the dualistic confusion.

Your last letter was more pertinent than usual—as was your letter to Will that you sent me a copy of.

You query: "What is the purpose of being awake in the world?" Is one to "go out and 'help' other people?" It's obvious, as you point out, that no singular individual is going to change the world (or the "establishment," or system, as you might say), awakened or unawakened.

It must be obvious that 1) if there is to be a possibility for change, it must start with you; 2) the only change that you could have direct control over would be your own. You state this clearly in your letter to Will: "The most important thing you can do for anyone or anything is to allow your own self to awaken."

So, the what-to-do is to awaken. The what-to-do, if anything, *after* awakening can only be known after *awakening*.

This means that the best thing that can be done for yourself, others or the world is for enlightened clarity to be present. Out of that unconfused, undeniable clarity one then acts. Any actions prior to the above are confused actions—from the standpoint of the "self," "others" and the "world."

The *purpose* of being awake arises from *being* awake.

READER'S RESPONSE TO "ADMIT ONE"

"Robert, it seems to me that in times past I was busy 'collecting' information; not only from you, but others as well. There seems to be a difference now. I am no longer collecting, but rather assimilating the 'material,' which is certainly consistent now.

"Talk about ending confusion; 'The *purpose* of being awake arises from *being* awake.'

"This sort of came into play with your haiku, last night:

'Only when awake—

the dream seen for what it is:

empty of meaning.'

"…it's all a dream, regardless of the path, myth, legend, or religion. It is a *most radical* idea that exposes these things. (Truth is a pathless land.) Prayer and healing (any attempt to 'change things') is merely, even in its best dress, a subtle form of religion, which is probably an attempt at manipulation, mind control, or a belief in 'the power of the mind.'

"There is no way that I could have lived with the Course in Miracles these many years (13), and not know what is in it. It is ambiguous! And you are right about 'reading into it what we are seeking.'

"There's no question that 'clarity' has been lacking here. I don't believe I've been without a lot of 'confusion' either.

"There has certainly been 'confusion,' which I attribute to years of mis-education: Dr. H. would probably refer to this as 'do-gooder' training. This stuff does not work! And especially in environments such as the ones I've known these last fifteen years.

"People who are entering AA are not looking for a 'spiritual awakening.' What they are looking for is a way to fit better into the status quo that did not work for them."

WHAT'S YOUR AGENDA?

As you note, I've used the word "dedication"; and I do sometimes use an alternate word, "sincerity."

There are those who seek to discern the ultimate reality who are *partially* committed to this engagement: they have other concerns which are higher on their list of priorities. In other words, they are more amenable to distractions. And there are others who are cognizant that unless we have ended our conditioned, existential confusion, all which we attempt to do will simply be an expression of this underlying confusion. For *this* one, the matter of complete clarity is the first order of business, and all the potential distractions are somewhere toward the bottom of the list of interests. Such a one is not just *partially* committed to the discovery of the *total* truth.

Likewise for some, their awakening will be thorough and profound from its outset. There are others whose awakening will be less pronounced, with some residue of unclear perceptions still to settle out.

It should not be surprising that for those whose dedication to the matter is preeminent, the immediate clarity (of the nature of ultimate reality) is usually more acutely present. Contemplating any matter, and contemplating it while being distracted, are like the different results of precision when operating with a sharp scalpel or a dull scalpel. Or, looked at another way, the operation is apt to be most successful when the surgeon is giving full attention, than when she's not.

REACTING TO SUFFERING

Actually, the feeling I've gotten, over decades of reading/hearing spiritual material, is that the suffering that is discussed is more generally referred to in the mental (psyche) realm than the physical. I think the teachers presume that mental (emotional) torment or pain is much more susceptible to eradication from consciousness than is physical, bodily pain.

But, in either case, the focus is on eliminating the subject-object bias; the idea that there is a corporeal entity, I, which is the sufferer. "No sufferer, no suffering" would be the equation.

✧

The issue which Gary Snyder raises ("Using such means as... even gentle violence, if it comes to a matter of restraining some impetuous redneck.") is among the most persistent (aged) in spiritual discussion (e.g., Krishna to Arjuna centuries ago): to what degree does the enlightened involve himself or engage in political/social considerations? A consensus of what the teachers have said on this subject, I would submit, is that such activity is not unjustified, but—in the long run—it is ineffective. (Krishnamurti has been particularly eloquent on this point.)

If I were to sum up my understanding of the message, it would be this: What do you have any obvious control over? Yourself. Use every ounce of your energy, first, to bring yourself to total clarity. When you are—and know without doubt that you are—thoroughly free from reactive suffering, then set about assisting "others" to relieve them of "suffering." You will know, at that point, exactly how you are to go about that—without any pre-conceptions as to the degree to which you need to engage in social/political activity.

In my purview, the greatest social/political service which one can render—and ultimately the most subversive to the system—is to assist others (on a direct, one-to-one basis) to come to a radical, life-changing realization of their true identity/nature. When I study the lives of the enlightened teachers, I note that they too dedicated their lives entirely to this activity.

But that was, in all cases, their second dedication. Their first dedication was to free *themselves* from their illusive identity as a "doer."

THINGS WORK TOGETHER

The medical director of a Canadian insane asylum, Doctor Richard Bucke, published a book a year before his death (at 65) whose title since minted a phrase, *Cosmic Consciousness*. At age 35, he experienced a realization "which ever since lightened his life," and almost thirty years later he had completed comparative research into fifty other lives exhibiting evident Realization. First published in 1901, this curious book was republished by E.P. Dutton in 1923, and again in 1969 (when the title phrase gained currency). He says of himself:

> What joy when I saw there was no break in the chain—not a link left out—everything in its place and time. Worlds, systems, all blended into one harmonious whole...

> I saw that the universe is not composed of dead matter, but is, on the contrary, a living Presence; I became conscious in myself of eternal life. It was not a conviction that I would *have* eternal life, but a consciousness that I possessed eternal life then; I saw that *all* men are immortal; that the cosmic order is such that, without any peradventure, all things work together for the good of each and all; that the foundation principle of the world, of all the worlds, is what we call love...

Without a "gut feeling" for this "harmonious whole," this "living Presence," how is one's centric energy to be freed from the grip of fear, to express unbounded love? Without a profound perception of "everything in its place and time," how is one to sustain trust that "all things work together for the good of each and all"?

If there were a principle of the universe, it would be that *anything* which any thing *does* is okay. Whatever. It's perfectly okay. Whatever *you* do in the next minute (hour, day, year) will fit in perfectly—from the cosmic view—with exactly what is going on. It is not necessary for anyone to do anything other than what they're doing, at any time. But if they should happen to do something different from what they're presently doing, that's okay too. Whatever is done—or not done—is an expression of the same actuality.

The expression of actuality is present in living, and it's present in dying. In order for there to be expression, which is change or movement, there must be the coming as well as the going. Your presence is not more important to this expression than is your absence. With all in this universe which has come to death, there is no hesitation in all the things which come to life.

GET TO "KNOW" SUFFERING

Emotional, or experiential, wounds abound. There are therapists who have made a career of counseling about these.

Basically, this is the essence of the "suffering" which Buddha spoke about: the word *dukha* is often *translated* as that: but it really means un-happiness, in the sense of dissatisfaction or anguish. What did Buddha point to as the source of dukha? Desire. The *source* of suffering Buddha spoke about is not "pain" (corporeal, or psychic) but the desire that pain not exist.

By the time we recognize and label any particular condition, it is already an actual fact—at least, in our consciousness. So, the desire for some thing not to exist which does presently exist, this is dukha, suffering; our word, today, would be dis-content.

So, in your case, you write that there is a recurring sense of guilt or remorse concerning some past event or experience.

Consider, firstly: We recognize some feeling or emotion which has arisen in consciousness. Selectively, we identify it categorically: say, as "joy," or as "guilt." We locate it on a scale of qualities or characteristics that ranges from "positive," on one end of the spectrum, to "negative"; or "pleasurable" to "painful," desire-able to un-desirable.

Due to our societal conditioning ("good" is better than "bad"), we hold the view that everything negative needs to be converted to positive. We identify our awareness of guilt as a "negative emotion." And so we try to change the fact of our conscious awareness of guilt. We endeavor to move our dissatisfaction from the place, on the spectrum, where we have designated it. We desire to deconstruct the fact which we have already established.

Consider, secondly: How necessary is it to identify by a categorical name or label any particular condition, or a perceived change in condition, which appears to exist in consciousness? Aside from an attempt to control, what purpose is served by calling up a job description such as "anger," "resentment," "compassion," "pride," etc.?

What is the need to assign (in any case) some fleeting state, noticed in awareness, to an imagined balance scale of Right and Wrong?

And here is the nexus where personal desire comes in: No matter where some conceived value rests on the scale, from whence is the source of the idea that it has to be changed? Does not discontent with 'what is' simply compound our "suffering"?

All things change, Buddha points out—of their own accord. During a single human lifespan, some things may appear to *remain* unchanged. Your recurrent sense of guilt and regret may never *cease* to recur, despite (if not because of) your persistent energy to negate or stifle it.

Buddha claimed, from his own experience, that there is a way to defuse dukha. Few, in our culture, have learned this way. Desire isn't only an issue concerning material possessions, but more importantly it's involved in our insistence that things be other than the way they are.

Even one's "dissatisfaction," with the way things are, need not be given a qualitative title; measured against a yardstick of personal preferences; and resisted attentively until some other "undesirable" emotion comes along to replace it.

"Freedom" means to *allow* 'what is' *to be*. Peace means truce in the war with what appears in consciousness.

We won't even, here, get into the matter of "who is the Doer" in *all* of this: Buddha seldom did; he tended to confine himself to simply pointing out the unsubstantial structure of dukha. Other sages have done so, as well, in their own words.

When Ramana says, "Accept with equanimity whatever occurs," that means in the mental realm as well as the material world. Guilt happens.

Response to "Get to Know"

"Thanks very much, Robert, for your input on my 'guilt problem.' Just what I needed to hear, the problem now no longer exists!

"It is so clear to me now: when there is no *resistance*, there is no *problem*. When a memory pops up now, I just let it come and go: no repression and no indulging. Before, I would analyze it, dwell on it—and that would then lead to a sense of guilt. Now, I view it as just another memory passing through consciousness.

"It is clear, now, that this can be true for *every thing*!"

Different Strokes

"Are you in any disagreement with what Tony Parsons says about nonduality?"

Not at all.

Just as no two persons can stand in exactly the same spot to view a sunset, so no two exponents of nonduality report their view from precisely the same perspective.

And generally the aspect of that view which initially made the most impression on each is typically the aspect which that particular teacher will tend to emphasize. In consequence, no two teachers give the same report, down to the last detail, though they've shared the same discovery.

In addition, different teachers adhere to different styles, probably as a development of what they've experimentally found effective in terms of transmitting this (counterintuitive) dharma.

The effect is that some teachers are more easily understood, by a particular listener, than are others. Or put another way, some listeners come more prepared to hear *this* teacher as contrasted to *that* teacher. The same, of course, holds true for the written material.

And, finally, there are some teachers who are most easily understood by those who have themselves already perceived the clear view. These teachers serve the purpose of removing doubt that the listener is indeed seeing through to the singular universal Truth.

As is obvious, of course, not everyone who professes to expound on nonduality has a thoroughly complete grasp of the matter. In such cases, dualistic viewpoints will inevitably surface in their pronouncements.

There are many effective teachers of nonduality speaking and writing these days, and Tony Parsons is the voice which some listeners will respond to best. On the other hand, someone may find him to seem unapproachable in their comprehension, while, say, Adyashanti may connect their dots.

The same message can be, repeatedly, delivered through different messengers. Focus on the comprehension of the *message*.

This Way to the Precipice

Someone said to Ramana, "I understand that you can give enlightenment."

Ramana said, "Yes. I can give it. Can you take it?"

There is a "shortcut." It can be pointed out to you. But "you" will die by taking it. "Can you take it?" Most enquirers can't. That's why Jesus said, "Many are called, but few are chosen."

You want to remain as you are, and yet to be "one with everything." When your body expires, *everything* that you know of will *cease* to *exist. Including* your self. Is there not *then* a condition of oneness?

How can you possibly be "one with all that is" while "you" remain as a separate entity? This is what is meant by "dying to the self." When the idea of you as a *separate being* no longer persists, "you" are no longer separate from all that exists.

So, the shortcut is well marked by the foot-treads of the sages: die to the idea that *you exist.*

This is not a palatable prospect for most people. So, the shortcut is visited only by those who feel free to "take it." The shortcut ends at a jumping-off point. The end of the search arrives quickly!

WAKE UP TO YOUR AWAKENING

Thanks for your report!

As you say, "It seems that most spiritual awakenings happen to those who are... ready to die." Yes, ready to die, essentially, to their attraction to "suffering"—what some teachers these days call the "drama" or "story" upon which the sense of self feeds for continuation. This death is the death of the old self-fixation, into what some term as a re-birth. Nothing changes in any external sense, just the awareness that what we had taken to be our identity is a misconception.

You said, "it was noticed that the 'fear' which has troubled and confused me for such a long time had disappeared." Where there is no identification with the old "me," what becomes of (old) "Norm's fears"?

The awakening, as I've said, is "a brief, quiet, simple shift in perspective": and you say, "Perhaps my perspective has changed." Don't underrate the significance of what you're seeing, by concluding something like "This couldn't be the awakening they speak of, could it?!"

"I perhaps have arrived 'at the edge of the river,'" you conclude. These perhaps-es suggest that you suppose that there is still something *more* to be *awaited*—a crossing. By supposing that there is some crossing that you haven't made, or need to make (or, even, can make), you create a chasm, a division, a separation

39

between "this" self and "that" omnipresence. This is specifically what Krishnamurti was cautioning about:

> You are seeking, asking, longing, to walk on the other shore. The other shore implies that there is *this* shore, and from this shore to get to the other shore there is space and time. That is what is holding you, and bringing about this ache for the other shore. That is the real problem—time that divides, space that separates; the time necessary to get there and the space that is the distance between *this* and *that*.

Adyashanti talks with hundreds of "seekers," around the country, each year. He sees many of them deny their own awakening.

> And isn't that *telling*? I think it's unfortunate that a person can spend hour after hour, day after day, year after year, lifetime after lifetime dedicating his life to enlightenment, and yet the very notion that anybody *attains* enlightenment is a taboo. We're all going after this; but God forbid somebody says they've realized it. We don't believe them, we're cynical, we have doubt, we go immediately into a semi- or overt attack mode. To me, it highlights the fact that people are chasing an awakening they don't believe could happen to *them*. That's a barrier, and the *biggest* one.

What might explain this tendency?

> People want liberation, but they are also terrified of it. If they completely let go, they fear they'll find a dangerous, deluded person underneath it all. The sense of Sin is alive and well in us. We think that there's something fundamentally black about our nature; that something monstrous will emerge if we let go. We walk around all day in this virtual reality, physically experiencing what the mind is telling us. If we stop, see through it all, and give it up, what will become of us? It's scary. Everything in the end is a defense against nothingness.

40

One of the Dzochen teachers, Tulku Urgyen—who says "I have known many, many people who attained an enlightened state, both male and female"—urges that you give validation to your present realization.

> Sometimes we may have doubts and hesitation when relating to the Buddha's teachings, but do not leave it with that. It is very important to validate what is trustworthy and what is not. My teachers mentioned four kinds of validation. First are the words of a fully enlightened being, such as the Buddha, whose statements are never unwise. Then there are the teachings by the great masters of the lineage, passed from one to the other until today. Third are the instructions we receive form our personal teacher. Finally to *decide* with certainty, we need the *validation* of our own *intelligence*.

Buddha did not await a lightning bolt to come down from heaven to validate what he was aware that he had finally realized. He simply got up from under the bo tree, and began to live his life as "the awakened" (the *meaning* of the word Buddha).

You write, "What you say, I have heard many times, but I didn't really 'hear' before." Now you have, and need not await another hearing.

"Nothing needs to be done, nor can be done," you have *realized*, "for a spiritual awakening to take place." This is a signal change from the *old* Norm. Don't *ignore* what you are seeing. This is exactly what the Buddhists call "ignorance." Ultimately, you have to rely on the validation of your own intelligence.

WHERE TO GO

There is no right or wrong answer, Joe, to this question of non-attachment to the relative world. Some feel impelled to cut as many ties as possible, others take no such actions and find that they are not hindered. Even from a practical standpoint, much could depend on the degree of one's obligatory responsibilities and unavoidable commitments.

It would seem obvious that where one is unencumbered by practical matters, there is greater latitude for the kind of contemplative introspection that generally tends to be conducive to an exceptional insight.

However, the awakening to the nondual nature of our existence has occurred in all kinds of differing circumstances.

In other words, a change in circumstances may or may not be tangential to a shift in perspective. And non-attachment involves more than mere detachment from material matters. As has been said, the final renunciation is of the self who would renounce.

The key factor is this: that which we have come to feel that we need to seek is, the nondual teachings assert, omnipresent. If that is true, not anything could be apart from or outside of it, nor could even exclude it (thus it is even said to be "within you"). In short, one comes to realize that this which we are seeking is actually inescapable. Why else is it stated, "That thou art"?

Why, then, would it matter where you are or what you are doing (or not doing), when you recognize that any and all movements are simply "That doing what it does"?

When such a realization is perfectly clear, the sense of being a separate, individuated self disappears into an abiding awareness of the Absolute. Where, then, is the self which needs to be in some particular place or activity or circumstance in order to attain the object of its seeking? No separation. No self. No seeking.

With Self-realization, some changes in circumstance may ensue; a substantial degree of non-attachment from worldly matters, for example. But the latter is more likely to be a development of the former, than vice-versa.

DECLARATION OF INTERDEPENDENCE

That cloud, up there, is quickly disintegrating, its whiteness (which we would identify as moisture) disappearing into the blue of the sky, into the atmosphere. Its molecules are changing form, generally speaking, from water molecules to air molecules. This oxygen may be absorbed by a plant, in the composition of the molecules of fiber. This fiber may be ingested by an animal, and these molecules may become the constituents of flesh. This flesh will yield moisture, and its oxygen.

All things being interdependent, a molecule has no independent identity of its own, and it embarks from no particular place nor returns to any particular place. It is inseparable from that energy which is manifested as change. You and that cloud, while different in form, are not different in nature. You are interdependent.

FOUR ESSENTIAL WORDS

Sum up the nondual teachings in a few words, you say?

David Godman did it, in a title to a book of Ramana's pointers: *Be As You Are.*

This is probably *the* most difficult matter to convey, except to those most deeply steeped in the nondual precepts.

First of all, the "as you are" begs the question of who—really—are you? When you genuinely know who you are, it's clear that you can never be other than what you have *always* been, and forever will be.

Even if you *don't* know who—or what—you truly are, you still will continue to be as you are (however confused or conflicted). This is the point the teachers are making when they say there is no such thing as free will; or, "You are not the Doer."

The Self-realized person has no problem being exactly as he is— spontaneously and transparently. He holds no notions of who he is supposed to be, what role he is assumed to play in other people's imagination.

But the unawakened person has every form of dissatisfaction with *being* what presents as who he is. This sense of being an imperfect product is an inevitable consequence of the I-thought, which engenders "others" to continually compare to, or who are perceived as the jury on how one "ought" to be.

The quote from Ramana is not *"Become* as you are." What you are in truth (as Buddhists put it) is "nothing special." There is not something you must become, in order to qualify as nothing special.

This morning, I noticed a full-page magazine ad: a corporation's logo—"Always Improving, Never Satisfied...It's our nature, never being satisfied."

It's really *human* nature, where "self" improvement would be a dead-end street, were it not an endless avenue.

If you say "be as you are," and you recognize that you simply *are* as you are, *being that* is something that you are a perfected master of.

When you have come to terms with merely being as you are, you are then disposed to allow *others* to be as *they* are, without feeling the compulsion to "improve" them.

To be as you are, is where peace and freedom are finally understood.

UNRAVELING THE PARADOX

Sometimes in my comments on the teachings of the enlightened sages, I make a distinction between "actuality" and "reality." This is basically in reference to what is regarded in the Sanskrit scriptures as the "Absolute" and the "relative," respectively.

Reality, in this case, denotes what appears to us to be real, in terms of the dualistically relative world of "things" (whether material or immaterial). *Appears* is the key word here: this is the realm where the word "illusion" or "dream" is often associated; all the "worldly" things are impermanent and changing.

Actuality is generally used to denote a condition which is permanent and unchanging, and words like "eternal" or "everlasting" are associated with it: more specifically the ultimate, indivisible (non dual) actuality that represents the Absolute (though it goes by myriad names; as Ramana has said, for example, "The Self, Consciousness, the Absolute and God denote the same thing.").

It is the continuous awareness of the immanent and transcendent presence of the Absolute actuality which is known as enlightenment; also known as realization, awakening, illumination.

That which we speak of as relative, of course, is dependent upon bifurcation, division, for its very identity: each "thing" is limited to its defined form, to being an entity which is separate from "others." Though a practical and useful distinction in terms of control of the subjects of our interest, this is the category of duality.

The Absolute, however, is regarded in the scriptures as formless, a non-entity, and therefore without limitation; this is defined as being without beginning or end—infinite in either space or time. Since, if there were two (or more) conditions that were infinite, they would necessarily merge into sameness, this actuality would be transcendent of the limitation we call duality; it would be characterized as non-dual.

Further, if forms—being impermanent—"come and go," there is implied a state from which they come and to which they go. In other words, the impermanent forms presumably arise from a permanent "field" or "ground" that can be present every-where and every-when that the forms arise, due to its ubiquitous, formless potentiality.

Given what has been said definitionally, though, a significant factor to bear in mind is that we are not speaking of an Absolute which is the opposite of the relative: the actuality and the reality, although we might assign them a different valuation in our consideration, are simply aspects of the same unfolding development.

The Absolute, or "ground of Being," infinite and formless, is without boundaries or restrictions of any kind; it is unconfinable and unrestrainable. There being no barrier to its presence anywhere in time or space, spiritual and religious teachings refer to it as omni-present: ever present everywhere, with no point in time or space where it is not. As the Vedas specifically say: "Nowhere is It not."

Therefore, the Absolute actuality surrounds every form; while it also permeates and saturates every form. So the scriptures clearly point out that all of the finite forms exist within the infinite—simultaneously with the infinite being present, as the essence, in all forms. Beingness is essential; as a "source" of any manifestation would naturally be essential.

This tells us that the absolute beingness and all relative forms are completely and irrevocably inseparable. As is said, "One is all; all is One." The Buddhist phrase puts it: "Form is formlessness; formlessness is form." In Tao, they call the Oneness-as-manyness-and-the-manyness-as-Oneness simply "suchness." Some, such as Krishnamurti, call it the "what is." All designations refer to the seamless and indivisibly overarching actuality that is permanently potential and transitionally manifest.

Of the transitory element, incidentally, Ramana speaks of the impermanent forms as "unreal" in contrast to the ever-present actuality, which he calls "real." Thus it is said that you, and the world, are "illusory" (in the sense of unreal).

The scriptures emphasize that this which is indivisible, "indestructible," and infinite has no "parts," except as relative (dualistic) *appearances*. It is this *mis*-perception—that the actuality of Beingness can be reduced to independent, autonomous parts—which causes us to think of the formless Absolute as a-part from its forms—such as apart from *you*, for example.

In other words, if we conceive of the Absolute being as a *part* of the Totality—rather than *being* the Totality—we then suppose that it is somehow apart from its manifest forms (in the way that Christians think of God as apart from man).

Hence, what these spiritual teachings are emphasizing is that the Absolute is *inescapable*; it must be closer than your very heart; and that must be so this very instant. In other words, it must already always be present as the infinite actuality in which you move—while at the same time fully present throughout the entire organism or form that exists or moves within it.

Enlightenment is simply a conscious shift from one's inherited limiting—dualistic—perspective to persistent non-dual awareness. As a consequence of this "realization" or "awakening," our "individual"—separative—*self-image* dis-appears into Absolute awareness.

And with this perceptual change, our values and behavior also change. While the relative, material world doesn't vanish, the appearance of separative forms is *transcended* and we respond differently to "reality," from the standpoint of what we perceive as the essential actuality.

This, then, is the same, single illumination which all the spiritual masters have shared. There is, after all, but one undifferentiated enlightenment, recognition of the nondual actuality as ever everywhere present—which it is whether you recognize it or not!

Your Insignificant Other

When we speak of the "sense of self," basically we are pointing to the "I-thought," the identification (recognized or unrecognized) of the "self" as the I-person of limited presence. In this perception, there is "me," and all else—outside the contours of the bodily organism—is "not me." Hence there are, always, at least two things: duality.

What you are calling "liberation" is a transcendence of the dualistic perspective (thus called non-duality). The bodily organism does not disappear in this case. Nor does awareness of the relative, material world disappear. There is still someone who is alive and alert, but who identifies with (where called upon) a presence which permeates and unifies all of existence: the awareness which "sees" is seeing its own substance wherever it looks.

When these eyes look at this body, it matters not whether what it sees is called "I" or by some other name (such as Self): what is identified is not limited to "this" as compared to "that." Irregardless of the manifold appearance in the material world, only one thing is known to ever be *truly* seen. This *I* is not excluded from, or apart from in any way, that *one* thing: nor is anything *else*. The "me/not-me" perspective has been transcended.

WHAT IS DEATH?

Throughout our lifetime, we're never more than one breath away from non-existence.

Even though we don't consider it as such, we actually experience this non-existence with as much regularity as the passing of the moon. In fact, if we are deprived of this non-existence for more than a few unbroken occasions, we "lose our mind"—go crazy.

Consider it. Each night, for an unnoticed period of time, you are involuntarily absorbed in deep, dreamless un-consciousness: not at all conscious of any earthly reality—including existence of the *person*. Whatever it is that is present in this condition is totally undifferentiated; it has no relationship to the world, or even the cosmos: all that we usually think of as "reality" has *dis*appeared completely. There is not so much as a "self" which remains to *be* aware of the absolute emptiness.

This likewise is the condition which is said to be present in the deepest sublime state of meditation: the "momentary" death of an identifiable self, along with a "transcendence" of the universe in its entirety.

This pure unembellished presence is closest, perhaps, to our word "awareness" (as preferred to "consciousness," since this implies being conscious *of* some thing—for example, self-conscious— and is generally associated with sentient impressions, in the waking state).

It is this condition of formless presence which is universally the organism's primordial—*pre* "existent" or fundamental— condition.

Upon this natural condition is superimposed our waking and dreaming experience; when waking and dreaming consciousness falls away, this remains as the empty screen upon which the individual's self-image had been projected. While waking and dreaming come and go cyclically, (what is called) pure awareness remains unchanged throughout. As Ramana Maharshi said, "Awareness is your [true] nature: in deep sleep or in waking [or dreaming], *it* is the same."

To distinguish this ever-present awareness with a word of its own, Sanskrit has *turiya*. Thus Ramana has said:

> "Our real state is what is sometimes called turiya...the real and natural state of the Self...the transcendent state....

> "It is not apart from anything, for it forms the substrate of all...it is the only Truth; it is your very Being....

"Turiya is only another name of the Self...the only reality: there is nothing else....

"When the individual being merges in the Supreme, it is called turyatita."

Turyatita, then, would be what we confuse with a finite (mis)conception that we call death.

Where we mistakenly identify our essence with the impermanent organism, the body, we suppose that the body "has" awareness— and that, in physical death, the awareness falls away from the body. Rather, it is that the body falls away from awareness...as it does in deep sleep. Ramana addressed this:

"Before considering what happens after death, just consider what happens in your sleep....

"When you sleep, this body and world do not exist for you—and this question did not worry you....Did you ask while asleep... where do 'I go' after death?..

"Why do these questions arise [to the limited "self"] now, and not in sleep? Find out!...

"The body which dies: were you aware of it, did you have it, during sleep?...

"Sleep is temporary death. Death is longer sleep [turiya]....

"There is no ground for even the thought of death."

Consider this. If you were to die in your sleep—where you do not even exist—would you know that you had died? The essential state would merely no longer be aware of the body, nor anything else which appears in waking (or dreaming) consciousness.

Ramana makes the further point that any thing which can appear and disappear is impermanent. The world, the entire universe, even self-identity appear each day upon awakening—and disappear again from awareness each night. The only thing which remains unchanged is our fundamental, underlying condition. There is that which does not appear and reappear, and therefore is ever-present.

As Ramana put it: "That which does not exist all the time, but exists at one time and not at another, cannot be real." In other words, only that which does not know death is permanent and therefore ultimately real and undeniably existent.

This formless awareness was present before the idea of a "you" even came into form, and will continue in *presence* as the illimitable and non-finite Self.

> "At death, the limited mind
>
> dissolves in the unlimited mind."
>
> – Anasuya Devi

re: Your Eight Questions

1. From the time we are infants, we are conditioned to view the world in relative terms: "this" object as opposed to "that" object. While this perspective has some practical value, it develops a divisive mindset: conflict arises between "you" and "me."

   The message of the teachers of nonduality is that it is possible to transcend the limited perspective of duality and to recognize that the separativeness (that we assume) is, at root, merely a conceived construct.

2. If we truly transcend the dualistic conceptions of a "you" and an "I," to whom does the perception of nonduality become apparent? In other words, what is the relationship, if any, of the "I" to the nondual perspective? There is a seeming paradox involved; but similar to seeing through the image presented in an optical illusion, the shift in perceptive awareness (to what is called nonduality) can be an instantaneous matter. Teachers of enlightenment, such as Buddha, have suggested the conditions which make this shift possible. I have studied what was said, deeply contemplated the paradoxical aspect, and discovered that the perceptive transition that was said to be possible is possible indeed.

3. The shift to nondual clarity is not an occurrence dependent upon time. What is viewed from that perspective has always already been present: so it is merely a matter of recognizing the true nature of what is everywhere present. Therefore, no "practices" or disciplines are necessary.

   And that which is recognized transcends all temporal and impermanent forms, such as religions or spiritual traditions. So, no "beliefs" are necessary, concerning this clarity, because "doubts" too have been transcended.

4. Once thorough nondual clarity is present, it is self-sustaining. For those to whom this clarity is not obviously present, they can rest assured that it is not a matter of profound concern; all of us ultimately return to the same condition, whether we are enlightened or unenlightened.

5. The nondual teacher most often referred to in my book,

Living Nonduality, is Ramana Maharshi. Though Ramana died in 1950, he is better known now than he was during his lifetime, since both his life and his pronouncements have been so instructive to those of us in the Western world.

My book contains 238 monographs on various aspects of Self-realization, written over a period of twenty years. Some who've read it tell me that it closed the circle for them, so I would suggest that an inquirer start there and see what unfolds from it.

6. Just as Buddhism, particularly Zen (and later Dzogchen), gained attention in the U.S. during the past half century, the precepts of nonduality (as embodied primarily in Advaita Vedanta) are expanding the spiritual horizon for those intent on getting to the bottom of the "ultimate Reality" question. Given that the challenge to human life on earth is predicted to reach its zenith within the next two decades, I suspect that an increasing number of people around the world will become serious about transcending "the affairs of the world."

7. I live day by day, and for me "the future" is the next day following. I don't begin a manuscript without the awareness that I may not finish it. But nearly every day I am writing something about nonduality. My second book will soon be in print, The Gospel of Thomas: The Enlightenment Teachings of Jesus. Meanwhile, I am working on a commentary [ed. note: published under the title *One Essence*] on the Hsin Hsin Ming, a poem of Zen instruction still revered fourteen centuries after it was written. Its message concerns the nondual realization.

8. We living humans have already taken the red pill, in that we consider ourselves to be self-motivating individuals in a world which seems more real to us than the one in our dream state. For such, the "empty" pill is now needed, the one by which we lose our sense of being a separate, isolated and independent entity or "person"-ification. Those who would know what lies beyond the earthly appearances will want to consider what is being said by the teachers of enlightenment. Rather than watching The Matrix, they might benefit from viewing Abide as the Self, a video about Ramana (narrated by Ram Dass).

At Cause?

In nature, things generally do not change their course unless something changes it for them: such things yield when appropriate. The course of the wind is choicelessly changed by the hill; the wind changes the course of the fallen leaf; the leaf changes the course of the beetle.

Was it the leaf that changed the course of the beetle, or was it the hill, or was it the wind?

The energy of the beetle yields, when appropriate, to transformation by the beak of the raven. What was the cause of the meeting with the raven, in this change of course for the energy of the beetle? Was it the wind? Or the hill? Or the leaf?

The Highest Good

The shift in perspective, which nondual awareness represents, is occasioned by the dissolution of the (separative) self-image—the idea of who we think we are. When our typical self-centeredness dissipates, in this circumstance, we become even more acutely aware of the perceived "suffering" of others around us. Knowing now that such suffering is not necessary (the basic principle of Buddha's teaching), one will notice a natural instinct to want to share one's own discovery with anyone who has an interest in hearing about it.

After all, what did any of the great sages do after their enlightenment: they were available 24/7 to be of assistance to anyone they could who genuinely sought inner peace. An interviewer once asked Krishnamurti, why do you do what you do? And his answer basically was "Compassion." With Self-realization, one's values change; and, as a consequence, one's behavior changes. How would I characterize that change in general: a flowing through the organism of a creative, and benevolent, force that expresses itself in a generalized (rather than person-alized) love. Ramana Maharshi said this: "A Self-realized being can not help benefiting the world. His [or her] very existence is the highest good." Whose "existence" is it but that of the Ultimate?

THE "TRIAD" ILLUSION

The Hindus speak of the "triad": a subject (seer), and object (seen), and the "relationship" that *appears* to "connect" them: in this case, seeing.

As you said, "When the seer is not there, there is no seeing."

You think of yourself as the seer, an *object* in relationship to other *objects* (such as the seen).

But when you see anything, is there any separation, any disconnection, between you and the seeing? Of course not.

And whatever it is that you see, is there any separation, any disconnection, between the seeing and what's seen? No, of course not.

So the seeing unavoidably links, or connects, the seer and the seen.

And the seeing itself, of course, is not disconnected from, or disassociated from, either the seer or the seen.

The seer, the seeing and the seen ("the triad"), in other words, is one unbroken phenomenon, or reality—one whole.

That is why Sailor Bob Adamson has written that there is no separate, or isolated, seer; nor is there anything separate, or isolated, that any of us has ever seen. There is just one, unbroken actuality: the overarching All.

Only The Absolute

The matter of the "witness" is not often addressed in spiritual writings, because of its subtlety.

To begin with, you ought to continually be conscious of the one ultimate condition: "All that is, is That"; all is the Self, the Absolute.

Therefore, it becomes clear that what is referred to as the witness, or "witnessing," is none other than "the Self, doing what it does."

Put another way, the Self is the ever-present witness and *anything* which could possibly *be* witnessed is merely another element or aspect of the Self. All that is ever going on, in witnessing, is that the Self is everywhere witnessing itself.

You know that this must be so, because that which (you are aware) is witnessing does not, of itself, ever interact with—and is completely unaffected by—whatever is witnessed. Likewise, the Self (or Absolute) has no need to interact—being already all things that exist—and cannot be affected by anything extraneous to its own presence, since not anything *is* extraneous to it.

Ramana has said, to put it simply, "Talking of this 'witness' should not lead to the idea that there is a witnesser [subject] and something else apart from him that he is witnessing [object]."

You are the Self. The Self is all there is. The only thing which you *could* witness is your self (as the Self) in another form.

Ramana gives as an example: the sun shines on the world. The sun has no interest in what goes on in the world; but the world could not exist without the presence of the sun.

Your awareness depends upon "witnessing"; but you (as you think your self to be) are not your awareness. The self that you think you are depends upon the awareness that is witnessing; but the self is not real, because it cannot exist outside of the Self; the witness is not real either, if it is also presumed to be other than the Self.

In other words, any witness (subject) of the self (object) is unreal, because there is no separate form as the witness *and* no separate form as the self. There is *only* That (always), only the Absolute.

So, be aware: whatever you think of as the witness is the Absolute. Whatever you think of as the self is the Absolute.

Non-dual. "Not two things."

One Names All

Once the awakening process is underway, one begins to re–examine, in a new light, that which heretofore had been perceived in duality. It's apparent that you're beginning to look anew.

The central point of nonduality is that there is only one recognition that you need to be continually conscious of, and that will be the key to all that you need to know. It is this: all that *is* (everything, whether we say it is existent or non-existent), is the one single, indivisible actuality. Any thing which is formed, formless, named or unnamable is, in the final analysis, that illimitable actuality in essence.

Confusingly, this all-inclusive actuality has been identified in a plethora of ways, over mankind's history. As just a few: God, Absolute, That, Self, He. Ultimately, it makes no difference what *name* is given to *anything*, since *all* things are merely expressions of the fundamental actuality.

However, due to our ingrained dualistic mindset, it is important to give some attention (at least initially) to this matter of referential wording concerning this underlying actuality. Consider for yourself whether some referential wording may not be more likely to lend itself to dualistic reverberations than others. Some, for example, have historically been associated with a dualistic conception of an entity that is inevitably viewed as apart from the viewer himself: He/Him, Lord, and God are examples of these, and the separative (dualistic) conception involved is clearly depicted on Michelangelo's ceiling in the Sistine Chapel; the anthropomorphic Jehovah, of whom the Bible speaks of his face, eyes, ears, hands, and his sitting and standing.

Even the Eastern term Self risks carrying a connotation of something similar to "my" self, which I think of as having a "mind" and intentions and plans, and so on.

For this reason, much of the classical Advaita writings utilize a more neutral term, such as That; however, even such a word leaves us with a choice that might better be regarded as *This*.

A more definitive choice, and one which is found consistently throughout all spiritual source works, is the word Absolute. So, too, the word Omnipresent.

But regardless of which term you feel comfortable with, it can be helpful to focus your attention on *one* referential term for the *one* actuality. This avoids such confusion, for example, as considering that "God is a part of the Absolute." Or such conceptions as "the Absolute is His expression." Or He/Self, Self/God, etc., which are subliminally dualistic expressions. *All* that is (by *whatever* name), is that *One* singular actuality. "Self" *is* the Absolute. "God" *is* the Absolute. "He" is the Absolute. (Or, Omnipresent—or whatever *singular* term you choose to confine your reference to.)

This expression, for example—"The Absolute must move within Self (God) if God (Self) is the All"—might be stated:

The Absolute *must* 'move' within the Absolute, if the Absolute is all that there *is*."

And this makes it clear that, ultimately, there is not *even* "movement" as a *separate* distinction *apart* from the Absolute. All that is (movement included) is merely the Absolute in its actual expression.

Or, as you recognized it, "This [the Absolute] is motion*less*." This consistent awareness of the overarching nondual actuality causes you to avoid such ingrained dualistic conceptions as "cause" and "effect." The Absolute *being* all that is, it would have to be *both* all possible causes *and* all potential effects. Put another way, where there is nothing *but* a singular actuality, cause and effect are meaningless, separative distinctions.

How much more simple (and effective) a key could we be given than to recognize, "*All* that *is*, is That"—and to be finished in one sweep with confusion and division?

This is what "clarity" means—clear, no obstructions!

Three statements by Ramana:

"The Absolute is the Self. It is God."

"The Self is God."

"The Self is the Absolute..."

(Did he contradict himself? Or is *all* One?)

THE UNBORN

Seventeenth-century Buddhist sage Bankei has said:

Everyone just learns the expression "unborn and imperishable" and goes on repeating it; but when it comes to *realizing* conclusively, and actually getting right to the heart of the matter, they haven't any idea of what the *Unborn* is.

The Unborn is traditionally another word for the Absolute, that which does not come and go, has no beginning or end. As you say, "To live by that understanding [of what the Unborn actually is] requires—for most of us—a real shift in perspective."

The shift in perspective, really, is to clearly recognize that you can never be apart from the Unborn. In Buddhism, the Unborn and what is called the Buddha-mind are equivalent, as in the way that Bankei has used it:

> You each received one thing, from your mother, when you were born—the unborn Buddha-mind. Nothing else.

He speaks (above) of the "unborn and imperishable"; so, the Buddha-mind is not something which we are at risk of losing. Nor do we need to, as you say, "rely on thought, ideas, opinions, beliefs, etc." to retain or even maintain it: what we do need to do is to recognize that it is the inherent consciousness out of which our movements or actions flow. That profound *realization* is evident, in Bankei's words, "when you just stay constantly in the unborn mind, sleeping in it when you're awake. You're a living Buddha in your everyday life [can't *help* but *have* Buddha-mind], at all times." This is known as Self-realization, also as Absolute awareness.

Once the understanding is clear that the Buddha-mind is ever present, is anything *more* required to "become" a Buddha? Bankei says no: "There's not a *moment* when you're *not* a Buddha. Since you're always a Buddha, there's no 'other' Buddha, in *addition* to that, for you to become."

As a Buddha, all that you do is a *product* of the unborn Buddha-mind.

The Uncaused

One throws a rock into the water and the water makes ripples which lap the farther shore.

The human who throws the rock; the rock itself; the water; and the far shore—all these are equivalent manifestations of the same actuality of wholeness. The rock, the water, the distant bank are as much a cause, in the event, as is the human. Actor, action, acted upon—all inseparable elements in the manifest expression of wholeness.

One comes to understand that all *things* (matter) are nothing more than *events* (energy), in their transient nature, and that all events are the same infinite, unbounded event. One thus recognizes oneself as the expression of all that is.

Put another way, that which is all there is cannot be the cause of anything, because that which is caused would have to be something other than, or beside, that which is all there is—and there is not anything that can be outside of this wholeness which is infinite.

Therefore, when we view anything as a distinctly separate entity ("I"), we are incorrectly identifying what it is that we are viewing. There is no legitimate way in which "I" can be separate from all that is.

In the same way that I am not separate from all that is, and the rock is not separate from all that is, the rock, the ripple, the far shore and I are all the same.

When this is clear to you, you automatically cease to objectify— to regard objects, or events, as apart and alienable from that which you yourself, by nature, are.

The Uncommon Denominator

Several people have asked me if I still had the sheet that I typed out, that I mentioned in my account of a pivotal moment in awakening, in *Living Nonduality*.

Once that inspiration had been typed out, I began to write some of the 600-plus monographs that I've written since. So that page got "lost" as just another page in my ring-binder.

Looking through some of those earlier monographs, more than 15 years later, I saw one that might be the original one. If not, it is probably very similar to what I'd have written.

The significance of it is not so much in what it said, but that (for the first time) these observations were appearing as truths which no longer were derived from some absent, enlightened authority: they were now purely and entirely truths that I knew first-hand, as revelation. I now knew that there was no question that I could ask, that I could not answer. (Many of the monographs written subsequently were to *concretely* answer some of the perennial questions.)

A "different person" *read* it, after *writing* it: a person who knew, without doubt, that clarity was irrevocably present; and for whom separation, as a perception, had unquestionably ended.

Ramesh Balsekar speaks of a similar moment, when he became aware (while translating) that his awareness of the Absolute truth was no different than that of Nisargadatta's.

Thought's Source

Basically, the spiritual teachings say that there is but one actuality, and it is Absolute in the reach of its presence—reaching into all of time and every cubit of space. Anything which has a formed appearance must, then, appear within the Absolute. These forms of appearance are called "*relative* forms of the Formless [the Absolute]."

Since the presence of these appearances (each or all) must be entirely *dependent* upon the presence of the primordial, or original, actuality, they are in no way apart from their Source. They, the relative existences, are *one* with the Source.

The Formless itself has no "thoughts," in the sense that humans call a speculation or an opinion or a doubt, etc., a thought. But would there be any such development as a thought—*or* as a human being who thinks—if it were not for the Absolute presence of the one actuality?

As a consequence of this uniting perspective, it is sensible to ask oneself, "*Whose* thoughts *are* these?" Ultimately, the source of all thoughts—the source of every present appearance—is the Absolute.

Consider that the very source of the cognizing being itself is the Absolute: so what, then, of its by-products? Whatever "actions" these thoughts lead to are *also*, in this broadest sense, the activities of the Absolute. In this sense, it is said: "All that is [done], is That doing what it does."

To the person who supposes herself to be a separate individual, these appear to be "her" separate thoughts. But to one whose identity is a fusion with the Absolute, "all that is, is That"— including the presumed thinker *and* her so-called thoughts.

So, one teacher might be heard to—correctly—say, "You are not the source of your thoughts"...if the "you" being addressed considers herself to be a separate individual or entity.

Another teacher might say, "You are the source of your thoughts"... recognizing that every "you" (and every "thought") is merely the Formless appearing as a form.

The "correctness" or "incorrectness" lies in the awareness of the being that is addressed, dependent upon whether that is (what can be called) *nondual* awareness or the *dualistic* mindset.

In other words, *both* teachers can be "right," if you understand the perspective from which they're speaking.

The pivotal question here, of course, is what is *your* awareness? Where nondual awareness is present, there exists no separate "me" who has (or does) anything: has thoughts, or thinks. There is only One actuality, not separable—in any real sense—into limited parts. Consider: in deep sleep, "you" are not there—*nor* are thoughts.

A questioner to Ramana: "Then thoughts are not real?"

Ramana:

> "They are not: the only reality is the Self [Absolute]....

> "Thoughts...arise from the Self....

> "They appear at one moment, and disappear at another. Wherefrom do they arise? Their source...must be the Eternal state [Absolute]..."

DRAMATIS PERSONAE

Truth is, indeed, stranger than fiction. There is a play being performed today—far too imaginative for television—and you will get to see it, because you have a part in it.

This is an improvisational play, but there are a few guidelines for its players. For example:

This play never ends. Therefore, there is no "outcome." No one can or will ever know the outcome, and so no matter what any of the actors do (or don't do), none will ever have any effect on its denouement.

Also, the actors and the playwrights are the same persona, and so the play is both written and performed in the very same moment—each and every moment.

Too, anyone can choose any role they wish, and can change their role at any moment they desire. However, it may be worthwhile to keep in mind that no matter what role they play or which changes they make in their role, this will not in any way affect the outcome.

A player can choose not to elect any *particular* role, in which case the director will determine the most appropriate role for that time.

All actors will perform their role both effortlessly and perfectly, because no matter what their action (or inaction), it is a brilliant interpretation of their role. However, no matter how skillful or pivotal the player, the other actors reserve the right to continue with or without the physical presence of any player.

This show, in truth, *must*—and will—go on.

THE SELF IS THE SELF

As you put it, "there is no thinker," from the standpoint of Advaita. It is, as you say, the Absolute (or Self) which is the doer of what's done: "action, thought and thinker are all the Self."

Another way this could be looked at, *as well*: "I am the thinker—but *who* am 'I'; I am That."

In other words, Advaita says recognize that "you" are not the doer of what's done: the Absolute (or Self)—being all that is—produces all that's done. On the other hand, one can acknowledge the appearance of *being* the doer, while at the same time recognizing that the 'I' is, in actuality, none other than That.

So, one could say "the Self has no eyes, ears, taste, etc." *Or* one could say, "the Self has eyes, ears, taste, etc., in it's manifestation *as* the 'I'."

It is this form of both-propositions-are-right that makes Advaita so paradoxical.

It is important that you comprehend the significance of the second kind of contemplation of the Self.

One confusion that persons sometimes have, initially, is the consideration of That—as the doer—being somehow apart from 'me' (because, "*I* am not the doer").

The point, here, is to recognize that you and That are not *in any way* two *different* realities: "Advaita" *means* "not two." This is why the sutras use the name-form of Self/self (Absolute/relative); the relative is the formless *Absolute*, in a (limited) form. Thus, "you" (a relative entity) are That (the limitless actuality). The Absolute in no way stands a-*part* from you: being un-limited, it pervades *all*—including the form regarded as "you"; "you *are* That," period.

If this isn't realized, you will maintain an *image* of the Self which is not unlike the image a Christian has of "God": a "spirit" which interacts with "man"—*two* entities.

It isn't that the Self is *causing* the "doing," as a force apart from what is done. It is that the Self is inseparably *in* the activity of doing what is done, because it *is* all that is *doing* what is being *done*. Contemplate this subtlety thoroughly.

For example, to say that "the Self is the knower" doesn't mean that the knowledge that is known is stored somewhere (such as a Christian might think of as "the mind of God"). It means that *any thing* which could possibly know anything (such as "you") *is* the *Self*. The Self "knows all" (omniscience) *because* the Self is all "knowers."

Thus, rather than saying "the Self is the witness," it is better understood that "every witness is the Self."

This is the point, where it is said that "the Self is not a doer": the Self is not a "witness*er*," it is all that is *involved* in the process of witness*ing*. Even the writers, of some of the materials you have been reading, are not clear on this matter of deeper understanding. That is why it is important for you to have *first*-hand knowledge, not *second*-hand.

A PARABLE

There is a story, concerning realization, that goes like this.

Two disciples of a particular order were making their way through the jungle, intent upon spreading their gospel. In a clearing along the river near where they had moored their boat, they encountered a native who was digging roots. The native said in surprise, "Who are you?!"

"We have come to tell you of an amazing man, who lived before our time. If you take this string of beads, run them through your fingers, and say 'Hail Mary, full of grace' with each word—every day for the rest of your life—you may someday be like him."

Impressed, the native sat down with the beads, and the missionaries coached him over and over until he could repeat the mantra by himself. Kneeling at their feet and thanking them profusely for their gift, he bid farewell to the two emissaries.

The missionaries returned to their boat, pleased with the outcome. As they were rowing a quarter mile from the shore, they heard a shout: "Wait! Wait!" They rested their oars and looked in the direction of the shore. The native came running across the water, and leaned over them in the boat. "I guess I must be hopeless! Can you tell me again what those last three words were?"

REVELATORY REVOLUTION

You're correct, of course, that whatever one's state of awareness, we have to each of us provide food and shelter for the body. And how we attend to this is what has been called "right livelihood"— in a relative world where circumstances are not ideal.

A suggested first consideration: to the extent that one is in confusion, all that one does is an acting-out of that confusion; to the extent that one has clarity, all that one does is an activity of that clarity. So the first item on the agenda needs to be this matter of arriving at clarity concerning the ultimate nature of our reality. When you know who, or what, is the true Doer of what's being done, this is the "right" foundation for subsequent "livelihood."

Then this consideration: ask not what you can get; ask what you can give. The lives of the enlightened masters tell us that when your wants and your needs are not two, you are likely to lead a non-competitive life, involving a freedom out of which emerges a fearless creativity; this becomes, without intention, a life of "service." And, like water reaching its own level, such service tends to be supported without even the need to ask.

You write, "There is no *me*." Then allow the Doer to do what needs to be done, while living in that clarity.

THE CAUSE IS THE EFFECT

Your (somewhat poetic) visualization admits of three elements, but you indicate that you understand that in actuality this "trinity" is an indivisible and indiscriminate One: "the three in reality are the One," in your own words.

This is often viewed, in the classical (Advaita) texts, as "the doer, the doing and what's done." The doing, of course, cannot in any way be separated from the doer; nor can the doer and its doing be realistically apart in any way from what is done. So, clearly, these three aspects are one consistent actuality.

Because we tend to break this truth into a linear exposition (so that we can cognize it in relative terms), we posit that the first element is the "cause"—within a passage of time—of the third element, and it is the second element which is responsible for the resultant "effect."

There are three things, you will notice, that the enlightened masters inevitably aver: from the standpoint of the ultimate actuality (or Absolute) there is no such reality as (1) time; (2) space (or distance); or (3) cause-and-effect. These are all, obviously, just *relative* concepts. (Give it some thought, and you can see why.)

So, what does this mean, in terms of the doer, the doing and the done? It means that what we place in the linear context of time is merely a (misleading) appearance. The doer is not *doing* the "doing," the doer *is* the doing. The doer does not *cause* what is done, the doer *is* (the same as) what is done.

Think of it this way, if you need to. *All* that IS, is THAT (Absolute). Therefore, *That* is the doer. Likewise, therefore, there can be no distinction made between what the doer *is* and what it (simultaneously identified) is doing. Nor can—since ALL that is, is That—a distinction be found between what the doer is doing and what one points to as "whatever is done."

Thus, if you were someone who insisted on relying on an image of "God," it must be obvious that this Omnipresence is everywhere present in the form of any and all "doers." Being so, whatever these doers "do" is an activity that is consequent to that Omnipotent power. Then, look around at what you presume has been "done": can you not readily see that it is a manifest appearance of this all-pervasive be-ing?

Therefore, no time is involved, because there is no "movement" in this *presence*: it is *simultaneously* present before the "cause" even *needed* an "effect"; being Omniscient, it "knows itself" as the effect as early as it could know itself as the cause.

The point is not how to see "three things" as one, but to see that the concept of three identifiable aspects is false, in the first place: there never has been other than a singular actor acting every action. How can this be? Because It is *all that is*. No *exceptions*: One-ness itself.

This Absolute totality is present *as* the doer; present *as* the doing; *and* present as whatever is the product of the doing: it is all an unbroken, simultaneous "event" (or phenomena).

This ultimately being so, our perception of cause-and-effect (God dependent upon time, as if time were a reality independent of God) must be an erroneous concept, a basically dualistic proposition.

Another point made by the sages: in the ultimate condition, there is no such thing as "movement" (sometimes phrased as, "Nothing ever happened"). Plumb this, delve into this, and see if you can comprehend why.

When you do, this will answer your other questions (about this relative, earthly realm).

IN THE PERSON OF DUALISM

Due to our habituated experience of sectioning and parsing the present reality, in order to manipulate it for effects in the daily world of relative needs, we tend to carry this inclination over into what would be our spiritual perspective.

To be specific, this can be noticed in the concern we express regarding the presumed relationship and complicated inter-workings of such selective concepts as "mind," "thought," "witness," and so on.

To one who perceives in terms of being a (separate) "self," that self's mind, thoughts, awareness et al are elements of a fragmented reality which needs to be "harmonized" with effort.

For the one for whom the image of being an isolated, separate entity has dissolved, the problematic ideas of "mind," "thoughts," "witnessing," "awareness," etcetera, disappear with it.

The point of the nondual teachings has basically to do with freedom and peace. There will be neither, as long as there is a notion that the present actuality should not be what it is: "My mind should not be in this state"; "It would be better if my thoughts were absent"; "Sometimes I am the witness, most times I'm not"; "My awareness does not seem to be what my guru says it should be..."

Can you see that such "better/worse" attitudes are dualism personified? The sagacious teachings urge us to transcend such designations, and to recognize that a singular, unbroken actuality is the essence of all that is occurring—good, bad or otherwise.

When you can be *present* with whatever seems to be appearing as mind, thought, awareness, witness and so forth, without *equivocation*, that is the freedom and peace that the rishis are describing. When there are not preferences for some particular state or condition over another, where can consternation arise?

The "Pre" is Present

Your question: If "you are not the doer," as the nondual sages say, does that mean that we are simply subject to fate?

Fate is defined as: "the inevitable outcome of events, as predetermined by a superhuman agency, or God."

We have been enculturated, for centuries, with the notion of a celestial agent (or agents, before ancient religious currents reduced it to the singular) directing the affairs of humankind and worldly events so that these are pre-determined. There is a dualistic premise to this conception.

As early as the Hebrew bible (so-called Old Testament), the first verses of Genesis ("God created...") depict God hovering over— thus distanced from—the earth. His persistent activity, from thereon, is to separate *this* element from *that* element (light from darkness, ocean from land, etc.—beginning with the "formless and empty").

Even into the New Testament, centuries later, this agent, positioned in a heaven, was described as acting upon—fatefully—the person of His own surrogate, Jesus.

The point of view of the nondual teachings is that there is not a god which exists "hovering over" the world and man.

Nor was the "world created" by such a personalized figure (Gen. 3:8, "walking in the Garden in the cool of the day"!), in the past tense.

That which is creating (and destroying) is present at every point in space and time: it *is* what is being created and destroyed. It need follow no particular preordained outcome, because—being unopposed by programmatic limitations—there isn't any outcome which can be wrong.

In other words, this Absolute presence is what is being done—in, by and as everything which exists (or doesn't exist). It would therefore *be* anything which could be predetermined, as well as anything which was not predetermined; the fated outcome *and* that outcome which was not fated. So, fate really has no relevance in such a context.

Even those who are relatively spiritually sophisticated have difficulty recognizing their conditioning which predicates a remote and willful instigator of particularized outcomes.

Ajata: "non-existence"

Vedanta, generally speaking, is the organized study (and/or interpretation) of the ancient Indian collection of spiritual literature known as the Vedas. A part of the Vedas, the Upanishads (possibly dating between 800-600 B.C.) describe a form of spiritual liberation that is called yoga; among the various yogas is *jnana*, which leads to samadhi—immersion of the self into the all-encompassing fundamental reality (called Brahman, or the Self). These (Sanskrit) scriptures were evidently secret, at one time.

A particular emphasis in Vedanta, known as Advaita, was the focus of Adi Shankara, renowned in India as a teacher circa 800 A.D. He stressed that the Vedas declare that Brahman is the all-pervading, nondual essence that animates every self.

Advaita Vedanta (or jnana yoga) is best known in modern times as the life teaching of the Indian ascetic Ramana Maharshi, who died in 1950; his theme was that the Self which you seek to be united with is already your own essential self.

Ramana's teachings actually went further than Advaita; they reflected the most refined form of Advaita, which is called Ajata. Basically, Advaita emphasizes that "All is One"; Ajata erases both the "All" and the "One" as definitional concepts. Any thoughts of "existence" are dependent upon sensate consciousness; the dead are devoid of both the ideational entities of the Self or of the self.

So, the teachings of Ramana reflect the "emptiness" or "void" of reality, which renders all analytical philosophies moot.

BASIC MATH

Having failed algebra (9ᵗʰ grade), I can tell you that if you don't absorb basic mathematics (as I didn't), you won't be positioned to relate to abstract algebraic equations.

Put another way, if you're going to engage in foreign-car motor overhaul, you have to come prepared with metric wrenches.

Spiritual teachers make a multitude of pronouncements, some of them seemingly contradictory. Because the mind of the seeker is generally mired in relative dualities, the sages mostly (at least initially) speak in relative terms in order to communicate anything at all that will be understood. To seekers who have finally perceived beyond relative considerations, they (then) speak from the standpoint of Absolute actuality. The challenge for the seeker is to recognize, when hearing the teacher's words, where the references pertain to the relative—limited—and where they are referent to the Absolute (unlimited).

The point of all such teachings is to direct (or lead) the seeker's point of reference out of the spectrum of dualism, so that one might "stand above" all separative dilemmas and perceive the nondual nature of all that can be said to be.

The fulcrum to leverage the seeker out of his divisive confusion, for such teachers, is to remind the hearer that any sort of subject/object relationship is dualistic. Nonduality implies the transcendence of subject/object opposition.

Why is this a fulcrum (or flashpoint)?: Because the supposed objects are really nothing more than a creation (figment) of the subject (seeker). When the subject comprehends his/her nonexistence (in a context which permits the possibility of a nondual actuality) conflict dissolves, because there is no *seer* to stand in opposition (apart from) what is *seen*. Seer and seen are one; subject/object polarity (relationship) disappears.

So, the elements of basic math that we are given, by these teachers, are that (for instance):

Actuality (our true nature, Buddha mind, et al) is nondual.

Subject and object are one: nondual.

With these simple, basic, universally applicable tools, it is possible for a person to realize true nature (Buddha mind, etc.) and be one with all that he/she is in presence with. (Not having ever been apart: see 1. and 2. above.)

However, if one does not apply these basic tools (principles) to all that he/she sees, hears, reads or studies, the essential elements are not available to unravel the mysterious equations which the enquiry presents.

Ask yourself, with the questions that you can frame in words: "Is there a dualistic *proposition* here?" (e.g.: "enlightened," "unenlightened").

Ask yourself: "Is there a subject/object relationship here?" (e.g.: "me," "enlightenment").

If you can recognize that dualistic thinking (divisive), "and/or" subject/object relationship (separative), is inherent in your *proposition*, you can assume that you are not apprehending the matter from the Absolute perspective that the teacher would encourage.

Where there is division, there is conflict. To dissolve conflict and confusion, simply notice where there is a presumption of separation in the matter under consideration. Ask yourself: From the standpoint of "one without a second," does such a division exist in actuality? When it is realized that it doesn't, conflict ends.

$$0 + 0 = 0$$

Immanent means Inherent

"All that you're liable to read in the Bible, it ain't necessarily so."
- Gershwin

Jesus was born and died in a land that was subjugated by the Romans, who (like the Greeks before them) promulgated the myth about gods who inhabit a kingdom above the clouds.

Jesus was said, by his disciples, to have ascended bodily into the heavens. When Christianity had been established in Rome, Michelangelo was commissioned to paint the ceiling of the Sistine Chapel; you've seen pictures of the naked male archetype almost in connection with the hand of God—this bearded old man who, to this day, represents the Creator in the imagination of most every Christian, "father of Christ" in Heaven.

This anthropomorphic image suggests the separate entities of "you and Him," not even capable of connection in space. (At the same time, religionists can schizophrenically hold a contradictory "belief": that the Supreme Being is omnipresent.)

This image, of a god somehow removed from earth, has so infiltrated our conditioning that it is difficult for most people in the West to think of Absolute presence as *immanent* (another word which Christians profess is descriptive of God). The idea that "you" and the "divine" are patently separate is at the bedrock of orthodox religion. But the promotion of this doctrine has influenced even those who do *not* consider themselves religious— or, conversely, *even* those who consider themselves "spiritual," in a non-theistic sense.

Because of this pandemic societal conditioning, even the seeker of cosmic "Oneness" can somehow envision himself as being *outside* of, or apart from, that ubiquitous condition. And this is the very perception which nonduality addresses itself to, and attempts to counter.

Simply put, "you" and the "divine" Absolute presence are not in any way separate; in fact, so inseparable as to constitute one indivisible actuality. For those who can surmount the conception of a distant "God in heaven," this is the essence of the realization which has been called both God-consciousness and enlightenment.

God does not *have* being; God *is* being. Your *being* is God as *presence*.

Real Equanimity

"Thank you for your clarification regarding the equanimity with which 'ultimate' reality regards all experiences. I was intrigued by your suggestion that 'bliss is another word for that equanimity.' That insight has shifted my orientation to ultimate reality! When I dropped the preconceived expectation that my true nature was a feeling of unshakeable joy, a burden was lifted. And I realized it was not only not a feeling of joy, it is not a *feeling* at all.

"Upon reflection, I can see that since the Absolute is unspeakable, many times the words peace and joy are used as pointers. My mind turned these *pointers* into concrete *descriptions of feelings*."

Congratulations, your contemplation of these matters has been worthwhile. The peace and joy, even bliss, which is spoken of is not some polarized status—such as its being in opposition to some other status. It is when desire for any *particular* status has evaporated that true peace—and the joy of knowing that it's present—prevails.

And this "choicelessness," as you've now noticed, is not itself a special status or a compensatory, or satisfying, *feeling*. It is merely a matter of being present with 'what is'—whether the 'what is' happens to be, at the moment, on the positive end of the spectrum or the negative end. Being "aware, choicelessly" is the *equanimity* which is the condition of the Self-realized.

From the standpoint of one's previous dissatisfaction and discontent with 'what is,' this all-*inclusive* awareness may be described (if necessary) as bliss.

Choiceless, of course, does not mean that we become incapable of operating in the relative, material world: you still choose organic granola, at the supermarket, rather than Sugar Puffs.

Part of the choiceless condition is the relinquishing of the idea as to how one (or others) *ought* to behave. In other words, the Self-realized person does not hold some imagined ideal to which one (dualistically) compels oneself ("I should be more like Suzuki Roshi." Well, you're *not* Suzuki Roshi.)

The choicelessness primarily is applied to the "shoulds, woulds and coulds" in our daily experience. Rather than "I should do" this, or "I should not do" that, it's a matter of being aware of what the organism is actually doing (or saying, or thinking)—or what others are actually doing—as compared to what we might wish the reality was *instead*: that is, being choiceless (as you said) "about how various things" are being expressed by ultimate reality, and not having *expectations* which undermine equanimity.

Choices/Conflict

Your interpretation is correct.

We make comparisons: "this" (better) as opposed to "that" (worse), and desires then arise. ("I want to retain this, and eliminate that.") Where *choices* are made, a relative (or dualistic) situation is being engaged. Where there is a sense of division—as in attachment to the outcome of a particular choice—there will be conflict.

The fundamental seat of conflict is embodied in the "I" as opposed to "not-I" perspective. Where the sense of being an individual, separate, "I" prevails, there will be conflict.

The dissolution of such conflict comes in recognizing the truth which nonduality suggests. The I-thought can disassemble into the source of its Being. Then the outcome of any choice, being made by this particular manifestation of the Source of all activity (this "person"), is seen to ultimately make no difference. "Clinging" to (the importance of) choices, ceases. One observes the choices that are being made, and their outcome, without concern, without feelings of conflict.

This is what is called "choiceless awareness."

Nothing Gained, Nothing Lost

One of the most common matters raised for teachers of nonduality is the one in your query. It represents a difficulty in grasping the fundamental thrust of the teachings.

What is the essence of the nondual teachings?: there are not two actual things, only the singular, absolute, ultimate Reality. There are not two states of existence, which come and go independently of the overarching Reality.

You have a preference for what state is present in consciousness. When the state which you deem preferable appears to be present, you say "I am in the (awakened) zone." When an alternate state of awareness is noticed, you determine "I am not now in the (awakened) zone." Is it not obvious that such a conception is the crux of dualistic thinking? Do you suppose an enlightened sage concerns herself with *whatever* state of awareness happens to be observed? To the jnani, there are "not two." To the *a*jnani, there is "this state" of awareness and "that state" of awareness—or more.

The jnani has no conception of having acquired anything—nothing has been added to what she always already has: therefore, not anything is ever lost. "Gee whiz, I was one with ultimate Reality awhile ago. Now I'm not.": if she were to say that, she would not have *truly* recognized her inseparability from ultimate Reality, at any time.

The subtlety of these teachings is that even when what appears to be a lack of "awareness" is what is present, that too is the ultimate Reality in its *ever*-present form. When the "non-me" awareness is noticed, that is It; when the "me" awareness is noticed, that is It. Every apparent "difference" is a manifestation of *That*.

Your present condition—whatever and whenever it is—is the condition of the ultimate Reality that the "seeker" would be in touch with. The seeker *is* the sought, and vice versa.

THE ABSOLUTE AND I

Of the many dozen of persons I've had one-on-one discussions with, your questions are typical. And the vast majority, like you (and I), were seekers for decades and had practiced meditation.

Most everyone who has any kind of a "practice" supposes that if they practice correctly and diligently, they will at some future time experience the Absolute presence.

Every spiritual or religious tradition asserts that the Absolute is omnipresent. Therefore, it *must* be here (wherever you are) now (whenever you are). The *notion* that sustains your practice can only lead your attention away from the Absolute presence.

If the Absolute is truly omnipresent, as the enlightened sages maintain, there is no way in which you can possibly be *apart* from that which is *always everywhere*. We do not come to "encounter" the Absolute, as if "I" and "It" are suddenly to become co-joined (despite the fact that this is your assumption). We can only *recognize* that the Absolute presence which we seek is utterly *inescapable*.

As long as you think of "I" on the one hand (a separate form) and the Absolute presence on the other hand (a form which the seeker is apart from), there will be *separation*. Transcend your conceptions of "this" and "that"—dualistic subject/object perception—and what remains is the *non*-dual awareness that is being sought.

Do not expect that Self-realization, or awakening, will be a "dramatic event." (When you awaken from sleep in the morning, it is not a dramatic event.) Phenomenal conditions or experiences come and go; what you are seeking is undramatically always ever present—it is not a "special experience."

Lastly, *because* Absolute presence is always ever present, abiding in awareness of it is effortless. We exert effort when we hope to gain something; you cannot gain something which you have, in actuality, never been apart from.

So, as long as you continue in the mode of "practice," you may have further "insights." But complete nondual clarity is not a matter of periodic "glimpses," it is a matter of seeing, once and for all, to the bottom of the (bottomless) well. Seeking *ends*, and "insights" are superfluous, because you recognize that "I" and Absolute presence are merely two ways of saying the same thing.

No Need for Beliefs

Your response makes it clear to me that you have carefully read my letter. I could not expect that you would comprehend all, of what I have to say, the first time around. So I appreciate your descriptions of the parts of the message which you *do*, at this point, understand. I want to reply to a couple of things.

First: you use the words "belief," and "believe." Belief is defined as: "to suppose to be true; such as a premise or theory."

Unlike other viewpoints, nothing that I say to you is to be "supposed to be true." I am relating to you what you can discover *for yourself* to be an actual first-hand—not second-hand—perception of the truth of *your own* existence. This *truth* cannot be *far* from *you*: it *must* be HERE, *NOW*. Since it is a *reality* in the *very moment* that you are reading this, what could possibly be *believed*? Do you need to believe that your nose is as present as your face?

You spoke of a "challenge" to your (present) understanding. I suggest that the nondual perspective will prove to be a challenge to your *beliefs*. Put *all* beliefs aside, at least temporarily, while you consider a *realization* that *transcends* a *need* for belief.

You say that, in the past, you've "spoken of oneness," but that your behavior was "contradictory," yet that it is your intention to take the *expression* of oneness "into daily life." And thus you will continue an "in depth inventory" and examine the "discord caused by misinformation," by analyzing some of the views presently held.

Basically, all that lies at the root of commonly-held misunderstanding is the divisive thought process that we are *conditioned* to, in our *self-centered* culture.

As infants, we are taught one word at a time. *Each* word divides, excludes, some "object" from some "other" object. "Mother" is mother because she's "not father." This process has a *practical* value, in the realm of (relative) *objects*. It is okay to play with a "lizard," but fatal to play with a "rattlesnake": a useful distinction.

But words, by their nature, set up dualistic oppositions. There is, most notably in this connection, "man" and "God": we may say that "I" am in the world, "God" is in heaven.

It is *distinctions* like these which both form and are formed by our *divisive* thought process. Granted, there is a practical use for this process, on the "survival" level of our material existence. But if we are to think in terms of "oneness," we must recognize that there has to be the capability for a different form of inductive process: a type of recognition which *supersedes* divisiveness.

You put your finger on this crucial understanding, when you commented: "I must begin to view my grasp of Oneness, instead of having to balance everything with an opposite."

What the sages are telling us is that, yes, on the relative (worldly) level, there are opposites: hot/cold, night/day, etc. *But*, for example, is night divided from (as separate entities) day? Is the (relative) "I," in the world, *separate* from the ground of Being, out of which all relative things are said to arise? Or are all things merely "different" aspects, in appearance, of the same underlying condition or "source"?

86

If there were no thoughts of "I" as an entity, and "God" as a "different" entity, would there be any thoughts or concerns about "separation" from God; or, similarly, "unity" with God?

This is what the sages are saying: *see through* the divisive nature of our dualistic thought process, and all *dilemmas* disappear.

Otherwise, as you can discover for yourself, wherever there is *division*, conflict will ensue. Put another way, to remove or resolve conflict, the divisive mind-set will need to be put to rest.

That is the virtue, or value, of the nondual realization: freedom from "suffering," as Buddha would put it.

So, if you get over the *idea* of coming to "unity" with the ground of Being, you simultaneously surmount its opposite proposition—that you were (ever) "apart" from it, from the beginning. It is as a consequence of *this* recognition that it is said, "There is nowhere you need to *go*, nothing you need to *do*." No "disciplines" *need* to be followed; not anything needs to be supposed or "believed." The fact of your "oneness" will be *self-evident*.

No More Floor-Painting

You write: "Your advice about not putting a lot of reality into any established self-image is well taken." And you seem to at least be hearing the point that comparing and labeling what manifests in the 'what is' (*could be, should be, better/worse*, etc.) leads into the gilded trap of self-improvement.

And you seem to have heard the message in the monograph about "letting go of the compulsion to emerge (from our questing) with an intact ego and an ideal outcome." That is, you seem to have heard the latter part, anyway: to have in mind any *ideal* outcome is to set yourself up for dissatisfaction with 'what is.'

But have you attended to the first part: that we do not emerge, in the nondual realization, with an intact ego—the "I," the self-image you spoke of? The sages are not advising us to "not put a lot of reality into" the I-concept: they are urging us to put *no* reality into this illusive conception of "individual" existence.

The matter of the folly of self-improvement efforts is not simply that it is a fruitless attempt but that it is empty of meaning. From the standpoint of the realized, there is in reality no separate self to whom any such benefits can accrue: all of this results from maya (illusion).

This is the petard for many who seek enlightenment: enlightenment will not represent an improvement in your self-centered condition; it will mean the absence of the idea that the self is somehow separate from the totality of all that is: thus the Absolute is rendered as "Self."

Your ending questions arise from a premise that there is "someone," some person to whom the answers apply. Now that you comprehend that self-improvement is a source of dissatisfaction and conflict (rather than a panacea for it), turn attention (attend) to the core of the spiritual teachings: you have never really been who or what you believe yourself to be. Assuming that the sages are telling us the truth about this, exactly what is meant?

It's *why* "the floor never needed painting in the first place."

BANKEI'S PROPOSAL

The first couple of paragraphs, of your writing on "one's eternal nature," makes sense. You speak of "going beyond duality...what we are to contemplate is beyond all limitations...resting in our natural state...In this state, nothing is lacking."

You also write, "It is our conceptualizing that prevents us from experiencing [this]....It's really very simple; and if one is looking for something complex, one isn't going to find it."

All this is basically summarized by your quote of Zen master Bankei: "Put yourself in the state of mind you were in when you came out of your mother's womb."

Then you advise a couple of things which you propose that a person needs to do, so this "natural or eternal state" not "be easily missed." The first directive is described as an "approach" to it, and then there's "the next step." You suggest that otherwise "I doubt that one can be in it at all times." And, you say, "one must first get a glimpse of this state."

The condition that you're referring to is presumably the "natural" state of the freshly-birthed baby (as per Bankei).

Is there something that the baby, resting in its natural state, needs to do in order not to "miss" it? How would the baby go about "approaching" it, "step" by step? What would "prevent" the baby from experiencing it "at all times"? Why would the baby need to "first get a glimpse of the state"—*resting* in it beyond all duality and limitations, with nothing lacking?

Doesn't my second paragraph, here, indicate that you are not taking your own suggestion to follow Bankei's proposal?

What does a baby—or you—need to do in order to be in a natural state, or eternal nature, except for resting in it?

"It's really very simple, if one is not looking for something complex."

PURSUING THE SACRED OX

The Ten Oxherding Pictures were created in 12ᵗʰ Century China, presumably for the teaching of Buddhist enlightenment to the illiterate. But they were accompanied by prose commentary, plus a verse in poetry (both excerpted here).

The Ox represents the Absolute, as well as the Self-realization of it. In the first picture is a young boy; in the final picture is an old man. So, while the implication is of the progression of a novice to a master, the development in each picture does not necessarily apply to every wayfarer in every particular detail. In general, the point is that enlightenment is an *immediate* realization (picture 4), and the balance of the pictures describe ways in which one gets *accustomed*, or acclimated, to the nondual perspective. Picture 10, in particular, relates to the *living* of it. (A worthwhile version of the text and pictures can be found in *Three Pillars of Zen*, by Philip Kapleau.)

1.

Seeking the Ox shows a boy on a trail in the forest, carrying a bridle. The first line of commentary advises us, "The Ox has never *really* gone astray, so why *search* for it?" The poem describes: "he treads many bypaths...heart-weary, he carries on his search." We're given a strong hint where the Absolute (as Ox) is to be discovered: "At evening, he hears cicadas chirping in the trees."

We've been conditioned to perceive in terms of "subject" separate from "object": "me" apart from the "Ox." Feeling a sense of division, we seek to heal this rift. It's possible to discover that the observer (me) and the observed (Ox) have never been apart from the beginning. That which hears (boy) and that which is heard (cicadas) are essentially the same. We will experience conflict until our dualistic mindset is transcended.

2

Finding the Tracks shows the boy focusing his attention on indicative clues. "Through the sutras and *teachings*, he spies the tracks of the Ox. He has been advised...that *each* and every thing is a *manifestation* of the Self....He sees in a tentative way." Poem: "Even the deepest gorges of the topmost mountains can't hide this Ox's nose—which reaches right to heaven." Another hint to the location of the Absolute: from earth to the heavens, there's no place where it *can't* be found.

He is committed, now, to following through on his intent to pursue the truth of his ultimate nature. But he's still thinking in terms of an "I" who will become one with "That." He hasn't yet recognized that if he transcends the subject (I) *and* the object (That), what remains is the nondual Reality.

3.

First glimpse of the Ox. He has entered a clearing where he comprehends that the Absolute must be *present* in the *same* place that he is: this very day, this very place; he cannot possibly be *separate* from it. Hint: "If he will but listen intently to *everyday* sounds, he will come to realization—and, at that instant 'see' the very Source. The six senses [in Buddhism, awareness is a sense] are no different from this true Source. In *every* activity, the Source is manifestly *present*...that which is *seen* is *identical* with the true Source." Poem: "A nightingale warbles on a twig; the sun shines on undulating willows. *There* stands the Ox. *Where* could he *hide*?!"

The seeking comes to an end with the recognition that the seeker *is* what is being sought. There is no need for "unity," because there was not disunity from the start.

4.

Catching the Ox. The supposition of being apart from the omnipresent Absolute has ended. He now truly understands what "nonduality" means. His habitual, dualistic mode of perception may persist, but he now sees it for what it is: separative, the root of division. Yet it continues to have a necessary, practical expediency in terms of coping with the relative, material world. It too is an aspect of the manifested buddha-Mind. With nondual awareness, he need not exclude discursive thought, but he needs to be mindful when dualistic propositions predominate in awareness.

"Today, he actually *grasped* the Ox...weaning it from its old [wayward] habits is not easy." He will want to be attentive whenever he's neglected to notice that all is One.

5.

Taming the Ox. Poem: "Properly tended...it willingly follows its master." The young man is shown leading the Ox (which he had bridled in the previous picture), as he becomes more accustomed to its Presence. The "I-thought"—the primary dualistic "self" distinction which is at the root of divisive mentation—is subsiding. Whenever notions concerning "me" or "mine" appear on the screen of consciousness, there is present awareness that, in actuality, there is no separate entity such as "I": all that is, including the perceived "person," is in essence merely a manifestation of the ultimate Source.

Even his wayward thoughts, he comprehends, need not be an object of concern. He has transcended contentious ideas concerning "right, wrong," "better, worse." He has abandoned the notion that anything ought to be other than what it is—what it "could" be, or "should" ideally be. And even *if* such thoughts as *these* arise, he impartially witnesses whatever condition is momentarily present without concluding that the actuality ought to be otherwise. Prose: "Enlightenment brings the realization that even such thoughts...arise from our True-nature."

6.

Riding the Ox, so connected that there is no "he" or "it" as conceived entities. His nondual awareness is as established as had, before, been his dualistic perspective. His attentive awareness is stabilized in every present moment, and is *effortless*—like breathing. "The struggle is over....Astride the Ox's back, he gazes serenely," not concerned with where the ride may take him. Poem: "In his heart, profound *tranquility* prevails. This Ox requires not a blade of grass." He needs follow no "practices," or observe any "disciplines."

7.

Ox Forgotten, Self Alone. The man's self-centeredness has disappeared; his self-image has evaporated. "I am" is the substance of his identity; no longer does he think in terms of "I am this," or "I am that." He acknowledges simply that the Absolute is animating his—and every "other"—organism. Personal ambition and the indulgence in hedonistic pleasures are absent. He no longer concerns himself with what he "ought" to do, or "ought not" to do.

"In the Dharma, there is no two-ness. The Ox is his primal-nature: this he has now recognized." Poem: "Only on the Ox was he able to come Home. Lo, the Ox is now vanished." There is just a solitary man in the picture, sitting quietly. "Yonder, beneath the thatched roof, his idle whip and idle rope are lying."

8.

Both Ox and Self Forgotten. The picture is the symbol of emptiness, a thin circle devoid of content. The identification of the organism with the Absolute is now so much second-nature that one need not even reflect on it. It is clear that this which would contemplate the nature of the divine is the divine itself. All things being the divine, nothing is special. Whether a person is "enlightened" or "unenlightened" has no real meaning in nonduality. The sage is aware that, ultimately, nothing really matters. "Delusive feelings have perished, and ideas of 'holiness' too have vanished." He is so empty of person-hood (or even Buddha-hood) that one "can discern in him no specific quality."

9.

Returning to the Source is a picture of the forest in its everyday natural state. The implication is that this is now what is unambiguously seen by our Wayfarer, without his making *distinctions* between "this" and "that."

"He observes the waxing and waning of life in the world, while abiding unassertively." He regards the fleeting panorama of all life forms as simply "manifestation of the Source.... Alone, he observes things endlessly *changing*." With choiceless awareness, he has no concern for what comes and goes.

10.

Entering the marketplace (with empty hands). Depicted is an aging man, wearing not even the robes of a Buddhist. If anything, you'd view him as a hobo. "He goes his own way, making no attempt to follow the steps of earlier sages. Carrying a gourd [for sipping liquor], he strolls into the market. Leaning on his staff [due to the liquor], he returns home. He leads inn-keepers and fish mongers in the Way of the Buddha." Poem: "Without recourse to mystic powers, withered trees he swiftly brings to bloom."

So, viewing the world as it really is—without having *ideas* about it—he lives "in" it, though not in the customary manner.

He is free to act as he pleases, without notions of "proper" or "improper." While he participates in the mundane world, that is not where his attention is centered. Thus free of strife, he is capable of revealing to others how separative concepts are to be transcended. He never claims to be a "healer," yet he puts an end to the anxieties of those who are confused; and the example of his unegoic behavior is the way he leads.

YE OF LITTLE FAITH

Darien:

Scientists, such as physicists, are hard-headed pragmatists. They do not base their propositions on principles (so-called natural laws) which cannot be demonstrated, at will, in the laboratory. At the most fundamental level of scientific knowledge, it is understood that every single subatomic particle—which is the "fabric of the universe," as one book title has it—knows what it "is supposed to do" (or not do). Scientists say that, as yet, they do not know *why* this is so; they can only, so far, say that it *is* so. This is "consciousness" at its most elementary level.

When your body begins to decay, every cell will, in its subatomic essence, know precisely what to do. It will regroup with other subatomic particles in another "intelligent" form. The point is that consciousness is in every minute part of your body (thus, the body functions in deep sleep)—even though you may not *suppose* that it has something to do with "your" perception. But when "you" and your body and senses and "mind" are no longer functioning, consciousness remains as it always has—unaffected. It is not *your* consciousness: but then, it never *has* been "your consciousness." You are in consciousness, consciousness is not *in* "you."

A Risky Business

Although *every* great sage has said it at least by implication, it is reported to have been clearly stated in the most memorable satsang in human history; the sermon on the mount. According to the gospel called Matthew (6:24), Jesus said, "You cannot serve both God and money," after saying, "Where your treasure is, there will your heart be also."

Instead he said, about even the most *basic* material needs, "Seek ye first the kingdom of god and its righteousness, and (or, then) all these things will be added unto you." His next seven words described not only the way he lived, but the way he advised everyone of the hundreds of persons within hearing to live *their* lives: "Take no thought for the morrow." Explicit enough?

Possibly the most memorable thing that Peace Pilgrim ever said was, "Ask (yourself) not what can I get, but what can I give."

From my own experience, I would say that if you took seriously (as was intended) the pronouncements in the previous three paragraphs, you will discover for yourself how basic needs will be met.

Was Jesus serious about urging the committed not to worry about money? When he sent his twelve closest disciples out to minister on their own, he "commanded them that they should take nothing for their journey.... No bread, no money in their purse" (Mark 6:8). Reportedly all survived (Luke 9:10).

Was Peace Pilgrim serious about thinking in terms of giving, rather than getting? She walked 25,000 miles (before she stopped counting) with only the clothes she wore and a few items in her pockets. She was once asked, "Did people in passing cars ever throw anything at you, while you walked along the road?"

96

"Yes."

"What did they throw?"

"Fistfuls of dollar bills."

The next church she came to, she dropped these in the collection box.

"And I truthfully tell you that—without ever asking for anything—I have been supplied with everything needed," (over a period of 28 years!)

Ox-Herding as Ongoing

The unfolding which the Ten Pictures are illustrating:

1. Dissatisfaction is all that we have ever known; it is this dissatisfaction which leads us to initially question, "What else is there?" The pursuit of such questions can be motivated by sincere intent, but at this point are often instigated by ambition: the ambition to escape the meaninglessness of life. And so, at the outset of the search for an "alternative" is a "gaining idea"; and wherever there is an idea of gain, there will be an attempt to control—for fear of loss. In conflict and confused, what will this searcher find but confusion and conflict?

2. But even with tentative, experimental application of the teachings of truth, one observes the unmistakable ending of fragmentary conflict: one's eyes begin to widen. Though one may still be needlessly reliant on guidance, he directly begins to see broad—astounding—implications in the simplest of insights. There are now cherished moments of liberating

transcendence. But he still has not answered for himself, "What else is there?"

3. There is now thoroughgoing commitment, if he could but understand what it is to be thorough-going. In any event, his life is now being ordered by unforeseen priorities. However, he is still in thrall to his conditioning, to conformity, and to habitual reactions such as doubt. His head, and line of vision, have not yet pushed above duality. Though *ambition* has dissipated, certain *ideas* are still retained.

4. The last *ideal* has died, in the light of attention; there is, therefore, now no hope of escape. All dualities are now the same: empty of meaning. Whether in pleasure or in pain, he recognizes that there can be nowhere—neither here nor there—that It is not. He tries to appear normal.

5. Whether with effort or without, he now cannot lose it: "gain" and "loss" are just words. "Realization" is merely the attentive living of life; and there is wood to be chopped, water to be carried. Contemplation is part of every mundane movement, unceasingly. Who is it that watches what?

6. The self (and its thoughts) now in its proper place, action—unlike previous reactions—is without the predictable subject/object stimulation. In the absence of the sense of self, one has no need for justification, and one answers to no distant teacher. Even the security of the *teachings* is relinquished.

7. While his contemplative life has the appearance of normality, it has nothing in common with conformity. Acting out of

emptiness, he has no encouragement for those who hope. There has been an "about face" from the discontent and agitation which was felt from the outset, and his utterance is the utterance of simplicity.

8. The body is but a form, the "self" is an idea, even "consciousness" is limited to a concept. Only one thing could possibly be identified, but its description is not distinguishable from its describer. What is "bliss," when there is not a word from the start? How is experience to be recognized, where there is no cause nor effect? Can "illusion" even be *illusion*?

9. There being no division, what need there be improved upon? There is but one actuality: not lacking one thing, it is in the embrace of all that is or isn't.

10. The finger that points to the moon is one's life; the pointing is without intention. No one need ask anything of a simpleton: he has nothing of his *own* to give, anyway. Those grapes in his basket were plucked from the roadside vine, and even they are his only for the moment.

"Take Up Thy Bed..."

For some time, the Indian nondual sage Nisargadatta—who spoke the dialect Marathi—had an English-speaking translator, Ramesh Balsekar. With the increase of the Westerners who sought out the teacher, Ramesh became a steady conduit of the teachings. As a consequence, he began to intuit what the sage would say—thus discovering that he himself was a realized being.

Lest there be any doubt, when Nisargadatta could no longer speak, due to throat cancer, he said finally to Ramesh, "Speak for me!"

After his teacher died, Ramesh continued the lineage. While in a period of teaching in Santa Barbara, a drug-and-alcohol-dependent young man was invited, by a friend, to a satsang. Wayne Liquorman (!) became so engrossed that he virtually sat at the feet of Ramesh for weeks—finally realizing his *own* awakening. But in the period before that (though having already abandoned his addictive ways), he lamented to Ramesh about his past debauchery. Ramesh pointed out, "It took that to bring you here."

His point was that there are pursuits, or activities, which don't get us to our destination but do put us in a position to make the trip. Buddha, for example, spent years in futile, extreme, exhausting ascetic practices—leading nearly to death—before he had been brought to a point of readiness for enlightenment.

Buddhism may or may not take *you* there, but it can ready you for the catalyst which does. Christianity may not take you there, but for some it has readied them for the epiphany which did. Likewise, with such things as the Course in Miracles, 12-Step Program and other inspirational disciplines.

Some of the vehicles which don't result in a profound awakening are *nearly* effective—but never quite nearly *enough*. Thus, some adherents spend their life on the brink of an awakening (Zen is particularly concerned with this situation), but still die in "ignorance" (unrealized).

The sutras, the scriptures, and the messages are suitable for those who are satisfied to take their authority second-hand. But for those who will settle for nothing less than Truth from the source of their own being, these crutches must eventually be laid aside.

It was not until Buddha abandoned his "teachers" and "practices" that he experienced enlightenment. It was not until Jesus forsook John the Baptist and spent forty days in contemplative solitude that he emerged as "one who speaks with authority." It was not until Krishnamurti renounced Theosophy that he was free to speak of a realization that relied on no tradition or doctrine.

"Truth is a *path-less* land," K said (not because it had a clever sound, but because he had learned from experience). Be a light unto yourself, Jesus admonished. Know thyself, Buddha advised.

When clarity is present, no book, bible or text need be relied upon for guidance. The source of all cosmic wisdom is as available to you as directly as it has been for anyone else in recognition of it.

The teachings of Buddha, Jesus, Krishnamurti et al were not intended to produce Buddhists, Christians, "followers" etc. They were intended to provoke *direct* experience of transcendental consciousness—*nothing less*.

Chattering Mind

As creatures, or organisms, we live in a relative, material world. The body needs to be fed, sheltered, and so on. As a consequence, on the physical level, we have to relate to the practical realities. You could be the saint most idealized, and yet this would still be the case.

So, on this level, Julie, the "me" does not disappear: the awakened person still answers to her name, pays her bills (or doesn't), etc.

Thus, it is not like there is no longer ever a consciousness of being "I"; it is that the awakened person does not lose sense of "who" (or what) this is which is *considered* to *be* "I."

Therefore the I-thought will, as you say, continue to appear and disappear in your awareness. We have been conditioned to this I-centered conception for many decades. Even after Self-realization, this conditioning does not dissipate overnight. However, with the presence of Absolute awareness, the recognition becomes—on the appearance of the I-thought (as isolating identification)—that the actuality is that the essential nature of the "I" is That, the Absolute (or Self, as it is also said).

Secondly. Prior to Self-realization, there is an I, on the *one* hand, who desires to end "mind chatter," on the *other* hand (subject/object: duality).

With Absolute awareness, there is observation of the appearance of mind chatter, without *concern* for whatever *is* factually present.

Where there is no I with attachment to preferences ("This mind chatter needs to stop"), what becomes of the volume of mind chatter? Dissatisfaction with what is present is what makes up the bulk of it. Much of this dissatisfaction is a consequence of (dualistic) comparisons. If you compare yourself to some presumed saint, this idealized expectation will lead to the dissatisfaction which you called "suffering."

For the awakened, there is neither "self" nor "other": dualistic comparison comes to an end.

Where, in Absolute awareness, there is "not two," preferences (aside from those practical and necessary choices to be made, as in paragraph one) also end: it makes no difference whether there is mind chatter or no chatter.

In other words, where the I is recognized to be a fictitious proposition, all of these other problems will be swept off the table with one profound realization. The I-thought is at the root of the problems.

VIEWING THE WORLD

The word *nothing* actually means "no thing; nonexistent; void of meaning." A *thing* is "an entity, distinguishable from all others." What creates the difference between one thing and another thing is the definition which we have assigned to each: "it is *this*, because it is not *that*." We conclude that each defined thing, having a "meaning," *exists*; a separate form, construction, concept or entity thus distinguishable from other things which we deem to exist. It is by this conscious intellectual process that each thing is invested with reality by us. (In fact, the word *real* is derivative of the Latin word *res*, which means "thing.")

We have a word that defines "the totality of all *things* that exist": *universe*. In other words, all of the things which we can cognitively define is what comprises the universe. Although our *world* is not separate from the universe, we have an exclusive distinction for it: this particular planet and every thing that accompanies it. So, the universe, world and all else "exist" *as such* because our cognized locutions have defined their "reality."

If our defining minds had never made their appearance, what could be said to be real? Well, no thing. Without at least one capable mind to define what is "real," existent, as contrasted to what is "unreal," or nonexistent, such designations as real or unreal have no relevance when applied to the universe (or anything it contains). In fact, the universe does not exist *itself* as any conceivable thing, in the absence of a mind to specially identify it.

So, from this standpoint, the world is not real, no matter how many minds conceive it to be so. The world is dependent upon our conception of it. No one to determine so, no "world" that "exists."

NO SELF TO BE SEEN

The (17 syllable) haiku is an amalgam of Zen and poetry: the noticing of Zen's principles in an ordinary scene or circumstance.

Zen masters, traditionally, have written a "death poem," when that development seems to be immanent, in which they attempt to summarize their teachings.

A particular poem, by the revered 13th century Japanese Zen master Eihei Dogen (who has stated "To forget the self is to be enlightened"), may or may not have been intended as a death poem—but it has perfectly summarized the basics of nondual teachings, in only six more words than a haiku has syllables.

No wind,

no waves,

the empty boat

is flooded with moonlight.

Attaining this way,

one's daily life

is the realization

of ultimate reality.

No wind. The absence of mental agitation; the confused and conflicted thinking patterns which infect the self-centered person, before enlightenment.

No waves. The absence of divisive behavior or activities which are a consequence of the separative distinctions inevitable in the dualistic perspective.

The empty boat. The organism persists, though absent a helmsman who attempts to steer. With no wind and no waves, this vacated shell now has ceased to rock to and fro.

Is flooded with moonlight. In Buddhism, the moon and moonlight are a metaphor for the nondual teachings and the ageless benefit of such illumination.

These teachings are paradoxical: although flooded with prajna (Absolute clarity), that which is flooded is nevertheless empty. Empty *because* enlightenment is the realization that (as a Zen patriarch, who preceded Dogen, has said) "there is Nothing from the start."

Attending this way. This "way" is absent a *way*: Krishnamurti is perhaps best remembered for the phrase, "Truth is a *pathless* land"; there is no "way" that leads you to encounter the Truth that is ultimate reality: you are inescapably immersed in it.

Therefore to expectantly hope to "attain" a Truth which is living you, is to imagine that a self exists separately from a Reality whose presence needs to be "gained." As nondual teachings consistently emphasize, "The seeker *is* the sought."

One's daily life. "Nothing special," Zen masters like to say. Dream up an ideal person; conceptualize this being's ideal behavior; imagine the ideal affect which this saint's blessings will bestow on mankind. Now, recognize that this ambitious destination is not a port sought by an empty boat. No wind and no waves results in quiet. An absence of self-interest results in an attentive day-to-day existence notable only for its freedom from strife.

Is the realization. *Is*; not "will be—if you achieve some conceived state or goal, at some future date." The "realization" is that in this very moment you are not—cannot be—apart from the ever-present Omnificence which is sought. An empty boat need haul no cargo to be flooded with moonlight.

Of ultimate reality. The word "ultimate" is sometimes used in the sense of "furthest"; but it really indicates "final," as fundamental: the dictionary says "beyond which it is impossible to go." Ultimate reality is inescapable; therefore, it is not "far" from "you": you and it are already One—whether that "is the realization" or not. But realization that this is the actual Truth is called "attaining this Way," this way of being flooded by moonlight.

"You Are the World" —Krishnamurti

As you said in your query, yes, "You are an object in your consciousness until you come to know your true nature."

From the time you were a child, you looked out upon all the things in the world as "not-me"—as *objects* observed by your self (as subject). Therefore, counter-posing all these *other* objects, was another object in your conception, your "self."

This is what Buddhism means by "dependent co-arising." The conception that there is such a thing as a world (*apart* from you) arises mutually with the conception that there is a self, or "you" (*apart* from the world). It is in your mind in which such dualities are originated. Just as the idea that there is such a thing as "right" depends upon the counter-conception that there is such a thing as "wrong," so does your conception of "you" depend on your conception that there is some thing that is not you (such as a world).

This is easy to understand, and it's meant to lead you to awareness of the duality and divisiveness in your conceptions. Also to lead you to consider: if the objectification of self and all other things in the world is misleading, or false, what then is the truth?

As you say: "It seems to me that when you remove the 'you', the perspective changes; and the world (as we knew it) no longer exists." That's an accurate observation, on your part.

Krishnamurti liked to say, "You are the world." Or, as you're putting it: without you, there *is* no world. That, definitely, is a change in perspective—from the dualistic (me/world) to the nondual (void, regarding both objects).

This is clearly your condition in the "primal state," which we experience each night in deep sleep: the 'I' vanishes, and the entire "content of its consciousness" (which are, of course, not two different things).

AWAKENING TO THE INSEPARABLE

Madhukar Thompson's commentary about the teachings of Ramesh Balsekar is an example of why clarity is of value concerning the relationship of the relative to the Absolute (and even, further, the value of the realization that there can *be* no relationship, in the *context* of the Absolute.) If there were such a thing as a "key" to enlightenment, I would venture to say that it involves this understanding—the comprehension of what the sages *mean* when they *refer* to That, the ineffable Absolute.

Sagacious teachers speak to the listener (at least at the outset) on the listener's level of understanding, not necessarily representing the *teacher's* level of understanding. To those who (at least at the outset) envision only that which is *relative*, they speak in relative terms. To those who recognize the Absolute, they speak from the standpoint of the *Absolute*. To those in transition, they may make alternate references, as a means of comparative illustration.

It is because of seemingly paradoxical—or "contradictory"— statements that sages are universally regarded (by the unrealized) as confounding. The situation is similar to hearing a joke which employs a double-entendre, and not "getting it" because you don't understand one of the two (or both) words that express the wit.

Thus Thompson relates that he early felt that Balsekar "contradicts himself repeatedly," later coming to acknowledge that Balsekar "switches between two distinct...standpoints: one which sees things from an individual [relative] perspective, and one which is rooted in the Absolute."

Thompson goes on to say that he eventually recognized that from the former standpoint, "the 'seeker' and the 'guru' exist as individual entities;" and that, from this relative perspective, "it is possible to list certain do's and don'ts regarding...any...aspect of life." This is the perspective of the I who "does" the do's and don'ts.

"This can be contrasted to the Absolute standpoint," he continues, "or what Ramesh refers to as the Enlightened standpoint." Here, "the seeker and...the guru...are understood to be mere... appearances...[manifestations, or 'reflections', of the Absolute] and are therefore illusory."

He begins to "get the joke": *"Aware of these two* standpoints...it [is] possible for us to review [the] teachings, with them in mind—identifying the *context* in which *each aspect* of the teaching is being presented."

Aha: "All aspects of the teaching can be related to *either* from the individual [relative] *or* the Absolute standpoint."

And he now begins to get a sense (by clarifying such distinctions in the teachings) regarding the implications of the specific references. "...in truth, what we really *are* transcends all phenomenal appearance [the relative], including the 'me' and 'God'—both of which are mere phantoms [from the standpoint of the Absolute] that never existed [except in the context of the relative]."

The *relative* is not "all that is": it does not "transcend" the Absolute. For something to be relative, it must be "separate" and measurable (limited) in/as time or space.

The Absolute, the teachers suggest, *is* all that is. It is transcendent of all things, not being transcended by any thing (unlimited), not even time or space. Being all that is, there is no counterpart, no "other"; therefore, there is not something else which it stands in relation to. The Absolute *is* anything which it could possibly be in relation to.

And that includes you.

No Past

You take a seat on a bench, in the twilight, and gaze at the horizon. But your attention is subverted by thoughts about a conversation of just a few minutes before. Recognizing this, you remind yourself that—whatever past you may think you have—this moment, which encompasses you, has no past. It is a fresh, untrammeled moment, free of influence because it is dependent on nothing. The past has no relevance to the vibrancy of this evening sky, you conclude, while thoughts of the earlier conversation evaporate.

Shortly, another concern surfaces in your mind, and you are aware, as quickly, that this thought, too, is relevant to the past and not to the present. You begin to trace back, in your consciousness, to where this distracting thought found its origin—and, in so doing, you carry yourself away from the colorful skyline but along the route of habitual return to the past.

There is not anything in this moment which depends upon your reference to the past for its reality—except for the consciousness of the self, which perishes without unmitigated continuity. The self cannot endure in the moment which knows no past.

BEYOND THE I

Yes, Ramana suggests that you ask the question "Who am I?" This ought to lead you to ponder, "Who is asking the question?" or, "To whom does the answer matter?" You may then begin to query, "Is there an 'I'?" Or, "If I say there is an 'I,' what *knows* this I?" (Hint: it must be something that is "beyond" the I.)

What is the true nature of the I, the "self"—beyond its appearance as a concept in thought? Ramana would say that it is the Self; the capital S designating that it is the something which is not confined to, or limited by, an I.

He does not urge you to "abide as the self" (I), but rather "abide as the Self" which is not limited to any particular, exclusive form (or I).

"I" is a form (in grammar, "first person"); what is "not I"—"you"—another form ("second person"); all else—"it"—the rest of the perceived forms ("third person"). Ramana means, as the "Self," what goes beyond all these forms ("I," "not I," or "it"), what is not confined to, or limited by, form.

Something is aware of "your self," "other selves," and "all the other" appearances. *It* is beyond the limitation of any of these forms. What transcends all forms? Might *that* be your *true* nature?

SAMENESS

Your latest questions revolve around the separativeness that is a product of the subject versus object presumption.

The point here is that if you consider yourself to be an "individual," an entity limited by its form, you (the "subject") will suppose that you are looking out on a world of "objects"—similarly limited to their forms.

The issue you raise is a good example. If you are the subject, your nightly dreams will feature "you" acting in relationship to "other" persons or objects—all as somehow apart from your "self." You will even, on arising, say: *"I* had a *dream"*—as if you were one particular *thing* and the dream (or dreaming) were "another" particular *thing*.

Obviously, dreamer and dream are one: would the dream have appeared without the dreamer? So, the point of this is that the "subject" and "object" illusion is an erroneous division.

And this divisive assumption is, of course, carried over into our waking life: "I am the seer, and nature is what is seen." Is the seeing organism somehow apart from nature?

So, you can comprehend how this leads into the matter of "you" being one *thing* and "choice" or "will" being another *thing*, "objectified" by (the subject) you. Do your choices or willfulness exist without you?

To this comprehension the enlightened masters bring the substance of their discovery: in actuality there are no two things; there is but a single, indivisible reality. Our illusion (based on appearances) of subject versus object is an unenlightened view.

This, of course, leads to your next query. This single indivisible actuality is spoken of, by the sages, as the Unchanging. Being single and indivisible, it represents "one" condition; it is "nondual."

A condition of "change" relies on duality: there is *this* state or situation which becomes another (or *that*) state or situation.

Since the Unchanging condition is recognized, by the enlightened, as the only *actuality*, the appearance of the changing must arise from that actuality. So "change" is an *appearance* that is manifested from the Unchanging.

In other words, just as the dreamer and the dream are in truth one thing, the Unchanging *and* change are in truth one thing.

All appearances (sages would say)—since all but the Unchangeable is impermanent—depend for their "being" on the Unchangeable. So all forms ultimately, at their root, are merely expressions of the same, one thing: both the seer (subject) and seen (object), dreamer and dream world, are the same *one* thing.

"Enlightenment" is when you truly recognize that "you" are that same One thing, and that your essential condition could not actually be otherwise. Then the "subject/object" bias disappears, and the presence of "oneness" is all that remains.

112

As Shankara said, thirteen centuries ago, "All is Brahman" (meaning the Unchangeable, or Absolute). As much as thirty-eight centuries ago, the Vedas said this as "That thou art" (That meaning the Absolute, Brahman, Self, etc.)

The Answer

There is a simple process by which you can answer all questions (these, and any other).

Ramana says there is only one question you need to answer, and it resolves all other questions: Who am I? He indicates that your true *being* is that which is present in deep, dreamless sleep.

This "self" will be discovered to have *no* questions: there is no "I" present which needs satisfactory answers of any sort. To your "*true* nature," nothing really matters.

He advises: "Ask yourself now, does this concern even *arise* in deep sleep?" If you can comprehend that it does not, then it is not a *matter* which *ultimately* will even need to be of interest.

And when you recognize that this true self is at one with the absolute, ultimate reality, you have discovered the conclusion to "Who am I?"

You have stated: "There is no I—or 'I am'—but just an image." Yes. And in deep sleep, there is not even an *image*.

So, any question concerning "What is the 'I', and what is meant by the 'I AM,'" are moot, pointless questions. Both I and I AM are mind-stuff, the consequence of a dualistic mode of thinking (as you indicated later).

Even though I AM has been suggested as a name for "God," in your deep sleep is there any such image as God? You, yourself, said: "The I AM is a creation of the mind." Moses did not say that "I am that I am" occurred to him in deep sleep.

Likewise: Did it occur to you, in deep sleep, that "there are three bodies: physical, emotional and spiritual"? Did your inert consciousness argue that "there are seven chakras in the spiritual body"? Or is this merely mind-stuff, created during someone's dualistic, waking mentation? You even made a comment: "the 'I' is freed in deep sleep, or when the understanding comes that 'I am boundless'." To an 'I' which has dissolved *into* the boundless, of what concern are any one of "three bodies"? And if the bodies go, don't the "charkas" go with them?

And likewise, dilemmas concerning Brahman, Vishnu and Siva. Did such questions arise to your unconscious being?

Next, as you point out: "This body sees only reflected light. Who knows of 'Pure Light'?" More mind-stuff, is it not? Does the body "see" *anything* in its mindless condition?

Finally: "Is the real and Reality the same?" In deepest sleep, your condition is presence, devoid of any qualifications: "real" and "unreal" don't even arise as propositions. Reality—with a capital R—might be a "name" for this condition; but what follows every name is an *image*. So, while your "true condition" is as real as it gets, Reality is an image—a conceived *category*—that attempts to paste a label on a condition which has no qualifications.

It is this boundless condition which is the substrate, the ground, of your being. When we awaken from deep sleep, this essential presence does not "go away": our waking (or dreaming) "mind" is merely superimposed upon it. So, while in your waking state

114

the "mind" identifies a "you," that "you" is still nothing more than that unqualified presence. When you recognize that this is the truth of what is so, you "know" (as in experience) 'who am I': 'I' am—at *all* times—that unqualified presence, despite any alternative images the "mind" creates.

THE ICE CREAM STORE

When clarity is present, your behavior will reflect that, and you will not thereby create problems. When clarity is not present, your behavior will reflect that, and you will create problems—for yourself and others.

The "presence of clarity" is a way of saying "the absence of ego," the ending of the I-centered outlook. The ending of the I-centered outlook is certain to cause a change in normative behavior, a definite change in the way we customarily live our lives. It is a change whose development we cannot predict.

Therefore, who (that wishes to cling to any "security" they know) would want to change their life in an unpredictable way?

No one, except those who are willing to give their "life" to live in peace—for themselves and others. Few are willing to sacrifice their ego, until suffering becomes unbearable.

The anguish you are presently experiencing is a "head pain" to alert you that clarity is necessary. The pain, in one form or another, will not dissipate until the prompting is heeded.

You *will* relinquish your ego-centeredness. Sooner. Or later.

At that time, you will cease to create problems for yourself *and* others.

Testimony to this fundamental fact is evident in the biographies of Buddha, Jesus and Ramana, among others.

These were human beings who recognized that peace could not be present until I-centeredness ends. Sooner. Or later.

For them, the proposition was clear.

Sooner.

What is your priority?

"Where your treasure is, there will your heart be also." "Man cannot serve two masters."

That this clarity is accessible was made evident in the uncommon lives of the clarions, and a few of those who followed them. How this clarity makes itself known was the subject of their discourses. And to whom is this information not familiar?

For example, who among us has not heard their universal message of non-attachment?

Do they say such things as "End your attachment to everything," and add "after Christmas?" Or "in 2015?"

Or, is the implied message, "When you want to end suffering"?

Now? Or later?

How did those free spirits answer that for themselves? "When I'm ninety?" "After I finish my book?" "After I'm impotent?"

Who would want to act immediately on such truths—unless they were eager for a change in the status quo?

And when will we be that eager, until we've suffered enough on the wheel of self/other?

So, wind the clock, or skip the wait.

Truth is not scheduled for tomorrow, for you to act on it. It's here today. So is *suffering*. Either is a matter of how we prefer to live our lives—or *not* live typical lives.

There are sacrifices to be made either way. Neither way is "right" or "wrong."

That's why the ice cream stores sell chocolate and vanilla. But they are two distinctly different flavors.

What you get is what you pay for.

The Imprisoned I

I do empathize with your situation. I am not naïve about what is taking place in prisons these days—from the inmate's standpoint. I must confess that I do not know how I would bear up under it; not as a model, of any sort, I suspect.

Unfortunately, if conditions are bad now, all present signs indicate they could get worse. And, from your observations, you say they *have* been getting worse. Do not suppose that your situation is not regularly in my mind.

I ask myself, at all times, how can a person best respond to these ugly worldly conditions—which (not just in prison) are deteriorating. This, of course, has been a perennial question for those sensitive to the inhumanities surrounding them. At the time when man first began recording concerns in writing, we have a record of this quest for a conciliation with the existential realities of cataclysmic life.

In some seven decades of considering the varied points of view on this subject, I have found only one means which has felt consistently satisfactory. This approach does not move one (from the negative end of the spectrum) toward the permanently positive end of the spectrum—because it is based on the observation that all *conditions* remain *changeable*, in the context of time. Instead, it focuses on 'What Is' being *what* it is, *as* it is. This is the only approach that I (and others, for centuries) have found that can bring basic peace of mind.

You write that now "every day brings renewal...I am confronted with that Inner spirit of this Outer man...I am viewing some of prison life's situations in my past; I'd respond with violence. Not now.

"What's changed surely is not prison, nor its way of being. Therefore, it must be my outlook on circumstances around me."

There is only one thing, frankly, which you have the lasting capability to effect. You would not be the first inmate to discover this.

"Prison life is questionable," you say, "and decisions are sometimes without time to think—but only respond."

The view that I spoke of above has to do with response (the real meaning of the word responsibility). It is our responsibility—the only responsibility which we have—to operate, respond, from the place of enlightened awareness.

What does that mean? It means, succinctly, *That* responding to That *as* That. It means, first, to understand (for certain) what it is that is responding—and to what.

These outward circumstances (*however* they are) are worldly and ephemeral. The presence in which they appear—come and go—is universal and timeless, eternal. Which then has significance, or reality, in the ultimate sense, the true or actual sense?

If the eternal presence is the actuality, then the impermanent appearances—the material aspects and passing events—must be manifest from (or within) That. Therefore, all of "this" is That unfolding as it is aligned to do. Not some *part* of it a playing-out of That's potential: the Source has *lent* presence to *every* thing which is.

This means that, in essence, the only thing which all appearances have in *common* is That.

From this standpoint, no one "thing" is any more relevant than any other thing. *You* are one of those things. *So* are all *other* things. It's *all* just That, spilling out—positive or negative—as it spills out.

When this *really* becomes *clear*, the "you" and the "others" disappear from the eye of the witnesser (which is all that remains). The witnesser is That, *viewing* That (me/others) *as* That.

This does *not* mean that what That (as the witnesser) views is now suddenly all A-OK. It *is* what it *is*: good, bad or indifferent— three of the distinctive forms in which That appears.

But what this *does* mean is that the person who realizes these interconnections now *responds* from a deep-seated sense of (so-called 'cosmic') awareness, in which there is no longer an *isolated* 'I' who is pondering a response relative to *relation-ship*.

You said that what has been changing "must be my outlook." The only freedom anyone really has is where to place one's attention. Attention to one's outlook is our sole responsibility. And when that attention results in a shift of *perspective* (from, we could say, I to It) that is called *real*ization. And it is from (or as) this *awareness* that we now respond, in our every act, action and activity.

Such a realization will not necessarily lengthen our life (or shorten our sentence). But it is the only prospect we have of getting the troublesome "I" out of this scenario that we *presume* has independent significance.

Open and Empty

The mind which is unconstrained—by ideas, theories, opinions, preconceptions and remembrances of the past—is an open mind...open as a field in which creation can manifest, rather than open as a trap.

This opening, or relaxing, of the mind is not an emptying in which there is a goal, an opening which is subsequently to be exploited for gain. This is not an emptying of the mind of all previous ideas so that they may be replaced by forthcoming ideas. This is not an opening of the mind, merely a stretching, to accommodate additional yardage of self-improvement.

The open mind, of which we speak, is a consciousness which is free of the limitations imposed by the bounded image of the self. It is consciousness which does not restrain itself to a fixed center. It is a mind of possibilities, rather than probabilities or certainties.

The Physics of Tao

You may not be familiar with Bell's Theorem, but you ought to be!

A theorem goes beyond a theory, in that it is provable. What has been proven, in this case, is what is known as—deceptively understated—entanglement.

Less than fifty years ago, physicist John Bell proposed an experiment which has subsequently been performed, then reconfirmed several times.

A simplified analogous depiction: An atom, in decay, emits pairs of particles. They will be of a polarization opposite to one another, and will be expelled to each side, beyond physical contact with each other. If the subatomic particle ejected to the right was polarized as positive (for example), you could zap it electronically mid-flight and switch its polarity to negative.

But by a construct of physical nature, such paired particles are required to exist in an oppositional polarity. The abrupt switch in polarity of the right-hand particle from the positive to negative will register a startling observation in your monitoring of the flight of the left-hand particle.

The polarity of the left-hand particle will spontaneously and instantly switch orientation (in this case, from negative to positive), in accordance with the effected switch in polarity of the right-hand particle.

How can one particle be apprised of an instantaneous change in the other, when both are zooming away from any spatial link between them?

In our sector of the universe, there is an established physical principle, that not anything can be propagated through space at faster than the speed of light. Yet, when experiments have been performed on particles separated a decisive distance in space, the determination is that this "phase change" is coordinated simultaneously, and cannot be a communicated message between particles—even at the speed of light.

The most apparent explanation is that the subatomic particles (which, of course, all matter is composed of—including you) exist in, and are inseparable from, a field or background of unlimited or absolute connectedness. Subsequent experiments are demonstrating that this interconnectedness pertains to particles of increasingly greater number; and in evolving size, even beyond that of an atom. In physics today, entanglement is discovered to be an operative reality in a widening panorama of phenomenon.

Entanglement is a physicist's label for interconnectedness; and the latter is a synonym for oneness. Entanglement is a proven fact. Anyone can continue to argue about the reality of oneness or undeniable inseparability: "That's just a theory!" But know, for yourself, that it is the *absence* of oneness (perceived as duality) that is now nothing more than a theory.

The Door Stands Open

If there was one quality that is relevant to enlightenment, it is sincerity. You have that, as revealed in your committed comment: "I'm not afraid of change [or "transition"], if Truth is found...[to] better understand this [First] Principle."

Having put into your own words my previous comments indicates that you have grasped much of what was said (which is all that could be expected). It will require some length, but I want to take your reply sentence-by-sentence so that I can respond in detail.

First, a general comment: you might find it helpful to (at least temporarily) attempt to think in terms which avoid the use of the words "God" or "Christ." These words, in particular, have an ingrained tendency to cause us to regard the Omnipresent in the context of a conceived *entity*. I personally prefer using the word Absolute to represent that which is infinite and eternal; for the sake of furthering discussion, I do sometimes use the word "God," but it is always—for me—as an alternate, where the word Absolute or Omnipresent, Infinite, could as readily be substituted. It doesn't matter what specific word you use as an alternate, but the more neutral, the better: the words "God" and "Christ" are just packed with *image*. The Vedas (for one) often use the word "That" to indicate what the words God, Absolute, Self, etc., point to. Freeing yourself of the *image* of the ultimate actuality (the Buddhists use the words Suchness, and Void) will be more *useful* in contemplating its *true* nature.

You have used the word Spirit, so let's allow that to stand in for That, Suchness, Absolute, etc.—assuming that we conceive of spirit as omnipresent Being, and not in the deistic sense of being another image in the so-called Trinity: "Holy Ghost."

"The Spirit," you write, "cannot be antagonistic toward us."

The Spirit being, by definition, omnipresent—*all* pervading—it is in no way *apart* from us.

"The Spirit is constantly flowing into us."

From the standpoint of that which is all-pervading, there is no such (relative) "reality" as "in" or "out"; being *all-pervading*, it is the *essence* of all things. It does not "flow into us" because, in an obvious sense, *we* are in *it* ("it" being infinite, and "we" being finite, to put it in relative terms).

> *"It's always expressing itself through us."*

Not ever having been apart from us, it is always expressing itself *as* us. As the Vedas say, Tat Tvam Asi: That thou *art*.

> *"This self-expression of Spirit is also the self-expression of man."*

Yes, "man" is "Spirit" expressed, or manifest.

> *"The I AM is individual and universal."*

Yes, "individual" in the relative context; "universal" or cosmic in the Absolute sense. But these "two" are, ultimately, one.

> *"Individuality merges into universality."*

Another way of putting this is that the relative (individual) is a "subset" of the Absolute; an "appearance" (Latin: made to appear) of the Spirit.

> *"All forms are rooted in the Spirit, which is the spirit of man."*

Yes.

> *"To practice the Presence is to awaken within as that consciousness."*

This Presence is what we *are* in essence; there is no need (or purpose) in "practicing" *being* what you *unavoidably* are. Comprehending this *is* to "awaken within" *as* that consciousness. The "consciousness" of the Supreme Being is *your* consciousness: this very moment.

> *"Spirit is 'God' in the soul of man."*

Spirit *is* man (or, put another way, man *is* Spirit): no need for a middleman "soul": Spirit, "soul," man—all *one* actuality, no *separation* or *division*. All one thing: "*That* is *all* that *is*."

You put it well: "The resurrection is the death of the belief that we are 'separate'." Call it resurrection, awakening or enlightenment.

"This death is to the illusion, and not to reality."

The illusion (which dies) is that of "duality" as a (false) form of perception. The *appearances* of a world or cosmos of "separate things" does not itself *dis*appear, but are now regarded in their true nature—as *manifestations*, appearances, of the One, unbroken, (and indivisible) actuality.

"Spirit did not die, (instead) man awoke to life."

Spirit, transcending time ("time*less*"), itself knows nothing of "beginning" or "ending"; "life" and "death" are characteristic of all relative, impermanent appearances. It is the *appearances* which *arise* from the Absolute (or Spirit) and *subside* in the Absolute; better put, arise as the Absolute (formlessness into form) and subside *as* the Absolute (form into formlessness). As Buddhists say, "Form *is* formlessness; formlessness *is* form." This indicates that "birth" and "death" are merely change in appearance of the Absolute.

"The awakening must be on the part of man, since Spirit already is life [awakened]."

The "awakening" is merely to *realize* that the so-called awakened "person" is none other than God *conscious* of its "self": "God-consciousness." Simple as that!

As you signed yourself, you are not "In Divine Light," you *are* Divine Light.

As you have persistently done, I'm sure you'll contemplate these matters in conclusive depth.

In any case, my "door" is al*ways* "open."

Non-Attach-ment

For those of us who are not living in a vacuum, nonattachment means the breaking of patterns. It is the severing of the tie that binds, from apron string to necktie. But the most fundamental nonattachment is to the *ideas* we hold about how things are, have been, or should be.

One example of attachment is the story told of two monks who are traveling on foot and come to a waist-deep river, which they must ford. A young girl is sitting on the bank, distraught because the river has risen since morning, and she can't get home. The younger monk, taking in the situation, sweeps her up in his arms and carries her across, placing her on her homeward path. Many miles later, he notices that the older monk seems distracted, and asks if something is troubling him.

"You know," says the older man, "that in our order we are not to have physical contact with females."

"But, Brother, I carried her for only a few feet. You have carried her for miles!"

Our most grievous attachment is the attachment to fixed ideas, to our ideational fixations. From this is born inflexibility, compulsion and manipulative behavior; it is the root of fanatic belief, contentious opinion and self-righteous judgment. It is the seat of knee-jerk reaction (which once led Alan Watts to muse that "the 'self' is nothing more than a tight asshole.").

Nonattachment is not a quest for "better" or "richer" experience, but for a true and fundamental perspective. It is a surrendering of one's attachment to the ephemeral.

Ramana Maharshi:

> "A man should surrender the personal selfishness which binds him to this world. Giving up the false *self* is the true *renunciation*."

A student of Ramakrishna:

> "Ramakrishna was a simple man, illiterate and uneducated—he was so illiterate that he could not even sign his name, let alone write a letter. He was humble in appearance and humbler still in mode of living, yet he commanded the allegiance of some of the best-educated and most-cultured men of the time, in India."

Realization is, in a sense, to "go beyond," to transcend appearances. It is not to get caught up in petty drama.

We must come to a recognition of a particular *deep-seated* desire, that of the pursuit of pleasure, of personal gratification in its myriad forms. This is perhaps the most sinuous of our attachments. The home is the locus of a catalog of satisfactions. Probably the two major technological deterrents to spiritual sensibility and tranquility are television and the computer. As an extension of human memory, the computer is a crypt of what is past: As an extension of human imagination, television is a handmaiden for fantasies of the future.

Images of what "has passed" and ideas of what "is to come" are the tendrils of the vine of attachment. If there is to be even a remote possibility of the cessation of sorrow and of anxiety—of suffering in general—then fascination with "past" and "future" must indubitably be dispelled.

This is to be a leaf on the stream. Otherwise, when you have put down an anchor, your voyage ends.

Nonattachment is in the palm of your hand. You will not be manipulated when you do not have anything that anyone covets, and when no one has anything that you covet. This is not a matter of *repressing* desire, but of allowing it to fall into disuse.

Fixations on time, pleasure and fear—by a self whose choices of reaction are control and resistance—are the ingredients for a lifetime of misery.

The difference between alert caution, and the paralysis of dread, is that *one* is concentrated in the moment; and the *other* is focused on the future or past. Fear is *divisive*, as Krishnamurti indicates:

"When you see a wild animal—a snake—and you withdraw, is that fear? Or is it intelligence...? But is it intelligence that operates when we *divide*...? When we make this division between you and me, we and they, is that intelligence...? Such division... *brings about* danger..."

Surrendering attachment to our secure patterns and comfortable choices represents a dramatic change of direction. "Great ships turn about by a small helm," says the Book of James.

Jesus was concerned not with men's theoretical knowledge, but with their informed behavior. Were it not for the dramatic change of behavior of Paul, Jesus' name might still be filed in the judicial archives.

To be present in the moment is to risk.

This road is passable, but it does steepen. If you are not intent in your direction, you may access the leveled detours. But if you do take the direct road, be prepared to jettison your cargo.

No Matter

Even as a fetus in the womb, awareness is present. The eyes are closed, and the environment is dark, but the organism still responds experientially to certain stimulus. Then the baby is born, the eyes are open, the environment is multitudinous, and the same awareness continues undiminished.

Throughout our lives, an unabated awareness monitors every activity or inactivity. Yet, the awareness itself cares naught what is seen, heard or considered.

All living things evidently share in awareness; even plants exhibit a responsive awareness to their environment. And awareness in any particular human shows no characteristics of being different from that of any other human.

As an organism, every single thing which you experience is experienced within awareness. And to the extent to which awareness itself can be experienced, it too is merely another experience.

It is not "you"—an *object* of awareness—which is seeing through your eyes, it is this ever-present be-ing. It is not *you* which is aware of thoughts—objects *in* awareness—it is, again, awareness. Any thing which you can think of that you are, is simply objectified in awareness. So, clearly, it is the awareness which is the you that perceives, not the objectifications in awareness identified as characteristics of your self. There is no self outside of awareness.

Whence the source of this awareness? Surely not you: it is not a "creation" which you had any control in initiating. It was in existence long before your organism was germinated, and will continue in existence far after "you" have disappeared as a fixture in awareness.

So, the sages say, recognize that *Essence* which is aware of "you"— and every movement, concept and experience—*as* you.

DRAMA REVIEW

Your letters are beginning to stick closer to the issues at hand here. This life is not a dress rehearsal. In only a matter of years, we will be reduced to anonymous ashes at the foot of an incinerator. Annihilation. Whether or not we are ready for it.

What you are trying to bring into the focus of awareness, meanwhile, is not something which will be found in the past. (And by "past," I mean anything that happened before your last letter.) *Past* includes memories or experiences, good *or* bad. How much time are we to *wisely* dedicate to re-warming events of the past—since what we hope to find wasn't *found* there? What is being sought is not a passing experience, but that which is permanent, eternal, time-*less*.

If what is being sought isn't present now, and always present, it is of no use to us *now*. What we're looking for is that which can resolve our confusion *now*, and put an end to this existential confusion permanently. It *will* be put to an end when we die. But if we have any prospect of living out the rest of our days without the conflict and suffering (for ourselves *and* others) that confusion ensures, we had best make optimal use of each irreplaceable moment. Everything mundane, worldly, that we focus our attention on has a beginning and an ending. Your body. Your thoughts. Your egoic identity. The entire "story" of you had a beginning and will end for you. If all that we can sense comes and goes, what does it come and go *in*? If what it comes and goes *in* comes and goes, then cosmic existence is truly a meaningless phantasm: the entire universe could disappear in a wink.

The other possibility is an unchanging actuality within which all that is changing is manifest: a condition which itself has no propensity to start and stop, which never comes nor goes, which knows naught of beginning or ending; eternal, infinite. The nothingness out of which all that comes and goes *arises*; and to which only the impermanent can *return*.

Out of this, "you" arose (say the spiritual avatars) and to this "you" return. You are, in effect, meanwhile, merely an extension of that ever-present actuality—one of the abundant things that come and go, giving vibrant life to that which has no form apart from the changeable.

That actuality is present as all things, including you. And "your" awareness is not apart from this actuality, as one of its manifestations or forms.

So, you are looking for yourself. You are that, in contemplation of That. Whether *or not* your contemplation resolves your egoic confusion, you are That; aware—however vaguely—of itself.

What you are intent on discovering in awareness, then, is your "true" self; the Self (as Ramana would have it) that doesn't begin where you start telling your story and won't end when you end your story. *Being* you, it won't be *found* in the past, or in pondering the behavior of others. Nor in studying the accounts of the apostles. It is as close to discovery as is the focus of your attention in this moment—*to what is presently aware.*

Connect with the underlying actuality, whether you choose to call it Holy Spirit, Christ or whatever. Merge with it. In order to merge, you must first yield. When ink merges with water, it yields its individual identity, its story as being ink. All that it *was* is annihilated.

You will be annihilated one way or the other. But, in one of the ways, "your" personal suffering is a reality only to the extent that the suffer*er* is a reality. The "sufferer" and "suffering" can end when the curtain rings down on the story that you identify with; or, as soon as you recognize who the real "doer" is...who you *are*, that is known by every name.

Assimilating Doership

As I've indicated in other monographs, the paradox of our spiritual nature is this: the infinite, formless Absolute actuality surrounds and penetrates—thus pervades and saturates—all of the finite, relative forms. Therefore, we organisms exist within the limitless Absolute—simultaneously as the limitless Absolute exists within us, as the indivisible essence and source of all things. The transcendent Being and the immanent being, that is, are consubstantial, in the same way that Jesus has been conceived to be both God and man.

So, the Absolute exists to the extent that it is present in all forms; all forms exist to the extent that they arise within the formless ground of Being. The Absolute and the relative, then, are a single inter-existent actuality.

The forms—such as these organisms—make an appearance that is dependent upon their Source; they express change; and they dis-integrate into their formless Source. All these *finite* entities are impermanent, insubstantial.

The infinite, formless ground of Being, from which all forms manifest in appearance, is ever-present temporally and spatially: there has never been a point in time or space where this essential condition has not presently existed. It is the everlastingly permanent and unchanging background whose actuality is always.

Therefore, Ramana refers to the latter as real, the impermanent appearances as unreal (or illusory).

Hence, if I am to consider the inherent identity of this organism, is it the unreal, fleeting appearance; or is it the indestructible animating and eternal essence? As with the title of Nisargadatta's book, I must perceive "I am That."

So, what is the source of "doership" here: this animated one-hundred-fifty pounds of protein, which can only plant a tree that it itself cannot create?

Or is the real doer That from which this body evolved, and through which the propagation and activity of change occurs?

The jnani's recognition is that this body is an expression of That. If it has a brain, the brain is a product of That. If there is a mind, the mind is an aspect of That. If thoughts occur in consciousness, both thoughts and consciousness are a manifestation of That. If thoughts precede action, the actions—whatever they be—are an effect of That.

With this Absolute awareness, what remains for the jnani is simply a passive, objective "witness" experience through which That is connected to what That is doing.

The jnani no longer takes concern, or responsibility, for what the organism thinks, says or does. There is not even enough sense of personal doership remaining to need to make the *distinctions* "I am not the doer," "I am not the body," etc. There is merely the uncritical, unattached observation of the unfolding in the unbroken movement of the panoramic, effulgent display.

This ends the self-concern for what "I" think, do or say—whether considered to be positive or negative. All this is regarded impersonally as "That doing what it does."

From the Bhagavad Gita:

> God is attained by all those who see God in every action...He who sees that all actions are performed by Nature alone, and thus that the self [person] is not the doer—that one sees truly.

A Ring of Truth

In general, all that you've said in your six (full) pages has a ring of truth to it. However, it somehow sounds as if it was "learned." The important matter is, is it "known"?

In other words, the important matter is not to know what the guru says about these spiritual questions, but to know for oneself the presence of enlightened awareness.

To say, for example, (or to know that one "ought" to say), that "there is no 'I,' there is only the indivisible Presence" may just be a matter of repeating what some sage has stated. The question is, has the "I" (as you know it) disappeared into the ultimate actuality, the ever-present Be-ing that knows of no parts?

There is nothing that you can learn that can effect this shift in awareness. In fact, to learn about some matter is to suppose that the learning will have some pay-off, some result, at some (future) point in time.

One does not need to "learn" that one is *now*, always has been and will be, the embodiment of that ultimate and *ever-present* Be-ing.

The "realization" is that this indivisible Presence is the only permanent Actuality; and therefore the sense of existing as an independent (and impermanent) individual is false.

This dissolution of the "I" image is the "transcendence" which is spoken of. Recognizing that "there is no me" is the recognition of what then *remains*. It is this *self-realization* which is all that matters—not, instead, that one knows the "answer" to a series of spiritual questions.

So, again, the only question is: is this awareness of the indivisible condition present so that it is the source from which action stems NOW?

BEHAVE YOUR SELF

"I am really 'seeing' differently," you say. You are also, according to your report, now actually *hearing* others, rather than being *focused* on your inner dialogue with your self.

As a consequence, you are noticing that you are responding differently to others; and this results in them responding differently to you. There is more healthiness/wholesomeness in these interactions now.

Such fruits reflect the fact that *living* the teachings is commensurate with a change in behaviour.

Quoting you: "You've sometimes said that one consequence of awakening is a noticeable change in behavior. Like what?"

The epitome of awakening is the evaporation of one's *self-centered* fixation and concern. A remarkable amount of energy is released, and now available for constructive purposes, which had previously gone into establishing, maintaining and animating your egoic self-image.

With the focus no longer on one's persona, you become even more acutely aware, sensitive to, the perceived "suffering" of those around you. Knowing now that the confusion and angst of the duality-ridden psyche is not necessary, you may feel the impulse to be present and of assistance (in whatever way possible) to alleviate the conflicted human's condition.

Years before Self-realization, a comment by Peace Pilgrim lodged in my awareness: "ask not what you can get; ask what you can give."

You know, when we encounter someone (in our self-centered condition), our first thought is, "What can this person do for me?" It is possible for that attitude to be reversed, and for one's attention to be on "What can I give to this person?" And of course I don't mean merely material giving, but what can I give that is invaluable: my time, attention, compassion, encouragement, etc.

This is a giving which is not extended *because* it's "helpful" (to my ego), or out of pity or superiority; nor because I suppose that I "should" do this, or that I will be "a better person"; nor because my church sect says that I ought to do this; or perhaps that it will result in recompense in return.

And what is it that can best be given by one who is acting out of Self awareness? There is that saying, "You can give a man a fish, or you can teach a man to fish." If you are able to be of any assistance in transmitting the dharma, I submit that is the greatest gift, the "precious pearl."

With awakening, Adyashanti has written, life "calls to us now in a new way"—what in Buddhism's tenth Oxherding Picture is portrayed as "re-entering the marketplace." Or, in Adya's words, "coming back down from the summit." Then, "Our greatest contribution to humanity [or individuals] is our awakening...we come back as a gift...without trying, without taking any credit..."

This, I think you can understand, can be a noticeable change in our behavior from our typical concern for "self" survival.

Who is God?

Due to our divisive (subject-object) habit of thought, the average person tends to envision God in two particular ways: As an entity unto itself; and, as standing apart from oneself. Thus: the *traditional* depiction of God as Jehovah, "up there" somewhere, to whom one raises one's eyes in supplication like a teenager asking dad for the car keys. Contemporary references to God as "Goddess" are the same kind of thinking, merely modified.

"Who sees not God everywhere," as Meister Eckhart said, "sees God nowhere." If the Almighty is indeed everywhere, that must include where you are standing. In other words, one who recognizes the nature of the *Absolute* recognizes that God is one's own personage. But this is not to say that the *Absolute* is confined to any particular personage. The shrub outside of your window is no less God.

The realization is not that you alone are God, but that you are— along with all else that is—God. To suppose that you were God alone would be to suppose that God is a singular entity, with the capacity to stand apart from other entities. Such is a notion which many orthodox religionists hold, which prohibits them from recognizing, and acknowledging, their own identity as God.

No one is more—or less—Godly than you.

BEING PRESENT

Thanks for your note and your comments.

> "It seems to me that one of the last realizations that needs to be hurdled, is that there is no need to 'communicate' with anyone about anything."

It looks like you're beginning to recognize that we need not think in terms of "converting" others, even if we suppose that we can "save their souls." To do so is to re-act, on the presumption that circumstances in "God's universe" are not as they should be. True "communication" comes about when you respond to an interested query by someone—sharing your experience when asked. The universe will get along just fine, whether someone seeks your counsel or not.

> "I'm starting to 'see' things the way they really are, rather than the way I would like them to be."

"The true purpose of Zen," Suzuki Roshi once said, "is to see things as they are"—not as how we would like them to be. He added to that: "And to let every thing go—as it goes." No attachment to an idea as to how any thing is "to go."

> "The Bible has outlived its usefulness (if it ever had any). It would do well to find its place amongst the world's mythologies."

The Bible is full of ideas as to how (heavenly) things could be, or ought to be. Myth never pretends to be about how things really are, or have perpetually been. However, even in cultures not exposed to the Bible, people have tended to focus on what could be or should be, in preference to finding contentment in what is.

"I am finally getting out of that box. I'm here with a great teacher, and it has me looking deeply at the most recent letters I've gotten from you....

"I'm gonna continue to work with these last few ideas we've been discussing."

I would not say that we have been discussing ideas, but practical and immediate means to "being present with what's present." An idea may or may not be acted upon; when we wake up to Reality, that in itself is to take action. You have already begun to go beyond the ideational stage, thus you are "looking deeply," and "finally getting out of the box."

OUTSIDE THE BOX

The "intuitive leap," which is spoken of, is (as *intuition* is defined) immediate understanding, beyond reasoning.

You're correct in your surmise (from experience) that mere ratiocination generally has a limitation when it regards nonduality.

For you to think of something, there must be "somethingness." Can you think, in terms of objectification, of "nothingness" without conceiving of it as "some thing"?

Nonduality is (to use a favorite phrase of quantum physicists) counter-intuitive: when nonduality is clearly understood, there is no intuition *apart from it* that is understanding it. To put it in your terms, the mind that is searching for That, is That itself. Why? Because anything which can be conceived (such as That) is the same That which is doing the conceiving. To put it in Advaita terms, you are That—because all things (whether some thing or nothing) are That. And since all things are That, you (as That) cannot conceive of any thing which is not That.

See why there are Zen koans?

I'm not trying to sketch something that is more mysterious than it need be. But nonduality is the original thinking-outside-the-box. The box is the limited conception of limited forms (material or immaterial). Take away all six sides of the box ("no mind," in Zen) and what do you have? No conceivable "thing." One might say that the insight has to do with subtraction, rather than addition; or looking at this from the standpoint of a mind that is empty of notions, as to what is to be discovered.

In practical expression, if you are contemplating any two, or more, things, you are operating in the realm of duality. ("Me" outside of That.)

If you are aware that this actuality (which the sages are referring to) is thoroughly indivisible and therefore does not admit of any separate "parts," then it is intuited that there is no individual "you" which could possibly be incorporated in It. The "search" ends, with the "searcher." This, then, is nonduality: an understanding which is *immediate*, and transcendent of reasoning limited to dualistic conceptions.

BURN YOUR BRIDGES

David Bohm was referring to a perception that is so new that it has never been old, when he said: "What we have to do, with regard to the great wisdom from the whole of the past (both in the East and in the West), is to assimilate it—and to go on to new and original perception, relevant to our present condition of life."

Morality is now dictated by economics, rather than the other way around. Consciences have been traded for corporations. An organization disseminating spiritual teachings may comment that its "many endowments" are its "insurance policy," and it is reluctant to utilize these reserves even though the effect is to "reduce the scope of what can be done." Yet it can ask of its adherents—who justify applying the same insurance-policy logic to their own reserves—"what prevents you from participating" in the "numerous" fund appeals?

Life itself appears to have resulted from *instability* in the cosmos, yet man disdains instability. The lives of Buddha, Jesus, Ramana, Krishnamurti—all—convey the message: burn your bridges behind you, and die to the past.

A "Way Out" Brother

The one-page "broadside" that you and the other inmates found, on your chairs at the Catholic mass, is a remarkable document. The signee, Richard Rohr O.F.M., is evidently an unordained member of the Franciscan Order.

His paragraphs which outline or describe six levels of consciousness—from "searching" to "enlightenment" ("non-dual transformation") indicate that he is familiar with more than merely the Catholic perspective on epiphany; and yet he is also aware of the root connection between "secular" transformational experience and that of the "religious" (for example, his phrase "the saint or enlightened one..."). The *final* experience, he states, is "habitual non-dual seeing" (or, what I would call Absolute awareness).

It would not be surprising to discover that this lay brother is acquainted with such as Thomas Merton's writings on Tao and Zen, and other open-minded Catholics like Father Thomas Keating or Brother David Stendl-Rast. He also may be well versed in the sermons of Meister Eckhart.

Interestingly enough, he might possibly be the most Self-realized person among the entire prison administration. In fact, for all we know, there might come a time when his writings are as well known as those of Merton or Eckhart. He is certainly attempting to point inmates in the direction of (at least inner) freedom from temporal authority, through his categories of "Intuitive Intelligence," "Understanding," "Wisdom" and "Transformation"— without using liturgical words for these phases.

BEING HERE NOW

You are asking for my assistance, but then you evidently don't do what I suggest.

There are, by now, dozens of books on enlightenment, with an increasing number published each year. You can likely spend the rest of your life reading about spirituality.

All of these (qualified) authors will, in the final analysis, tell you the same thing—the very advice which I have continually given you.

The reader (you) clings to the point of view that there is some information he is lacking that, once supplied, will put him in touch with the essential actuality which is described as the Self, the Absolute, Brahman, etc.

Put all the books aside. *Focus* your *attention*, during your waking consciousness on this question: Where could this actuality, this Being-ness *be*, which I am seeking?

You have read enough to know what these teachers and I have consistently said: The Being-ness which is sought is *omnipresent*; that means, *ever* present *everywhere* at every *moment*.

Is this news to you? Have you not read or heard this stated, time after time, by now? How many more times must you hear it?

If what you are seeking is infinite, eternal and *all-pervasive*, as every instruction says, where could you possibly go or be, that It is *not*?

Wouldn't this Presence *surround* you—no matter where or when you were; such as, this very moment?

If this formless Being-ness is infinite, meaning that it has no borders confining or restraining its Presence, wouldn't it permeate, *penetrate*, saturate every object which it unrestrainably surrounds?

If you have comprehended this much from your investigation, can you not comprehend that the Being-ness which you are seeking, must be not only the inherent essence—the *be-ing*—of every object you see, but it *must* be the essential, actual condition of your very *self*. You could not and would not *exist* if it were not for this universal and originating *all-encompassing* Presence!

So how *far* do you need to go, and how *long* do you need to look, in order to recognize That which—by its affirmed existence— cannot possibly be anywhere other, or at any time other, than *precisely* where you consider your *self* to be at this *exact* moment?

You *are* That (never heard this?). As long as you continue to presume that you are *not* That, you will continue to read and question.

You are expecting to *encounter* what is *Present*. If it's "always already ever-present" (ever heard that?), what are you—being present yourself—ever to encounter?

Pay *attention* to what has been said. *Contemplate* only this, and distract yourself with no more reading. You will see that you and Being are not separate, regardless of whether it *feels like it*, or not.

"AND GOD SAID..."

As to the question regarding where the dualistic perspective began to influence mankind's collective conditioning, on the broader social scale one could look to the beginning book of the Hebrew Pentateuch ("five books"). Legend has it that Moses authored Genesis through Deuteronomy, but scholarly science places his birth near the end of the 1300's B.C., and the writing of these books dated after about 1000 B.C. (and then not completed for at least another 500 years).

In any case, the book of Genesis (nee "generation, as in origin") is not considered to be history but merely legend that may have originated as much as a thousand years before Moses' time. Anyone who has a copy of the Old Testament will find the first three chapters to be of interest, when you consider how many people have read this account over at least the two and a half millennia since an unknown writer penned it.

The fable starts, "In the beginning"—and, as such, may relate to your question about duality and our subsequent conditioning to it.

Within the very first few verses (replete with chronological contradictions), "God's" initial actions are those of separation. This is a cognizing god, much like your father would be if engaged in creative tasks. After all, this is a god who walks in the garden in the cool of the day.

Man (Adam, in Hebrew) is set apart from God right from the start: he is dissuaded from partaking of the tree of knowledge of duality—"good" and "bad" (evil)—whose fruits, if touched, will result in death, mortality.

Adam's other half Eve ("life," in Hebrew) views these laden branches as a means for gain ("wisdom," in this case). And the serpent observes that, knowing good from bad will make one like God.

So throughout, the theme is of separation, category by category. Nowhere is seen the possibility of the inseparability of the divine and mundane.

We come into the world, this story goes, naked and unashamed, but quickly come to distinguish "this" from "that" ("naked" from "not naked," etc.).

The climax then, by Chapter 3, is that man and God are decisively estranged; human male and female banished from God's *presence*, now outside (with entry barred) the realm of sacred being.

The god, in this story, creates forms and is himself a form, an object. This is a god who, later on, worries that other objects, idols, might replace him.

When man, life, and the essential Presence are envisioned as separable forms—and this is portrayed from ancient times as divinely-inspired holy writ—this must account, at least in part, for the basis of our society's dualistic mindset.

YOU *REALLY ARE* NOTHING

You already are convinced that there is *"One"*: you. But who, truly, *are* you? A limited "individual" and an Infinite actuality cannot reasonably co-exist as two different entities.

Are you basically an external emanation from the ineffable One? Paul Davies, referring to a stellar explosion, says, "among the shattered debris of the star are found the elements... the raw material out of which...life will form. Thus our bodies are made from the ashes of long dead stars."

And of that debris—those ashes of matter, the raw elements of which your body is comprised—the physicist Joliot-Curie once calculated: the nuclei of all your atoms (which compose 99.9% of an atom's mass) could be packed together into the volume of a minute speck of free-floating dust—the kind you notice when sunlight streams through the window of a darkened room.

Even then, how unique are "our" raw materials? Physicist Heinz Pagels: "The truth is that the entire material universe, with *all* its variety, is entirely made up out of quantum particles which are completely identical." Physicist Nick Herbert echoes: "All quons, in the same state, are exactly alike....There is no difference whatsoever between electron #123 and electron #137."

In fact, your identity is ultimately even more indistinct than this. Herbert: "The quantum world is not made up of 'objects'. As Heisenberg puts it, 'Atoms are not things.'"

The material particle itself is nothing more than an indeterminate bump in a field of empty space. Hermann Weyl explains:

According to the [field theory of matter] a material particle, such as an electron, is merely a small domain of the electrical field within which the field strength assumes enormously high values, indicating that a comparatively huge field energy is concentrated in a very small space. Such an energy *knot* (which by no means is clearly delineated against the remaining *field*), propagates through empty space like a water wave across the surface of a lake; *there is no such thing as one and the same substance of which the electron consists all the time.*

So who are you? Not even "real"?

Physicist Werner Heisenberg: "The atoms, or the elementary particles, are not real; they form a world of *potentialities* and *possibilities*, rather than one of 'things' or 'facts'."

What is "not real" has not even "substance." Fritjof Capra: "Atoms consist of particles, and these particles are not made of any *material* stuff. When we observe them, we never see any substance; what we observe are dynamic *patterns* continually *changing into one another*...interconnections in an inseparable cosmic web....These patterns do not represent probabilities of 'things', but rather probabilities of *interconnections*."

The only "substance" which you can really have is your *interconnectedness* with all others.

The Taoist Wei Wu Wei: "To know that one's self has no objective quality whatever—has absolutely nothing objective about it, is devoid of any trace-element of objectivity—is surely to know what one *is*; which, in metaphysical terms, is just the 'absence' itself—the very absence of an absence, the total lack of any objective character or nature or quality."

Transmutation

The two things a spiritual teacher hears most often are: "I only have an intellectual understanding of Self-realization"; and, "I had the experience of no-separation at one time, but I lost it."

Firstly: you have to start somewhere, and an intellectual understanding is where we start. An intellectual understanding can be better than no understanding at all.

In addition, many people's "intellectual" understanding is actually a much deeper understanding than they are prepared to recognize.

But in most cases this is merely an indicator that the seeker is attempting to be in contact with Omnipresence while leaving the seeker outside of it. An analogy would be a human being who is seeking to know what it would be like to experience the effect of gravity.

So, if all spiritual teachings have asserted that the Absolute is infinite and eternal, there is no possibility that you could ever be outside of it, or apart from it. The seeking, then, ends with the recognition that what is being sought is actually inescapable. The being which is seeking Being need not look for it outside of one's own awareness. Whether one is a seeker or a finder, neither has escaped being.

Thus, when the seeking has ended, an "intellectual understanding" (the point of view of a "seeker") transits into Self-Realization: being is the experience of Being.

Similarly, with the second proposition above, if it is truly and thoroughly recognized that you cannot have ever been apart from that which is infinite and eternal, it must be clear that, in making this discovery, not any thing has been *added* to you; nothing has been "gained" that was not present all along. In terms of Being, you cannot now "have" some thing of which you have not been apart.

If you have really *had* this experience of no-separation, you know that being/Being is the same. Similar to the earlier analogy, occupying a human body and experiencing gravity are not two different things. You have not, at some moment, "acquired" gravity, and so you cannot "lose" it.

You have not, at some point, "come into contact" with the infinite and eternal Being; you cannot *add* its presence to you. Having never, at some moment, "gained" this, you cannot at some moment have "lost" it.

To conclude that you have done so, is an indication of supposing that you had been "outside" of the Absolute, stepped into it, and somehow contrived then to step out of it. You have not, at some point, engineered your way into what you have always been inseparable from, and so any idea that one could "lose" the condition of "no-separation" is simply an incomplete comprehension.

SHARED SECRET

There are few people, as you may be aware, whose day-to-day lives are not engaged in one or another form of conflict. But a person here or there—perhaps you know one of them—has directly cut through all of the confusion, and penetrated to a point of profound clarity.

Those who are effective in any endeavor will commonly share their secret with you: "Persistently do the most important thing first!" And throughout three dozen centuries of man's history, those most revered for their wisdom have variously agreed on the first important priority: clarity. Total and unequivocal clarity.

This clarity has been appended many names: enlightenment, liberation, awakening, realization, illumination—to elicit just a few in English.

Its price has consistently been given no upward limit. For just one example, this was doubly emphasized:

> "Like treasure hidden in a field; when a man found it, he...in his joy went and sold all he had and bought that field....

> "Like a merchant looking for fine pearls; when he found one, of great value, he went away and sold everything he had and bought it." (Gospel of Thomas)

What did these exemplary discoverers gladly surrender for this joyous treasure, this illustrious pearl of greatest-value? All. Everything.

The Meaning of Clinging

Please observe this for yourself, in nature: not any of the material (nor immaterial, such as ideas) things that we consider are elements of our lives are permanent. As Buddhism stresses, "all things change." Change—impermanence or inconstancy—is, in fact, the only element which is constant, or reliably consistent.

If that is so, what sense is there in forming any kind of attachment to, or dependence upon, any of the elements of our temporal, finite existence?

What we regard as a pleasure is destined to change; what we perceive as a displeasure is bound to change with time. Yet we structure an entire lifetime around fixations on our established desires and aversions. Even our desires and aversions, during our lifetime, tend to change.

The consequence of our fixations on attempting to maintain our desired pleasures and avoid inevitable displeasures is that we hope to control the element of change—which clearly is resistance to the inevitable. Our failure to affect our resistance to change is the foundation for chronic discontent; our normal, underlying state ranges from stress to festering rage.

This is the pattern of life which the Buddha generalized as the category of suffering. Its resolution is in what Krishnamurti (and others) described as choiceless awareness. This is not a matter of ignoring, discounting, or attempting to reject whatever is present. It is a matter of suspending hopes, ideas, and beliefs or preferences for whatever is present to be anything other than what it is.

THE *IS* IN "WHAT IS"

"This should be different than it is."

Such is a thought which we hold regularly, and generally without even noticing it.

By the time this thought, or idea, has occurred to us, that which we are critiquing is already an evident fact.

You cannot change the fact which has been observed, you can only wish it were otherwise or attempt to offer some form of resistance to it.

The development which "should be different than it is" may relate to me; may relate to others; may relate to the world; or to some other aspect of life in general.

The greater the number of notions one has about the way things *should* be, *could* be or *would* be, the greater the anguish and disappointment with the way things actually are—with me, you, the world or the surprises of life.

You, in existence in this moment, and whatever else is actually present—in this moment of existence, as a noticeable reality—are inseparable.

Whether you react or do not react to the present fact, or circumstance, does not change or reverse the fact itself. What *is*, is not appeased by your supposition of what ought to be instead.

You and the factual circumstances of your life (good, bad or indifferent) are an indivisible reality: neither resisting or clinging to any situation makes any existential difference either way.

To simply be present with whatever is present is for the momentary reality and "me" to merge into one harmonious movement of indivisible wholeness.

True Practice

Prior to getting the point of the nondual teachings—still a "seeker," not a "finder"—the full truth of what the enlightened masters have written, or are saying, obviously is not yet evident to us.

When finally the "Aha!" moment has come to pass, we can now go back and re-read those same spiritual texts and a completely different, and "new," dimension of the teachings is fully realized.

Prior to awakening, we read about or hear about some particular discipline or disciplines, and may engage in such a "practice."

Once realization is present clearly, we come to comprehend that the real "practice" the teachers are emphasizing actually has to do with how we live our life, not some superficial system or methodology.

Krishnamurti, for example, speaks of "meditation" (one of his most common words) and "choiceless awareness" in the same breath.

In my own case, from the time I wake up in the morning until I fall asleep at night, there is a constant meditation. This is not some sort of effort to maintain a certain state or to control, change, or express a particular condition. It is a matter that can most simply be stated as *being present with what is present*. In my post-realization re-reading of the sages, it was clear to me that this is what is truly meant as meditation—not some artificial, contrived activity.

You'll know when *this* meditation is your meditation when it is noticed to be completely effortless, and entirely without any idea that it is going to "benefit" you in any way.

When you are doing what you are doing (or saying, or thinking) without any idea that it would be "better" if you were doing something else, that is a true practice.

THE NAMELESS

Your comprehension is clearing. But there is still an element, in your last letter, that can be addressed.

You say that when aware of peace and joy, that is when your true nature is a reality. And you say that when you "have given credence to a separate me, the I-thought" (and you notice the "suffering" which is consequent), there is the "believing in a false reality.... I have left my true nature... and need to reestablish my orientation to it."

Both perceived states—joy and suffering—are basically a false reality, in terms of Absolute awareness. The "I," of perceived positive/negative experience, is a feature of both (opposing) states.

To begin with, "joy" and "suffering" are among the myriad (dualistic) names that we have overlain on 'what is'—on whatever happens to be a present condition. Both are ideas, or concepts, *about* some manner in which the Absolute is appearing. The Absolute itself has no notions of "positive" interpretations versus "negative" interpretations. It is the "I" which generates interpretations.

Your true nature is in transcendence of the dualistic (I/not-I) self-conception. As *such*, there is not concern for whether *I* experience "joy," or *I* experience "suffering." Whatever is being experienced will be experienced with equanimity. Put another way, the 'what is' (that is "you") is merely aware of the 'what is' (whatever happens to be present), without qualification.

Your "true nature" is another name for the ultimate Reality which none of us can ever be apart from. Therefore, you cannot "leave your true nature," nor can you "reestablish it." (*You* never established it to begin with.)

If you are equating "joy" with the "bliss" of which Ramana speaks, I submit that bliss is another word for the equanimity which is the characteristic of our true nature—in transcendence of both "positive" (joy) and "negative" (suffering) polarized (dualistic) conceptions. It is being at one with 'what is,' without a need to name, to evaluate, it.

WATCHING

The sun is waning, at the ridgeline of the distant gray hills. A cat is sitting quietly, doing nothing. It is black, with a white throat and face, like a Catholic priest. Front paws folded beneath it, and atop a rounded, silvery boulder, it appears as warmly comfortable as on a cushion.

The boulder is halfway down a green, grassy slope, amongst a number of small oak trees. At the foot of the hill is a road, active with the suburban homebound. The cat turns its head in the direction of a barking dog, rises on all fours to leisurely stretch an arching back, and resumes its sitting posture now slightly turned. Sitting quietly, both of us are merely observing.

THE CONTROLLING IDEA

Our temporal world is a projection of what is in our hearts. There will not be outer peace until there is inner peace.

The root of the problems of mankind is in the individual, each individual. More fundamental than the question of whether humans act on more wrong ideas than on right ideas, is the question of why humans act on the authority of ideas at all. An idea is a plan to control change—that which cannot lastingly be controlled.

What is the element of the human psyche which desires to control, and why? The seat of our fear is in the preservation of each individual "self": this goes beyond merely the instinctual preservation of life, it is the assertion of our individuality. It is the assertion that there is a meaningful division in reality, an idea which fosters comparison, opposition and conflict. This idea is at the heart of mortal consciousness, and each individual acts out of a lifetime of this divisive idea—save for those few who do not react to change as if it were a subject/object relationship.

Surrender Impatience

You say that there's nothing left for you now but surrender.

Have you surrendered to expectation? Or is this "surrender" an element of a gaining idea, quid pro quo?

Surrender, in the spiritual context, is an emptying out. For a new perspective to be present, the old perspective must evaporate. The old perspective says that I—as a persona—will remain in *place* while something new (Self-realization) is *added*.

No, no. We're talking, in spiritual terms, about subtraction, not about addition; creating a vacuum so that the something new has a place of occupation, or complete presence.

Buddha sat down under the bo tree, exhausted, disappointed, and dis-illusioned with the spiritual search. That was the emptying out. "Sitting quietly, *doing nothing*," something completely new became a presence felt. Had impatience not been an element of the *surrender*, emptying of the persona's preferences would not have been completed.

Surrender says to the unfoldment, "Do with me whatever you will: enlightenment or non-enlightenment, I have given up on asserting my preference." This is the transcendence of the duality of supposing that one condition is better than another; or that some moment in the future will be more sacred than this moment in the present.

This is surrender of the *self*-interest. No "gaining idea," as they say in Buddhism. What could you *gain*; it's all right here, right now. When one takes one's attention off of "elsewhere" and "else-when," we discover that what we've been looking for is what's been looking. And that isn't "me."

TROUBLES FLY

There is a housefly here with me today, an ordinary housefly. Well, maybe not so ordinary.

It is late afternoon in dwindling September. The loose, leafy branches of the big oak tree, on the other side of the path, are crowding each other to loll in the warmth of the sun, jostling each other to feel each touch of the cooling breeze. And a raven performed a somersault in this delightful sky today.

This fly could have chosen to sit anywhere: on one of the cushiony fallen leaves near my chair, on my tote bag or atop my warm thermos. But it has spent a long while, of its short life, on the backs of my hands today, which have mostly been at rest on my legs.

When I have risen for a stretch, it has relocated, with visible irritation. When I have poured from the thermos and drank from my cup, it has remained stubbornly on the second knuckle of my ring finger. As I write, it rides along atop my thumb.

I don't mind the company, as long as who sits with me is generally quiet. And this fly seems to be sensitive to that. I am, perhaps, more restless today than it is. But, then, there's no competition between us.

Surrender

The scriptures speak of non-attachment, and so we first think this applies to property and relationships. But then we come to conclude that the real arena is non-attachment to more than our wardrobe and record collection, or dependence on our parents. It has to do with opinions, ideas, expectations, even such things as desire. Eating only gruel and wearing a black cowl is not what it's all about.

We're not talking about desires like preferring chocolate cake or plaid shirts, or the impulse to roll on the floor with your child. Consider one's attachment to popularity, to having things go one's way, to wanting to be a reincarnation of Christ, or established in the Parenting Hall of Fame.

Likewise, when the sages speak of surrender, the last thing we think of is surrendering our preferences. Surrendering our image of how we ought to perform in the world is a good place to start: surrendering to how things are actually unfolding in the present, as opposed to how we presume they conversely "could" or "should" unfold. To *yield* is closer to what surrender is intended to mean.

Starting Where?

A half dozen spiritually-oriented people can sit around over a two-hour lunch, all the while exteriorizing about the sorrowful plight of the world that an anonymous entity called "they" perpetuates; this can lead to nothing more than a generalized conclusion that a worldwide revolution is in order.

When and where can such a revolution begin? Can it begin this very moment, right where I am, with a deeply internal inquiry that heals the vast, personal division within?

The *Biggest* Picture

You are how old, Delin? Sixty four?

How much longer is it safe to assume that you will live? Another forty years? And that's looking at the outside limit.

Pick up the newspaper any day, and you'll see that someone went out the front door, to go to the supermarket or whatever, and never returned. So it's possible, on any day, that you might have only one day left.

Given the fact that you, your world and all your relationships could vanish at any time—how important are all these matters that you're concerning yourself about?

You do not even know, for sure, that you *have* any future. And if you don't have any certain future, there's no real importance to the *past*.

All you have that is of any true, immediate, value is this impermanent present. In the moment that is present, you can recognize that the things which you are taking so seriously do not—in the big picture—matter at all!

Seeker's Reaction: A Fable

The seeker laboriously weaved his way up toward the summit, where he hoped to join the enlightened master stationed atop.

His foot caught in a crevice, and he wanted immediate help. "Anyone up there?" he called out.

"Yes!"

He explained his dilemma. The answer came down, "Just let go!"

He looked at the thousand-foot fall that would await him, and the rocks below.

He cried out, "Anybody else up there?!"

Reflected Image

Let us say that I hold a belief that generosity is a virtue—and I, due to my conditioning, wish to be known as a virtuous person. I strive to perform acts which are socially esteemed as generous. With the accomplishment of each of these positive gestures, I add another pleasurable memory to my collection of self-improvement experiences. This montage of past activities creates a picture in my imaginative mind, and it is this picture which I identify with, as to who I am. Included in the image, which I hold of myself, is the aspect of Generosity: "Yes, I am a generous person."

Were I to see that, always, I am only what I *presently* am (regardless of whether I am deemed generous or *not*), I would need have no attachment to a continuous image. In this present moment, I might act generously or not generously; in a previous moment, I may have acted in the same way or the opposite way. But I am always who I truly am, in any given moment: I am not an image, I am not the living extension of one of society's pet beliefs; I have not constructed a framework of ideal behavior and then attempted to stretch my skin over it.

Have you looked closely at what comprises the image of your self? Can you see the outline of those elements which are considered "positive" and those which are considered "negative"? Can you see that while you may have been regarded as "greedy" in the "past," there is nothing which externally dictates that you must act greedily in this present instant? The sense of "self" is entirely an image, which projects fixed behavior—as defined by the memorable past—into the present (and "future"). When we are free of the illusory image of the self, we are free of reactive, neurotic and inflexible behavior.

The image of the self is best not preserved, but pickled.

Unlabelled

At the end of a cul-de-sac, in a quiet residential neighborhood, the doorbell rings and I answer the door. There stand two blond girls, about five or six years of age, wearing long gingham gowns; the bigger girl wears steel-rim glasses.

They carry between them a wicker basket which has two handles and is lined with red plaid flannel. They set the basket down in the shade before the door, and it contains a few grapefruit, small yellow squash and a pink geranium cluster which they have evidently picked.

"Would you like to buy some flowers or vegetables?", the small one asks.

I pick up the geranium. "How much for the flower?"

"That would be...umm...three dollars," she answers.

I replace the geranium. I pick out a yellow squash and a small grapefruit. "How much for this?"

The girls look at each other. "Uh, a dollar and a quarter."

"Hmm, that's an expensive squash," I comment, reaching in my pocket for bill and coin.

The older girl considers this. "Yes...it is. But the grapefruit is a gift."

When I proffer the dollar bill and the quarter, the younger girl asks the other, "Which one do I get for my piggy bank?"

"The dollar, of course," the older girl says without hesitation. "And I'll take the quarter."

When they arrive next door, I hear the old man say—jokingly, I presume—"Can't you read that sign?—No Peddlers!"

I hear the older girl ask, "What's a 'peddler'?"

When you don't consider yourself to be anything in particular, you're not restricted by labels.

ONLY THAT

All right then, Hanneke, let's say that there *is* a "you" and "me." No problem with that.

But the question that the nondual teachings are asking you to penetrate is this: what is the true nature, the ultimate Reality, that is *commonly* the identity of "you" and "me"?

You and me are impermanent forms; all such forms come and go. There is a Presence in which all forms arise, and into which they will disappear; this Presence does not come and go.

Ramana has put it this way: that which does not come and go, which is eternal or everlasting, is the only thing which is "real"; all else is "unreal," merely a passing appearance.

All forms—e.g., you and me—owe their original "identity" to this ground of Being. So, from the standpoint of ultimate *reality*, who are *you*? Who am I? What difference is there, in that context?

That is what is meant by, "There is nobody," no "thing" or entity. Therefore, one comes to realize that there is no "me." And, given that realization, there are no "others."

This is not to say that the *appearance* of a me and others even needs to be absent. The realization involves recognizing "who," or "what," these are appearances (or manifestations) *of*. That (Beingness) thou art—*thou* applying to you, me and all others.

RELIGION'S CONTRADICTION

Perhaps you weren't serious about what you wrote, but it offers fruit for contemplation, in any case.

Ask any doctrinaire Christian to elucidate the fundamental understanding of the nature of God: they will reply confidently "omnipresent, omniscient, omnipotent."

Despite this, the doctrine simultaneously treats this God as an entity (such as "He," or the "Lord," etc.).

That which is all-present is, by definition, present in everything that occupies space, at every moment: therefore, (always) "in" every thing.

Being *in* everything ("essential"), this immediate presence is in a position of awareness of what is being done (or not done) by all of that which it is in: thus all-knowing.

Being *elemental* to all that is being done (or not done), it is automatically and inherently all-powerful.

Therefore, there is no requirement for some separate or distinct entity to exist "somewhere" ("a" Deity). This is "religion's" contradictory confusion.

The actuality is far more "miraculous" (or "mysterious") than the conception of a Zeus-like Jehovah, a cosmic Superman.

You write: "God (being omniscient) can predict the future trajectory of every snowflake, the sprouting of every blade of grass, and the deeds of every human being."

What *need* to *predict*, when this Presence is the essence which animates every single activity, including the interaction of every subatomic particle?

"But being omnipotent, He can do anything he *wants*, including behaving in ways different from those he'd predicted, making his predictions fallible.

"He thus can't be both omnipotent and omniscient."

Why would this Presence have "wants" in terms of desired or undesired behaviors, when it is the universal *source* of *all* behaviors—including so-called fallible ones?

It is because of conundrums, like you've stated, that confusion is inevitable in the orthodox mind. As you said at your outset, here's where doctrinaire "contradiction arises."

THE DAY'S BALLET

In the shaft of sunlight in front of my chair, on this quiet day, there are clustered some dozen, or so, insects in the air. They seem to be a type of small fly or large gnat, and they continually pulsate—on wing—around and about each other. At any time, no one of them is more than about a foot away from any other of them, nor ever closer than perhaps a quarter of an inch. They form a kaleidoscopic, changing pattern in the air, rising and falling as a group, an idle engagement for the eye of energy which contemplates them.

They are in relationship to one another, habitually; and that relationship undergoes constant change in space and time. And this will persist throughout their brief lifetime, relieved, somewhere along the way with mating—which is perhaps all that the dance is about. Their progeny will carry on the performance. Beyond that, it has no special meaning. Or, one could say, at best, that being without meaning *is* its meaning.

And our human life is not separate from that.

REINCARNATION

According to the reports, Buddha was enlightened; Ramana was enlightened; Nisargadatta was enlightened. We have no way of knowing with certainty what Buddha may have said (if anything) about reincarnation. We do have, on good authority, what Ramana and Nisargadatta taught about this matter.

Someone said to Nisargadatta, "We have been told about karma and reincarnation..." His response: "Leave it all behind you. Forget it." This is a dualistic concept, he said.

Ultimate reality was not born and never dies, he says; that which is born or re-born is within the relative dream—of impermanence. "There is no such thing," he says of reincarnation. Even its premise of evolving perfection is false: "You are already perfect, here and now." In addition, reincarnation would have to be a process in time: ultimate reality is time-less, transcendent of time.

Ramana, too, asks: Did ultimate reality create such an imperfection that reincarnation is needed to correct it? And: Ultimate reality does not "come" from somewhere; how could it "go" somewhere?

A questioner said: "You (teachers) say that I must be reborn." Ramana replied: "No, I don't say so."

Questioner: "Do you not uphold the theory of rebirth?"

Ramana: "No...remove your confusion that you will be reborn."

As for Buddha, would it not be likely that he would point out that if one had such a desire as reincarnation, it is *desire* which one needs to see to an end.

For your own part, in your deepest sleep, the self or the body are no longer a reality. You are neither alive nor dead, so far as you know. Continuation, or lack of it, is not something you need to concern yourself about. The teachers would tell you that you already exist, as ultimate essence, as anything which you could possibly reincarnate as.

In thorough nondual awareness, such a question does not even persist.

Remember Ramana, on his deathbed:

"Leave you?! Where could I *go*!"

Here Today...

The dove, like a fluffy grey softball, was lying dead on my patio this morning. A few birdseed, from the feeder nearby, still clung to its beak. Had it died of old age? Had it eaten something toxic?

I recalled seeing a dove sit motionless on the ground, under the feeder, the day before.

I put its limp body in a plastic bag and took it out to the dumpster.

Later, a single dove sits on the wall, past the patio, looking into my window at me. Judging from its size, I wonder if it was the male of the mated couple which used to sit together in that spot during the evening.

Had he seen the body earlier, on the patio? Does he realize that she has died? Or does he think, perhaps, that she has flown away and left him? Is he wondering, "What did I do? Is it something I said? *Didn't say*? Did I do something wrong?" He continues to look at me blankly.

There are some things that happen that we have no control over, I silently assure him. "Don't take it personally, okay?"

REALISM

If I take what you've described (in great detail) to be true, your spouse is demonstrating by his actions that he is not only inconsiderate but unloving, by social standards.

You seem to be aware that involved in your assessment is an element of idealizing: *ideally*, he ought to be acting (toward you) in *this* way, and not *that* way; he ought to be more sensitive to your needs, more consistently.

You appear to also be aware that such idealizing applies to yourself as well. You have a preconceived idea as to how you ought to (ideally) respond to this situation (which gives evidence of being a chronic condition). So, you have ideas not only about how he ought to behave, but about how you ought to behave in regard to how he behaves.

And you also, apparently, are aware of a couple of other fixational ideas. One, this dissatisfaction—to the point of antagonism—should not be occurring between my spouse and I. And two, we should remain together as a couple despite whatever else is occurring between us.

The fact is (according to what you've said, Miriam) that you perceive that your spouse does not treat you as if he loves you, to the degree of your pained dissatisfaction; and you conceive that the two of you ought to remain together *only* because to do otherwise would be to admit a mistake.

I'm reminded that while Gangaji was visiting Papaji in India, a man complained to Papaji thus: "I rent a room above a repair shop. The noise disrupts my meditation, and even disturbs my contemplation. What should I do?"

Papaji turned to Gangaji: "What should this man do?"

Gangaji went on at some length, to the effect that he needed to turn inward, transcend the worldly experience and reach the inner bliss where even the sense of sound is recognized as a gift from God—or some counsel along these lines.

Papaji turned to the man and said, "If I were you, I'd move."

Further, Krishnamurti was, at one time, sharply criticized by outraged religionists (in India) when he publicly advised a woman to divorce her neglecting husband. A "spiritual leader" ought to be *upholding* the marital vow, he was chastised.

I was the child of a married couple who were so alienated that I don't recall ever seeing them show affection or intimacy toward each other. My (unhappy) mother would not divorce my father, because of her Christian beliefs that to do so would run counter to the Christian ideal. Was home life a satisfactory experience for any of us? No.

Life is short, and this is not a dress rehearsal. If I found myself in the situation that you so graphically described, I suspect that I would admit that I may have been mistaken in my choice of mates; and/or that perhaps my expectations and my standards of ideal behavior had contributed to the dissatisfaction I experience. And if I continued to feel unloved and disrespected by my marital partner, I would likely move.

SPECIES IMPERMANENCE

There is no particularly good reason to believe that the human species will not become extinct. *Homo sapiens* is, after all, the only *remainder* of the *genus* of humankind, which anthropologists say has numbered at least two other variants.

Whether man's extinction is a climax to nuclear mechanization, or to strangling of his natural environmental habitat, or to overpopulation and consequent genocidal warfare, the precipitating circumstances are a moot point.

Man's collective folly lies in not recognizing his impermanence. A species of beings who individually deny impending death— even in old age and illness—and pray to avoid it, humans can hardly be expected to concede the perish-ability of their entire, domineering genus.

The fact is that it is more than vaguely possible that, inevitably, there is no real hope for the millennial tenure of mankind. Even were the world of humans to reform their self-destructive proclivities overnight, nature might still impose its own timetable upon the span of our golden age.

Were there any hope for man, it would be in recognizing his fragility and intransigence. In facing the reality of our collective death—in the same manner in which one may calmly contemplate one's individual mortality—the same reorientation in awareness is possible for the viewpoint of humanity, as it is for each human who personally surrenders to the imperative of the universal "what is." *Being* what it is, there is not anything to be gained by compulsively and frantically grasping, resisting and controlling—even where there is concern for one's physical continuation.

This awareness frees one not from the inevitability of mortality, but from the arrogant delusion of immortality, and permits one to relinquish the death grip on fantasies of a future age—golden or leaden. The awareness of which we speak is attentiveness to the abundance and wholeness of the moment—which is all there is, and therefore lacks nothing.

When there is a perception that not anything is lacking, there is an understanding that there is not anything which is mandatory that we achieve. We can then, at least, die serenely.

Whom Ever

According to astronomers, the cosmos had its beginning at something on the order of 13-14 *billion* years ago. According to biologists, the human species made its debut about two *million* years ago (give or take a year or two!).

If the history of the cosmos were reduced to one 24-hour day, the entire "history" of man might be missed upon the blink of an eye.

During the period of the entire history of man, it has been only within the past couple of hundred years that the tools of our physical sciences—with which to observe the macrocosm and microcosm of our universe—have been accessible.

Prior to that, not even the privileged few—not to mention the man in the street—could cite hard evidence to substantiate the true, demonstrable nature of existence.

Religionists had proclaimed that all that we see has been created. The scientific enquirer has only recently been able to answer the question: created of *what*? And the cutting-edge of these discoveries has trickled down to the man in the street like a wake, reaching from the boat to the shore with a lapse of about fifty years. In other words, the general public has barely the faintest appreciation of what physicists are reporting today as the true nature of our reality.

For example, take any piece of matter—a chunk of human flesh will do—and examine it. You will find that its uniform consistency is cellular. Break one of those cells into component parts and you will detect molecules. When, in time, a molecule is examined closely, it will be revealed to be an aggregation of atoms. Split an atom into its myriad particles, and you will notice interacting constituents that can best be referred to collectively as "sub-atomic particles."

Now, look closely at one of these particles, and what do you observe? Your first surprise is that there is not anything material— no substance—to this particle. Its form is no more concrete than a whirlpool in water.

Like a whirlpool in water, its very presence has no framework in which it is independent. In the way that one normally thinks of a particle—like a grain of sand—it cannot actually be defined as a separate entity. In fact, subatomic particles are so inter-related that the consequence is a behavioral field which operates by a set of laws that are fully incomparable to the physical laws of the macroscopic—seemingly "material"—world (the so-called "laws of nature" which we have supposed to be universal).

So, consider this. Most people you talk to today are still under the impression that the things, which they suppose they see, are composed of dense atomic *matter*. But even each atom is almost entirely comprised of what we consider to be "empty space"; only a minuscule portion is particulate. And these "particles," themselves, represent intermittent patterns of a presence so abstract that the closest comparison is "pulsating energy"

This, my friends, is the true, underlying nature of *your* "chemical make-up," of the composition of your body.

And not only is every gram of you formed of these immaterial quanta, but none of these quanta are independently discrete. What we view as empty space, or "air," is a latticed network of (identical) quanta (an electron "outside" of your body is entirely interchangeable with an electron "inside" your body). So, the quanta in the air that presses on your skin is in interaction with the quanta that *forms* your skin. And *these* "exterior" quanta are in interaction, like overlapping wave patterns, with quanta across and throughout the entire universe—not excluding any form of space; including that in your cells.

The physicists' question—created of *what*?—can now easily be posed (by those who understand quantum physics), "created of *whom*?" You and the created universe are indivisibly interconnected, cause and effect.

The Reality is...

Your letter was well-thought, and it looks as though you've been doing some meaningful contemplation. This is what often happens when we sit still and shut up. "Be still and know..."

"I have spent the afternoon lying down *considering*...what is there that is *not* energy...not It...if energy *is* all there is..." This is the kind of revelation which one can only arrive at by oneself; no one can give such "information" or Truth to you—except as *second-hand* wisdom.

You say that such discoveries previously were "not something I would have given any thought to," but "I seem to be seeing things now that I must have *missed* previously." This should be an indication to you that your contemplation is on a "firm" footing.

And bear in mind that no matter what illumination comes to you, two things will continue to remain unchanged: the world will not become a perfect place to live; and you will not become a perfect person. Imperfection, all around, comes with the earthly territory.

Not only does it appear evident, as you say, that we are on the verge of the collapse of the American empire; but it appears to be, additionally so, that we are on the verge of the collapse of global ecology. In all cases, I agree, it would be wise for people "to recognize the existence of...the *reality* of the 'invisible'." However, all of this just goes to emphasize the cosmic bottom line: Nothing really matters.

Transformation of Thing-ing

A "self"—which is not real—posits that it is the generator of "thoughts"—which are no more real.

The "self" is an idea *about* something; which is the same as saying that it is a concept. 'Thought' is an idea about something which the self repeatedly engages in—which is no less a concept.

"Self" and "thought," both, are what Ken Wilber refers to as "propositions about reality."

"All conceivable *ideas* [concepts] are embraced within the term 'delusions'," says Yasutani, "and, as such, are a hindrance to the realization of your Essential nature."

When one can find no limited "self" which is the purported originator of "thoughts," what becomes of (dreaded) "concepts"? There can be no concepts where there is not a self to conceive them.

So, rather than focusing on the cart—"thoughts," "mind," "concepts," etc.—look to the horse: that's where the action is.

Yasutani again: "You can never come to enlightenment [the end of subject/object delusions] through...conceptualization. Cease clinging to *all thought-forms*! I stress this, because it is the central point of all Zen practice."

Wilber again: "Since this [enlightened] experience of the 'real world' is obscured by our concepts *about* it—and since these concepts *rest* on the split between the subject that knows ["self"] versus the concepts that are known ["thought"]—all of these [spiritual] traditions emphatically announce that Reality can only be experienced non-dually; without the *gap* between the knower [self] and the known [thought]..."

Subject/object perception is virtually the *definition* of dualism. So, all of these teachers are insisting that this particular pattern or habit of postulating must be relinquished. To do so is inevitably the death of the conceptual self—the perennial *subject*. When the subject [self] dies, what becomes of the object that is at the seat of its delusions [thought]?

When the self has died, "everything" dies with it: "Thus [awakening] is called," notes Wilber, "Void, Sunyata [featureless], Empty, Agnoia [Unknown]; which means only that all thoughts and propositions *about* reality are void and invalid [to Reality itself]." Nothing left to think *about*; no one *left* to think about it.

This relinquishment results in, Wilber states, "not one 'view' among many, but the absence of *all views whatsoever*." Goodbye to the view of the object [thought] by the subject [self].

So thought is not "an important topic which needs to be examined and re-examined," as you suggest. You comment, "The fact that thought is divisive by its very nature should not be overlooked." And you add, "Thinking is *thing*ing."

When you stop *thinging*, when you've finished with dividing all that you see, as subject, into named objects—self-thought-mind-concepts-reality-emptiness-void—all are recognized as one, insubstantial no-thing.

Then, even goodbye to considerations as to what is 'dual' and what is 'nondual.'

That's the ending of thought, of the "known."

When in Doubt...

You are correct: if a person has doubt that Self-realization is present, that indicates that it is not present.

I am reminded of the words of Ramana:

> "The jnani (Self-realized) has no doubts (about) himself....He has no doubts, to be cleared....

> "So long as false identification persists, doubts will persist... Doubts will cease only when the (individuated identification) is put an end to. That will result in realization of Reality. There will remain no 'other' to doubt."

Even though Self-realization is not fully present (and your conclusion that this is so, is an indication that it *is* so), "Laura" has had a "glimpse" of something which has already effected noticeable changes. So, it is not a matter of self-deception here.

But the decisive factor is, as Ramana says, "So long as false identification persists..." The glimpse, as you say, was of Oneness. Yet, in this case, false identification persists: there is a "person" who has had an "experience"—this is a dualistic conception, not Oneness.

There also remains a person who has definite ideas about how that experience should be developing for that person. The person concerned is the "subject" end, of the subject/object duality.

Full Self-realization leaves no doubt about the actuality of Oneness, of nonduality. And in Self-realization the subject/object polarization is transcended, so that the false identification of the subject self and objective "other" (material, or immaterial such as "special" experiences) no longer engenders separation, or what amounts to the denial of Oneness.

The dualistic self-identity leads to separation in our lives, and this separation can be a *catalyst* for full Self-realization. The *glimpse* of Oneness (Christian mystics call it grace) can be a revelation that the condition of the jnani is realizable. "Person," "experiences," and "expectations" will be seen as empty of meaning when Self-realization is completely profound.

TRULY NO PREFERENCE?

You write, "My *feelings* are just energy 'passing' through awareness. There is no preference, because it is all the Absolute."

Having written this, presumably it is a truth you apprehend. So, how can you then go on to raise problems for yourself?

There is Julie, which experiences a particular feeling (or category of feelings). She can comprehend, in this case, that (as an aspect of the Absolute) energy—which can be characterized as "this" or "that," "positive" or "negative"—is passing through awareness. There is no idea, in this instance, that the energy (in the form of particular feelings) ought to be other than it is: "no preference."

Yet, in some other situation she is not content with the characteristic of the energy passing through awareness.

Why not then recognize this discontent, or dissatisfaction, as simply *another* form of feeling—or energy—passing through awareness?

In the first instance (where there is no preference for the manifestation which arises in consciousness), is there not "peace" with what's present—a lack of conflict?

In the second instance (where there is an idea that conditions ought to be different from what they are), is there not an uneasiness, a discomfort?

So, what does this tell us about which of these perceptions merits a consistent focus of attention?

Situation 1: The I-thought (self-conception) is not noticeably present in awareness. There is no problem, because it is recognized that "all is the Absolute."

Situation 2: The I-thought (and discomfort it raises) is noticeably present in awareness. There is no problem, because it is recognized that "all is the Absolute."

You write, "There is no preference." If there is truly no preference, where can a problem arise?

Is "All the Absolute" in some cases, but not in others?

Transcend the Terms

There is much confusion, in the spiritual writings, around these terms. The different sources have differing definitions in mind.

You might think of "consciousness" (as does Krishnamurti) as having "content." The ego is "conscious," in this case, of the content of the psyche (the "mind" and its "thoughts").

You can think of "awareness" as not being limited by egoic content; not being limited to any particular or special object of awareness. You are aware (peripherally) of more than you consciously focus your attention on. Here's how Nisargadatta has phrased the distinction:

"There can be no consciousness without awareness, but there can be awareness without consciousness, as in deep sleep."

It would be fair to think of the "witness" as a condition that is a connection between consciousness and awareness. Since there is witnessing during the waking state (but not in deep sleep), it is dependent upon consciousness. But the witnessing state, that is spoken of by the sages, is removed from egoic inclinations. It is an objective, neutral observation, or awareness, of what is presently existent in general: a non-restrictive perceiving of 'what is' present before the preceptor.

But what is typically being said is that your true essence goes even beyond the witness. The witness, the witnessing and the witnessed are all one unbroken actuality. It is this One unbroken whole which is your true nature, or essence.

All of these definitive classifications—consciousness, awareness, witness, etc.—dissolve when Self-realization is present. As Ramana would say, in the final analysis, only the Self is real. Consider that all distinctions (*including* the distinction of "Self") will disappear when you close your eyes for the final time.

That which remains, that which is transcendent of change, is your true nature.

THOU AS THAT

Now that you are considering developments with the possibility in mind that all is "That doing what it does," look more deeply into the fuller implications of this.

At the present, you are attempting to view "That doing what it does" while "you" stand apart from it.

To better understand this issue, consider that in much of the enlightenment literature (e.g., Bhagavad Gita) it is said that "all occurs in you." This *can* be interpreted to mean that all phenomena (material or immaterial) depend upon consciousness for their "reality"; therefore, in this sense, all that occurs, occurs "in" you.

But the intended meaning of this expression is that *you* are *That*, you are the boundless Absolute; you, being *all* that *is*, are the entire cosmos and every phenomenal thing (formed or unformed) within it. Therefore, *all that is* arises and recedes within you *as the Absolute*.

You *are* the "That," in other words, which is "doing what it does." You and That, being the same One Absolute actuality, it is not "you *and* That" which is intended to be suggested. It is you, *as* That, which is doing all that is done.

This is the *non*dual realization. To suppose that "you" (or any "other") are observing or noting "That, doing what it does" is a dualistic conception. You *are* That, therefore you cannot be standing apart, uninvolved (or only relatively involved) in what "is being done."

When the expression "all that is, is that doing what it does" is clearly understood, it is likewise understood that "you"— supposing yourself to be a "separate" entity—are not doing anything at all. As is also said, in fewer words, "you are not the *doer*." The relative "you" (*imag*ined self) is the doer of no thing. The Absolute You—*as* That—is the doer of *all that is* ever done: because all-that-is rises and falls within the *true* You.

There is no I

Under the best of circumstances, in a direct discussion, a listener can be brought to comprehend that the egoic self is merely one of the many forms that appear as manifestations of the absolute Self.

The consequence is that sometimes the listener exclaims the recognition, "Then the *I* doesn't exist."

In some cases, the listener will be silent for a moment; then their next sentence will begin, ignoring completely the insight which had been arrived at, "Yes. But *my* problem is that..." blah, blah, blah.

For some, on occasion, the I-image hears its death knell—"There is no I!"—and a burial soon follows. Rather than a "Yes, but" following the insight that the "I" is a misidentification, there is— in rare cases—a reflective acknowledgement: "Yes. Yes!"

A semi-retired man telephoned in the evening. "There's begun to be a connection with what you've been talking about." His report concerned a bit of his background: he grew up as a member of a minority group. Whenever he wasn't invited to a party, or whatever, he "took it personally"; his "ego was hurt." This led to resentments that he'd noticed all of his adult life.

Earlier on this day, this familiar situation was prompted to recur, by a typical incident. "But, for the first time, there was nothing 'personal' there to suffer any more. I've been feeling an immense freedom."

He had seen through the image of "who" it was that could be "rejected," no longer attached to his egoic "reality." He simply noticed his reactive tendency, *and* his dissatisfaction to see that trait reappear—without either a victim, an accuser nor a judge anywhere in sight. What was witnessing the troubling incident—the "why *me*?" reaction; the *secondary* reaction ("Here I go again!"), *and* even his release of the habitualized pattern— was itself unaffected by all the turmoil that was being witnessed.

He was not viewing all that was present from "my" standpoint, and the consequence is that there was no "me" there to suffer.

The Passing Scene

Life is like looking out of the window while sitting in a train. You have no control over what appears in view.

There's even the moment after the train has paused, when it imperceptibly begins moving again. The appearance is that the train is motionless, but the scenery outside the window is moving. That, too, is a view that life sometimes gives us, a falsely relative view.

We make no attempt to control the scene observed outside the train, knowing that wishing that it was something that it isn't would be useless.

And so it is, for the person who relaxes into Absolute awareness. Whatever passes across the screen of consciousness, whatever the organism experiences, is viewed dispassionately. The viewer acknowledges that all things change, and merely witnesses the changes impartially.

Hidden Truths

Agreeably, there is much that needs to be said about *spirituality* in Christianity (which few know about) as contrasted to *religion* in Christianity. As biblical scholar Bart Ehrman put it, let's get

182

back to the teachings *of* Jesus rather than the teachings *about* Jesus.

Throughout history, there have been those who have spontaneously awoken to nondual awareness; this is commonly called enlightenment. Among those (for example), the evidence indicates, are Buddha, Jesus, Ramana Maharshi, Krishnamurti—and others.

While the nondual perspective is radically different from the dualistic perspective, what the enlightened sages have realized is the same universal, transcendent truth which all share in common. Thus, the similarity in the language of their (paradoxical) pronouncements.

Even in the New Testament, there are sayings attributed to Jesus that are most transparent and meaningful when paralleled to the enlightenment teachings of such as Buddha or Ramana.

This never became so apparent until the unearthing of the Gospel of Thomas. Some of the quotations ascribed to Jesus—which some scholars believe pre-date the New Testament—can only be sensibly understood in the context of the Eastern emphasis on Self-realization. So, one can make the case that *truly* spiritual teachings were the product of Jesus; religious teachings were the product, originally, of Paul and Peter—who promulgated ideas *about* Jesus, rather than the ideas *of* Jesus. Not surprisingly, what appear to be the *original* words of Jesus—having to do with *Self*-realization—were left out of (what was eventually compiled as) the New Testament by the organized, self-perpetuating "church." Any reasonable amount of research into recent biblical scholarship leaves little question about all this.

Interestingly, this scenario can be revisited in church history centuries later. The German Dominican friar Meister Eckhart indicates (in extant writings) that he was the subject of a spontaneous epiphany regarding the Absolute nature of his own being. The sermons that emanated from his own mouth are replete with expression that could be taken from the accounts of Ramana or Buddha, or what "Jesus said" in *Thomas*.

And not surprisingly, as a consequence, the Church called him before a proceeding of the Inquisition, and subsequently disallowed his teachings. He was re-stating the doctrine of Jesus, in preference to the doctrine *about* Jesus.

So, if one is to concern oneself with *spiritual* truth, as it relates to what in the *West* is known only as religious dogma, one could most fruitfully examine available material on the Gospel of Thomas and, as well, on Meister Eckhart. [ed. note: Karina Library Press published Robert's *The Gospel of Thomas: The Enlightenment Teachings of Jesus* in 2010.]

SILENT MIND

In the diversity of spiritually-oriented material that's available, there can be found fuzzy notions, which amount to the mythical. There are catchwords whose meanings go undefined. To the reader, they can suggest that there are ideal states of being, whose attainment is possible. The seeker may go on, for years, comparing his actual state with the idealized state that he has been led to suppose is a requisite goal, thus focusing his attention on what "might be" rather than on "what is."

A person who is not perturbed by his present state, even though it's not the ideal state that the spiritual material seems to project, may rightly be said to have "equanimity" or a "quiet mind." To the extent that his state reflects an absence of comparative and dissatisfied mentation, this could even be described as a "silent mind."

This does not indicate that the person has no awareness of, or thoughts about, what his actual condition *is*—but that he has no problem with it *being* what it is. His mind is silent, so far as concern for the matter of his existent state is entailed.

If we now speak of a mind that is "devoid of thought" (devoid means "entirely without"), this might serve as a poetic extrapolation; but—in terms of a silent mind—it would actually mean that he is devoid of thought that is condemnatory of what he is currently experiencing.

In other words, a person who has a "problem" with any vagrant thoughts that occur—who is disturbed or agitated by what is acknowledged to be factually present—could scarcely be considered to have a silent mind. If that person were to have an objective of attaining a state "devoid of thought," his supposition must be that this *desirable* state will put an end to thoughtful awareness of the state he considers to be problematic.

A silent mind is not occupied by appraising perceived thoughts as "good" or "bad," "better" or "worse"—and then pursuing a proposed objective by which all vagrant thoughts cease to exist.

To seek a "solution" to the "problem" of thought, in attempting to efface it, is the dualistic way. To transcend the *concern* regarding any thoughts which appear—to *have* no problem with that—is the hallmark of a silent mind.

Here is substantially the point, in this context, that Robert Powell is evidently making:

The analytical mind that makes an effort to transform itself into the Silent Mind is merely projecting from its hearsay about the Silent Mind. It is the projection of an 'idea'; therefore this operation is still wholly within the field of the analytical mind, and so can never lead to a transformation.

THE ANCIENT PRESCIENCE

What mystics have known, for millennia, by inference, scientists are now able to confirm by technical research. Mystics, though, are guided by nonduality, while scientists are restricted by duality: which is why every (separate) answer merely leads to another (divisive) question. ("What is the smallest particle? A quark." "And why is a quark the smallest?" Et cetera, et cetera.)

Physics breaks reality into minuscule bits and then looks for what "unifies" them—when they never had discrete, independent existence to begin with. Puzzlement still continues today (as a June 2005 article in *Discover* magazine illustrates) over an experiment that is nearly a century old.

> Almost 80 years ago, scientists discovered that it *is* possible to be in two locations at the same time—at least for an atom or a subatomic particle, such as an electron. For such tiny objects, the world is governed by a madhouse set of physical laws known as quantum mechanics. At that size range, every bit of matter and energy exists in a state of blurry flux, allowing it to occupy not just two locations but an *infinite* number of them *simultaneously*.

It is only thought, conception (concepts), which creates the mystery—through fragmentation, isolation. Two "electrons" are merely named, individuated elements of the same fundamental energy. And no "energy" stands apart, in actuality, from its environment, from the place or location it's found. Nor are there any "places" in the environment which are, in fact, apart from each

186

other: there is no non-place abyss between any two "locations." So, electron-energy-location are all one unit ("system").

Substitute "person" for electron, and you have the context in which most mystics spoke.

It's all one thing, from the start.

Yes, Doctor, there *are* two "things" in different "places" at the same "time"—but only from the standpoint of dualistic differentiation.

So, an attempt is being made to understand the "miracle" of omnipresence in terms of (dualistic) cause-and-effect. Yet, a miracle—by definition—transcends understanding in terms of cause-and-effect.

Is mysticism unscientific? Or is science, so far, incapable of penetrating the inferences that its re-search reveals?

BLUE HAZE

Inverness is an hour-and-a-half drive north of Tampa, near the Gulf of Mexico, and is one of those small cities with a main street, a courthouse square and a few shopping malls that spill over outside of the city limits.

It is a week before July Fourth, and a swift, drenching afternoon rain has left behind warm, sultry air and a few billowy clouds. It is Friday evening, and the television sets of America have clicked on—even earlier than usual, judging from the one I can hear in the motel room which neighbors my room. I decide that it is an opportune time to go out for dinner.

Driving back from the restaurant to the motel on an alternate route, and looking for a suitable place to take an evening stroll, I see a sign which directs me to the most pleasant city park I recall having ever seen.

Whispering Pines Park apparently covers many acres of this generally flat, expansive and uncrowded section of rural Florida. Abundant with filmy pine trees and sub tropical vines and vegetation, it is a remarkably beautiful woodland, in the light of the setting sun. And it appears to be surprisingly well kept—no litter to be seen—with sparsely few "No..." or "Don't..." signs.

Parking my car near the unguarded entry gate, I walk a quiet paved road which leads to an Olympic-size swimming pool, complete with lifeguard on duty. A sign reads, "Pool capacity: 87." Counting children and adults, there are eleven persons in the pool. Though the park is fully equipped, with kept tennis courts, racquetball courts, volleyball nets, and all, the only additional sounds of human activity emanate from a distant softball field.

The night is warm and luscious enough to want to take off all your clothes, and yet there are no annoying insects in the air. Birds are still warbling, and the crickets have begun their song. A few lightning bugs are now to be seen. Past the pool, a wide, inviting path, marked "Jogging Trail," leads into the fragrant woods.

This is a trail you could jog in your bare feet. Soft pine needles have been washed by the summer rains across the white sandy path, and someone has gone carefully ahead and marked with spray paint the occasional gnarled roots or natural protuberances which might wrench your foot.

Indeed, the softness of the cool sand and moist pine needles speaks sensuously to my feet through the soles of my sneakers, and I sit for a moment in the path to remove both shoes and stockings.

I walk the approximate two miles of the jogging path, startled that such a small town could provide such a profoundly relaxing public park. And I do not encounter another single soul on the path! Certainly there is a population of some thousands within a few minutes' drive of this uncommonly gracious woodland— many of them living cheek–by-jowl in their boxes in town. Can the cathode tube have enslaved them all? Can "Jeopardy!" and "Perfect Strangers" have alienated them form the beautiful reality which is just beyond their windows?

WHERE NO DUST ALIGHTS

Seng Ts'an, the Third Chinese Patriarch (or Dharma-heir of Buddha), was the reputed author of the celebrated Zen teaching poem, the *Hsin Hsin Ming*. The Sixth Patriarch, Hui-neng, was at least as renowned, for the imprint he left on the enlightenment teachings.

According to a legendary story (which he himself is said to have recounted), Hui-neng (638-713 A.D.) was young when his father died. Living in the vicinity of Canton, he worked as a woodcutter to support his mother.

Upon delivering firewood to a customer one day, he overheard a man reciting aloud a segment of the Diamond Sutra. Hui-neng was illiterate, but he immediately understood the meaning of what he'd heard: "My mind at once became enlightened."

Wanting to know more about the source of such wisdom, he traveled for nearly a month to reach Tung-shan monastery in the north, whose Roshi was the Fifth Patriarch, Hung-jen, who presided over about a thousand disciples.

When he met the Zen master, Hui-neng was asked "from whence he had come." Upon replying that he had come up from the south, Hung-jen noted that people from his area were normally illiterate; how would someone from the south be able to comprehend the teachings? Hui-neng responded that "north and south are not different, in Buddha nature."

Impressed, the Roshi permitted Hui-neng to live in the stable, and to work at pounding rice and splitting firewood.

Some eight months passed. The Roshi, expecting to live no more than a few years, announced that he would pass his robe and begging bowl (thus appointing a Sixth Patriarch) to whomever wrote the best verse showing "what the essence of Buddha-mind is," the point being that "the man who has realized the essence of Mind can clearly speak of it."

All the monks anticipated that the winning poem would surely be composed by the head monk, Shen-hsui, so no one else bothered to attempt.

Shen-hsui sweated over a verse for four days. Doubting its success, he took a lantern and at night wrote a verse that was posted on a corridor of the Roshi's assembly hall.

> Bodhi [enlightenment] is like a tree [gradually attaining form];
>
> Mind is like a mirror bright—
>
> We polish it day by day,
>
> So that no dust may alight.

(In other words, with the effort of "practice," one might someday become enlightened—when "perfected.")

Shen-hsui did not sign the verse, reasoning that "if Roshi approves it, I shall then tell him that it was done by me."

Hung-jen deduced who wrote the verse, and asked the head monk if he'd written it. So as not to embarrass him, the Roshi told Shen-shui in private, "Your stanza shows that you have not yet realized: one's Buddha nature is neither created nor can it be annihilated." He suggested the head monk try again, in a few days.

Two days after, Hui-neng heard one of the monks repeating the verse that had been posted, and was told for the first time about the poem competition: "I knew at once that the composer of it had not yet realized." Hui-neng had never been to the assembly hall, so he asked the monk to take him there. He dictated a verse to the monk, and it was posted:

Bodhi is not like a tree;

Mind is not like a mirror bright—

Since there is Nothing from the start,

Where could dust alight?

Hui-neng's point was that all things in the universe are the manifestation of Buddha nature; there is nothing we need to do to "improve" on that which is already perfect, in its formlessness; both the "mirror" and the "dust" are merely expressions of the same ultimate essence.

Knowing that the head monk might seek retribution for the impertinence of the challenge, the verse was left unsigned. But the Roshi recognized that only one person in the monastery would have been able to compose it. Hung-jen sent for Hui-neng, and in private gave him the robe and the begging bowl, saying "Who sees intuitively his true nature, is a Buddha."

Because he knew that the head monk would seek revenge for the affront to his station, the Roshi urged Hui-neng to flee to the south while it was yet dark, saying "You are now the Sixth Patriarch."

Once established away from the monastery, Hui-neng was a vigorous teacher that "Buddha nature is nonduality." He is reported to have delivered his Platform Sutra ("sermon" or teaching) to an audience of 10,000 (thus he needed to speak from a platform). Even two years before he died (at age 76), he is said to have enlightened a monk who had sat zazen for 30 years before coming to him.

Less than a month before his death, he told his disciples, "I soon intend to leave this world." All the monks wept, except one. Hui-neng observed of that one, "You have attained awakening, in which 'good' and 'not good' are identical." To the others, he remarked, "You have not yet understood.

"If you knew where I was going, you wouldn't be crying: my nature is without birth and without destruction, without going and coming."

He concluded, "I shall depart from you now, do not weep....If you are without coming and without going, without judgment of right and wrong [dualities]...this then is the great way."

It is recorded, "After finishing speaking these words, the master quietly passed away, at midnight."

An example of his Platform Sutra teaching: "It is in our mind that a 'Buddha' exists. Our own nature is the true Buddha."

For those who comprehend the full meaning of his words, he said, "You will always be in the same place as I am."

How It Should Be

What is the bar to enlightenment?

Ideas.

For a start, consider these five ideas, any one of which the seeker is likely convinced.

1. It won't happen to me. Only someone who comes to enlightenment with a dramatic and unique background story like that of Buddha, Ramana, Krishnamurti, et al, is visited with the grace of transcendental illumination. I am of too low of a caliber to become enlightened.

2. It won't happen today. I haven't put in enough years of meditation; deprivation; study; penance; puja; denigration—or something—for enlightenment to be bestowed on me.

3. It won't happen here. Perhaps on my next trip to India; or while in the Self-Realization Fellowship temple; or during a spirit-quest in the mountains; or while at the feet of my guru. But not *here*.

4. It won't happen this way. It will only happen by shaktipat or diksha; or suddenly while repeating my mantra; or after completing the Blue Cliff koans; or in a flood of effulgent white

light; or while in a state of "no-thought"; or accompanied by cosmic bliss; or while in some state I haven't even imagined yet.

5. This is not it. This is not how Adi Da says that it happened with him. I have no feeling that all the planets are within my skin. I still feel like I'm here on earth. I felt no jolt of radiant energy coursing up my spine. I still can't read minds or predict the future. I don't seem to be beaming love rays. No one has certified my enlightenment. This is too much like ordinary life.

LIFE AND DEATH

The point, of what you've read, is that the fetus in the womb does not concern itself with such questions as "What will be my condition when I am no longer alive?"; nor even such a question as, "*Am* I alive?" And, so far as we can tell, a *baby* does not deliberate such questions, either.

In fact, you yourself are not concerned with such questions during your deepest sleep each night. Actually, you do not concern yourself with *any* questions when your sense of being a "someone" is absent in this deep-sleep state.

So, obviously, the dualistic notions of "being alive" or "being dead" are acquired after, as a consequence of our developing the concept of "being someone," being an individual self.

What would your awareness of "life" and "death" be before you took your first breath? What will your awareness of "death" and "life" be after you take your last breath? What is your awareness of "life" and "death" when you are in your deepest sleep? We can say in the latter case, "None"; and because that is our experience, we can contemplate that this non-awareness of life and death may likely be the same condition which prevails before we take our first breath and after we take our last breath.

Thus, if there is no sense of an individual self (which lives and dies) in the fetus, in the corpse, or even in our sleep nightly in between these states, how *essential* is it that a sense of being an individual "someone" be consciously maintained?

Where the sense of being a separate self is *not* maintained in consciousness, what is it then that is considered to be "alive" or could be considered to be "dead"? In other words, when there no longer is a conscious sense of being a separate self, there no longer is a sense of a self that is "alive" or may someday be "dead."

This is to transcend the dualities of such concepts as self/not self, life/death, and so on. That is the relationship of what you've read, to the nondual teachings. It's not anything more complicated than that.

Not Up For Grabs

No one is saying the things that are unpopular, in spiritual terms. There is no market for it. The "wisdom" that can be bought, is paid for by those who are affluent, and those who are affluent are generally ambitious. Their interest is in knowledge, for knowledge is power.

Knowledge can be easily and readily attained, and it gluts the marketplace. Knowledge is transmissible from person to person; wisdom is not apart from the person. Wisdom is to be found in this moment, and there is no currency for this moment, as it is the investiture of all.

We must look without for knowledge; we must look within for wisdom. And deep within, there is but emptiness and stillness—raiment that goes unnoticed in the marketplace. There is no market for raiment which cannot be seen by the envious eye.

The Departure of Death

It is sunny again today. The red-tailed hawk has spent another long day of fruitless hunting. The ground squirrels in the field, below, are alerted by the predator's shadow. The pasture grasses are at full height and dense, providing optimum cover for the prey.

It is toward the end of the day. A tract house sits near the field, and groups of Brewer's blackbirds are foraging, by turn, among the short and shaded grasses of the lawn.

The hawk comes quietly to rest nearby, toward the top of the lacy jacaranda tree, which has been among the last to leaf out.

The petit finches are pulling up tiny tufts of lawn grass, which are carried to the eaves of the house, where they are fashioned into nests. The female blackbirds too—who are dusky, in comparison to the larger and blacker males—are probably with egg; males and females now travel together in pairs.

One pair of blackbirds leave the lawn, one after the other, and alight on a low branch of the jacaranda, contentedly to preen. Then they descend again, one after the other, to the lawn, to resume their evening feeding. Amid their flight, death overtakes the guardian. Dissecting the path from branch to lawn, the hawk swoops between the descending blackbirds, and snatches the male out of the air. The startled female returns to the branch, where she watches and anxiously clucks.

The young hawk lands on the lawn, perched atop the body held between its feet. One set of talons have been wrapped around the blackbird's neck, the other set hold the struggling ebony feet and wings tight to the body. As the hawk balances atop its catch, talons slowly tighten into the neck and lower body of the prey. The blackbird remains motionless, while tiny tufts of feathers are freed to the breeze like smoke.

The hawk, in this brief time, has been looking aloft, considering to which nearby branch the body can be repositioned. Without a change in posture, he abruptly lifts his wings and carries his prey across the lawn to the leafy sycamore tree. The female blackbird continues to await her mate, and to cluck.

Hidden from enquiring eyes, up in the sycamore tree, there is the heavy flapping of wings, then the silence of death momentarily departs.

No Secret

The "disciplines" that you ask about are referred to as "esoteric." This is defined as "intended for an inner or select group of initiates." In more extreme cases, it is called occult: "purposely concealed from view of outsiders."

The thrust here (as in priesthoods) is that "I have something that you don't." The "something" is generally understood to be familiarity with the true actuality of our human (in relationship to divine) existence—as if this was a big secret ("arcane" is the preferred word.) In order to be privileged to share this secret, you must undergo a ritualized course of instruction: any information you garner along the way must continue to be kept secret from all but the elect few. Does it sound like a juvenile enterprise? It is.

In whatever dressing, this secret is purported to explicate the transcendence of the infinite and eternal and its immediate effect in our worldly affairs. The implicit promise of the unveiling of such secrets is that our individual life will be enhanced.

These are, clearly, teachings with a dualistic premise.

Can that which is infinite and eternal—by whatever name—be absent from HERE and NOW? Can that which is regarded as all-pervasive not be seen or found in everything which exists—*including* its seeker? Even the Dominican friar Meister Eckhart made no secret that "who sees not God *everywhere*, sees God nowhere."

Keeping the "individual's" true nature—as the Omnipresent—"secret" is equivalent to "selling water by the river." The descriptive word for it is "arrogance." If you have "spiritual" teachings, you openly share that which can alleviate someone's suffering; this is known as compassion.

YOUR QUANTUM JUMP

In the film *Mind Walk*, the physicist (Liv Ullmann) explains that we are not only *composed* of atomic particles (thus these quanta are *in* our body) but that these particles emanate from, and *surround*, our body...and thus interact with the body's environment, such as the air, the table upon which you rest your hand, etc.

As Heinz Pagels has noted, concerning the "quantum tunneling effect," this means that quanta effortlessly pass through solid barriers such as a cup or a wall: more exactly, "the electron has a certain *probability* of appearing outside of the barrier...particles really *do* materialize on the other side of the barrier...like a marble passing through the wall of a cup." And, so, such quanta appear inside, outside, and around your own body.

Further, Fritjof Capra relates, "nucleons are, in fact, *emitting* and *absorbing* 'virtual' [that is, short-lived] particles all the time... Every nucleon is surrounded by such a cloud of virtual mesons, which live only for an exceedingly short period of time...on the other hand, when two nucleons come so near to each other that their meson clouds overlap, some of the virtual particles may not go back to be absorbed by the nucleon which originally created them—but may 'jump across' to be absorbed by the other nucleon."

And, as David Peat says, "An instant before the jump, the elementary particle is occupying a given region of space. An instant later, it is somewhere else. And, according to the quantum theory, no physical process connects these two states of being... At one instant, the particle is inside the nucleus; in the next, it is traveling away at high speed. Nothing happens in between!... To put it bluntly, there are no *processes* that make the nucleus disintegrate. As we have already learned, a quantum jump simply happens."

Therefore, according to this information, a continual particle exchange simply happens, between you and your environment. Put another way, "parts" of "your" body, and parts of the body of the person sitting on the bus next to you, are being emitted and absorbed by each other "all the time." This is an uncontrolled natural phenomenon, which is even more intimate than a handshake or a hug—and it's done without effort, and even without awareness.

Furthermore, consider this aspect, as related by physicist Nick Herbert: "The mechanism for this instant connectedness is not some invisible field that stretches from one part to the next, but the fact that a bit of each part's 'being' is lodged in the other. Each quon leaves some of its 'phase' in the other's care, and this phase exchange connects them forever after."

This "phase" or "being" that is referred to might also be termed "essential Intelligence." It is in us, around each of us, and it connects all of us in each instant, and "forever after."

EXPECTATION

A female and a male pigeon have landed on the cross arm of a telephone pole. Sitting within a couple of feet of each other, they preen themselves for awhile in the sun. Soon the rooster rises, stretches his wings, and flies away toward the south.

Presumably, he did not tell her where, or why, he was going. Perhaps she has a good idea of where he might be heading, and could follow there herself if she wanted to. She stopped her activity when he left, and seemed clearly to be aware of his leaving; but she does not, apparently, lament, "He didn't tell me where he was going!", or "Will I ever see him again?", etc.

After a couple of minutes, she too leaves the perch, flying away to the north. The rooster will not have known, specifically, where the hen went, or why. Presumably, they may meet again some time later, maybe at a familiar feeding or watering spot, or at their nest under the frond of a nearby palm. If there happen to be young pigeons in the nest, apparently either mate is capable of caring for them until—if ever—the other mate returns.

If—and when—the two pigeons ever see each other again, their relationship to each other may resume. If, from moment to moment, their relationship to each other does not continue, likely neither of them either expected that it would or wouldn't.

LIFE IS BUT A DREAM

Eastern sages (such as Ramana Maharshi) sometimes like to refer to what they call the three states of human consciousness: waking, sleeping and dreaming.

The *sleeping* state and the *dreaming* state are distinguished from each other (in a scientifically-acceptable way): "sleeping" refers to "sleep so deep that it is free of dreaming; no conscious awareness is present"; "dreaming" refers to the condition in which "awareness is present, even when not consciously recognized."

To the Western reader of the sage's words it usually seems that the significance has to do with sleeping as an analogy for "ignorance" (of, say, either possibility of "enlightenment" or "unenlightenment"); dreaming as the condition of un-enlightenment; and waking as the presence of enlightenment (such as in the phrase, "an awakened master").

However, something more subtle may be alluded to, in such a reference.

In deep sleep, you are conscious without any awareness of being conscious; in fact, there is no awareness of a "you" that could maintain an awareness of consciousness. There is simply the presence of an unidentified (and unidentifiable) consciousness; but a consciousness which is ever-present for instantaneous action (such as sitting bolt upright if jolted with an electric prod). It is this *pre-cognitive* consciousness which is said to be the base of our true nature, timelessly (and universally) extant.

In a limited way, you could say that this condition is "ignorance"; but it is more accurately "oblivion": there is no mind of discernment in which there could either be ignorance or not be ignorance.

In dreaming, the consciousness (of deep sleep) can be said to have manifested in form, part-icular—or person-alized—form. Though waking awareness may yet be absent, there is a self awareness in which the subjects of the dream are in some relation to one's self—that is, with whatever the mind of the dreamer associates, or identifies, itself with. However subconsciously, the images in the dream have a connection with the dreamer's "real life," wakened perceptions or conceptions. In some dreams, one can even be aware of being a sleeper who is dreaming.

In the framework being discussed *here*, the waking state is simply a continuation of the dreaming state—under slightly altered conditions of conscious awareness. In other words, the mind which was engaged in abstract images and free-floating scenarios now focuses—when the dreamer's eyes open—on immediate appearances and sensations. The physical appearances which the eyes engage, upon waking, are now immediately assumed to be "real"—as is "my" (and "your") activities around them. *This* real world—and me "in" it—disappear again when I go to sleep. In *deep* sleep, this world (and I) were no more a fact than a dream.

In *dreaming* sleep, the images are merely a precursor to the waking dream (with its open eyes and thoughtfully-focused attention). The abstract images and free-floating scenarios of the sleeping dream become the "concrete" images and "living" scenarios of the waking dream; our humorously illogical and subconscious reflections become seriously logical and conscious thoughts. The dream was "unreal"; the drama is "real." In the dream, the importance of me and you (and our activities) *ended* when the

202

eyes opened; in the wakened state, such importance *began* when the eyes opened: now you are conscious of your "self" and even conscious of your consciousness.

In deep sleep, both the "unreal" dreams and the "real" world disappear, as equally nonexistent.

So, by worldly standards, the devotee boasts of an "awakened master." But the sage, who may once have been awake, looked upon the "unreal" and the "real" and is dreamlessly asleep.

LIVING THE WORDS

In regard to your questions, it matters not to me how the Course in Miracles came into existence. When I look at any implied spiritual material, what I am looking for is to see to what extent nonduality is represented; and then, if it is, how unambiguously— that is, does it generate more confusion, or greater clarity?

To a certain extent, one can excavate nondual teachings in the Koran, or in the Bible (Old *or* New Testament). But there are many other passages which have more to do with relative concerns than with the Absolute perspective. As a consequence, I personally don't spend much time with such texts, or recommend them.

I find no problem with someone referring to what the Course says, or what Jesus says, etc., etc. The question is: what do you say? In other words, are we *dependent* upon these texts for our wisdom; or is the wisdom ours—first-hand—and the texts something we might quote because they are supportive of a point we are trying to elucidate?

More importantly: are we *living* the teachings we quote?

IDEAL OR REAL?

What is meant by "idealism"?

There are conceptual, or imaginative, thoughts which occur to us which are termed "ideas"; these generally are the basis for an intention, whose execution may or may not be practical.

Connected with this intention is an expectation that the performance of the idea will result in a change in some situation.

Obviously, a change in a situation has the potential to either be toward a "positive" outcome or toward a "negative" outcome.

Due to our capacity for hopefulness, our tendency is to desire an *improvement* of the situation, as its outcome.

When we are fixated on controlling, or manipulating, the outcome of the activating idea so that the outcome does not become negative, the *idea* has transformed into an *ideal*; a standard not limited to what we envision *could* be, but rather what *should* be.

Such a presumptive attitude is, though usually not a conscious one, at the root of one of our most stubborn of expectations: I should get my way.

Clearly, where this expectation of the ideal outcome is *my* idea while it is also *your* idea, conflict is inevitable.

But even if this idealistic attitude is held only by yourself, disappointment and dissatisfaction is a continual result, because you will not consistently get your way.

What is usually unacknowledged in our initial idea is that the situation, which we would endeavor to change or improve, is itself an established fact: it has existed, is now existent, and—despite our hopes—has the capacity to continue to exist. The idealistic notion that we bring to the present reality is that "it shouldn't be the way it is!"

When we transcend the idea of what "should be" and what "shouldn't be," we are simply present with what *is* present, positive or negative, without idealism.

MAIN EVENT

Intruding between the browning hill in front of me, and the clear robins-egg blue sky behind it, is a slip of white. Like the tip of a head of cauliflower, this grows slowly up into view.

It is remarkably tight and dense for any cloud accustomed to this horizon, and it is cold-white like an iceberg. On a hot day like today, when even the bracing breeze cools only temporarily, it's a refreshing sight.

During a one-minute watch, you would observe no discernable change in its form; yet, at the end of five minutes, you recognize that it has noticeably changed—like the surprising growth of a kitten.

Now late August, the red ants scavenge the shattered dry grasses for fragments small enough to gather. Though an available segment may be longer than an ant's entire body, one manages to straddle it and drag it south along the path toward the nest.

A rabbit is only occasionally to be seen, no longer a naïve bunny: remnants of rabbit fur earlier were to be found in the precinct where coyote prints abounded, and rabbit tracks are scarcer here now.

A handsome snake has made only a single, memorable visit in these past few weeks. Black, with yellow dots toward its tail, and several feet long, it silently crossed the trail a few feet ahead of my chair.

The leaves of the poison oak are crimson when they drop to the ground. Pointed, shiny green acorns fall into the ruffled bedding of leaves beneath the oak trees.

The cloud formation has now taken the dimensions of a castle, towering several stories above its footing somewhere behind the hill. It is majestic. Its twin spires begin to crumble toward the west, its gray recesses highlighting the chalkiness. This is the cloud of the illustrator. One may wait another summer for a repeat performance.

Meanwhile, take in each moment as if it were your last breath.

NOTICING THE I-THOUGHT

One need not be involved in any kind of a chronic "practice," because spiritual practices presume that they will lead to a preferable consequence at some point in the future: but what you are striving for must be here now, or its not an everlasting, infinite Presence; therefore concentration on a practice is a needless distraction.

There is, however, an attentive awareness, to what is present, which can be of service to the seeker; it can assist in focusing one's attention on the separative distinctions which plague our thinking processes.

Thoughts appear successively on the screen of consciousness, and one can be attentively aware of such thoughts. The primary thought, in profusion, is the I-thought: "I," "me," "mine," and its various alternates.

Since we tend to think in word phrases, the preponderance of our thought phrases involve "I," "me," "my," etc. A person can be attentive to the occurrence of the personal/divisive self-identification, and notice that this conditioned propensity is at the very root of our dualistic perspective.

The I-thought is presumptive: it presupposes that there is an individualized self, a separate entity, which ought to be the overarching subject of attention and concern, that consciousness must invariably and exclusively identify with.

As one monitors the screen of consciousness, the arising of the I-thought, in any form, can be an occasion for questioning the underlying presumption of such a thought: *is* there, in actuality, such an entity, such an autonomous form, as a "self"?

One need make no effort to eradicate or to change anything which appears on the screen of consciousness, but to merely be reflectively aware of it: is this self-centered identification and emphasis necessary?

The sages insist that there is no such actuality as an independent self: then, "whose" thoughts are these? What is the source of the origination of all which appears in consciousness; what is the source, for that matter, of consciousness itself? Am "I" something other than this consciousness? Is this consciousness in any way apart from the infinite, eternal ground of Being?

So, the awareness of the presence of the I-thought and the reflection on its source (who *am* I?), can be a worthwhile subject of contemplation throughout one's waking hours—without making a compulsive activity out of it (I must do this, or else).

The important element here is that "I" am not "watching" my "thoughts"; there is an occasion for continual contemplation, here, that *"I"* and my *"thoughts"* are originated in (or by) the same universal, cosmic source—the infinite and eternal source of all manifestations. The watcher and the watching and the watched are merely aspects of one unbroken Whole.

When the I-thought appears, the dualistic thought process is at work (*I* shall watch my *thoughts*). This can be the impetus for the reflection "Who, or what, *is* the watcher, the watching and the watched?"

FANATIC CHARACTER

For what amounts to practical purposes, we are all initially encultured, conditioned, into the dualistic perspective. From the very beginning, each human organism has specific needs to fulfill, in order to survive and function. Our society, parents in particular, encourages self-sufficiency, which is essentially "me" oriented; "others" are viewed as a means for me to get what I suppose that I need. Even on the occasion when we do things for others, it is with an eye to provide some benefit to ourself.

However practical, this self-centered (or self-ish) orientation has a negative aspect, in that it leads to conflict. The relative world is conceived as composed of *me*, and all *else* that is not-me. Derived from separative distinctions in the environment of what I view as not-me, I determine "who" I think I am. This conclusion as to "who I am" is the kernel around which my subsequent self-image is formed. Any resultant threat to my self image—whether inwardly or outwardly—is a cause for conflict.

Society is composed collectively of basically self-interested "individuals," acting together to achieve certain mutual objectives. These objectives are, of course, influenced by the habitat of the societal collective, for each of the specific mutual interests. Each grouping develops an identity, as to "who" we think we are. Those who relate to our group self-image are "us"; those who don't so relate are not-us: "them." One of the words we use for this collective self-image is "nationalism." Other such words are factionalism, racism, ad nauseam; "ism" meaning character-istic condition.

The nondual teachings emphasize that conflict and self-image are proportional. When the "me" distinction is eliminated, the "us" distinction loses its basis. Conflict on both the individual and collective level is abated. When personal self-interest has been displaced, an effect on both inner peace and outward peace is a consequence.

904 Park Road

That symbol of peacefulness, the dove. Two of them. Male and Female. Facing each other, about six inches apart, resting on the thick green shag of suburban lawn.

Earlier, they browsed together and ate their fill of the birdseed which had been strewn across the grass in the morning. Content, without a need, they sit to one side of the terracotta birdbath. They sit in a warm, lingering-evening sunny spot, as the shadows of nearby rose bushes lengthen.

She is just a mounded handful of grey feathers, with a few flecks of black, with black beady eyes. He is larger than she, more prominent and visible in the stubby grass. Both are perfectly at ease, thoroughly relaxed. For a long while they are unmoving, only occasionally turning the head slightly for a change of view.

They are contented to merely be where they are, doing what they're doing—which is not anything. Rare birds.

"Give us *this day* our *daily* bread..."

QUENCHING THE THIRST

The message that the Advaita teachers bring to us is quite simple: recognize, truly and thoroughly recognize, that our dualistic perception creates a sense of reality which is false. And then the dissolution of this dualistic perspective changes our relationship to everything which we now view as relatively problematic in our life.

As simple and affirmative as this potentially liberating message is, and as sobering as its implications are, to follow through with that recognition (and to allow the dualistic perception to dissolve) is often met with resistance by the professed seeker of spiritual truth.

There are a number of reasons, some obvious, why this would be so. And, in many cases, the existence of this resistance is not consciously acknowledged by the seeker herself.

However, in some instances the seeker of spiritual truth is mindfully aware of a feeling of resistance to releasing the hold on, the attachment to, the dualistic mind-set.

Naturally, the conscious acknowledgment of the existence of this perceived resistance renders the dilemma easier to resolve.

First of all, do not concern yourself with the supposed "obstruction" that this sensed existence of resistance presents. In other words, do not create further diffraction by "resisting" the resistance. Rest assured that many who have found liberation from the dualistic mind-set were initially resistant to allowing its *dis*-appearance. Here is a recent "thank you" letter I received from someone who felt a sense of despair at his conscious resistance:

Hi Robert,

As I was heading towards the door, at the conclusion of our last visit, I remarked that I wanted some 'time to contemplate' the matters we had been talking about. And you said: 'You're not going to find anything out *there* that isn't right *here*.'

Odd that such a simple statement should *resonate* as it has!

I take your meaning as 'there is nothing to get.'

It is a subtle shift of *perspective*—from identification with a thought-constructed *persona* to clear seeing as *no-thing*.

And from the all-encompassing perspective of no-thing, your statement could not be more true! There is nothing to get—here, there or anywhere. Nothing to add. Nothing to subtract. No modification necessary, or possible.

Thank you,
Ron

Rather than putting energy into reacting to the conceived "obstruction," focus your attention on the dualistic conditioning which erects limitations and barriers.

Specifically, notice throughout your day those occasions and circumstances in which conflict—of any kind, outward or inward—occurs. Look closely, at each instance of conflict and divisiveness, for when the "I" individuation, or ego-centeredness, enters the equation. Let that subjective "I" awareness remind, each time: "Where there is division, there is conflict." Or, conversely, "Where there is conflict, there is division."

Given the amount of conflict you will likely experience in even just the weeks ahead (the occasions of what Buddha meant by "suffering"), you will probably become painfully aware of the (wasteful) price we pay for our enforced attachment to the dualistic and divisive exclusion as a "separate" I.

"Resistance" itself is not a problem. Being complacently satisfied with the un-wholesomeness of a fragmented, self-involved existence is the *real* barrier to recognizing the truth in this life-changing perspective; a truth that the Advaita teachers proclaim is available to all who thoroughly thirst for it.

ENLIGHTENMENT AS AFTERTHOUGHT

Krishnamurti one day used the word *mediocre* and pointed out that its Latin roots mean "halfway up the mountain."

And the Ten Oxherding Pictures are intended to depict the spiritual path from its start to its finish: one is enabled, therein, to determine one's degree of perception by identifying with one of the aspirant's conditions along the way.

By picture three, the young man has more than simply glimpsed the Ox he is tracking; in picture four, he has actually gotten a hold on the Ox. But that's not the complete story: he's only about half way to the tenth frame, where he is living his life through the eyes of enlightenment.

To continue to view things from the standpoint of the relative as is *convenient,* or to alternately view things from the Absolute standpoint when *that* happens to be more convenient, is not what the sages are teaching. The man of equanimity and freedom in picture ten is not half enlightened. You are not "One with everything" as long as you are cheating on your wife, but the person Jim Smith as soon as you learn that you have cancer.

Put another way, you do not say that it is God's will when you are in bed with another woman, but not God's will when a lesion appears on your lung. Such explanation is "not good enough"— which is the meaning of *mediocre*.

Enlightenment is not a consequence of half-way, half-hearted or noncommittal, measures. It is a matter of discovering Truth, and *living* that Truth without equivocation.

Do some people do otherwise, and "fool themselves"? Yes. That's why Krishnamurti was addressing this matter of the mediocre.

It's your option, if that's what you really want to pursue.

A FEW GRAINS OF SALT

The definition of a myth is "a fictitious account or belief, or person spoken of as though existing, often involving gods or heroes."

We think of mythology as basically the "religion" of Greeks and Romans, but it also infects the Hebrews' Jehovah and the reputed Son of God professed by Paul of Tarsus, and Islam's Prophet who was carried away to heaven. The Hindus have their blue-skinned Krishna, and Buddhism has its hermaphrodite Kannon.

Mythical characters, of course, perform mythical actions— which, being fictitious, have not been proven and are un-provable. Thus "as though existing," a legendary son of God is "believed" to have walked on water.

In the enlightenment literature, there are also accounts that—if not miraculously dramatic—can evoke an imagined "promised land" flowing with nectar, and bathed in glowing white light.

To be less poetic, the impression one can get may lead to expectations that are erroneous in the context of enlightenment.

There are variations on the few themes that I'll outline below, Martin.

Probably the most pernicious are unrealistic ideas, one acquires, concerning what is anticipated. This can sometimes lead to fear of what might develop. But more commonly, it results in dismissing what is being insightfully perceived. ("This is so *simple*: this can't be It!")

There is also the matter of comparing oneself with a particular larger-than-life spiritual figure and concluding that you are not cut from such a holy cloth. Or, in order to discover what that guru discovered, you need to emulate this "master" by making yourself into a carbon copy. (Christians blithely call this "imitation of Christ"; and imitation can never be the genuine article.)

And also it's worth considering that enlightenment may occur despite having a practice, not because of it. You might hear about those whose practice preceded their awakening; consider the number you don't read about for whom it was the other way around.

While you can prove to yourself whether or not nondual realization is possible, some of the things that are said about it do not necessarily apply.

Do It Now

"Is there a meditation you recommend?"

In the mind of most people, meditation is associated with a goal-oriented program. *Contemplation* generally reflects a freer focus of attention.

There is a Buddhist tradition where one sits, the night through, in a cemetery. A practical correlation of that could be to spend an entire waking day contemplating that *this* day may be the conclusion of the days you'll experience.

In truth, you do not certainly know if you will be alive tomorrow. Check a newspaper and you'll find a report, on any given day, of someone who went out their front door, not knowing that they would not again return.

One morning, contemplate that the next day you might close your eyes for the final time.

As you bathe, as you do your exercises, as you eat your breakfast, and then engage in the day's activities, be mindful that each movement you make, each sensation you experience, each encounter you have, even your every thought may never again be repeated.

The warmth of the sunshine, the blue of the sky, the bird overhead, they may not be viewed again. That child with the bright eyes, the woman with the attractive figure, the couple relaxing on the park bench, notice them carefully knowing it may not be repeatable.

When you open the mail, consider your friend's letter which you may never answer; when you set your wine glass back on its shelf, consider that you might not reach for it again.

Throughout the day, from morning till night, consider at every moment that this may be the last day you'll experience.

FEAR AND CONFLICT

In fantasy's magical kingdom, a mouse is transmuted into a coach horse. But, as we know, *this* world is not the embodiment of the magical kingdom.

If this were a magical kingdom, one might potentially wake up one morning and, forever after, never again find oneself in any instance of conflict with another person. How ideal!

Do you suppose that you will ever—short of a visitation to the magic kingdom—find yourself in such a perfect state of grace that you will not be directly antagonized by another individual?

If, contradictory to your usual circumstances, you note that you are in reaction—anger, resentment, defensiveness, hostility, resistance, etc.—to some person or thing, what ensues?

Guilt, shame, regret, embarrassment, etc.—are these appropriate responses?

Is it really of value to recall what *could* instead "have" been done; or what Ramana Maharshi *might* have done, under the same circumstances?

One of our typical fears *is* the fear of conflict itself. We are disturbed, in our composure, not so much by the confrontation as it unfolds, but by the fact that a confrontation has occurred at all. But if I do not harbor a conflict about conflict, I shall not get *secondarily* upset about having gotten *initially* upset. After all, I am entitled (as a fallible human) to, for instance, be angry. I do not need to make a *career* out of being angry, but neither do I

216

need to justify my humanness—to myself or to others. I am who I am, and I therefore do what I do: and I need not blame others for that, nor castigate myself for that.

Most importantly, I do not need to hold out an *image* of myself— either as perfect *or* as imperfect. Moreover, I need not *fear* conflict—*nor* my response to it. Relieved of the tension which sustains it, the pattern which may dissolve is the pattern of fear. In a conflict, *both* parties are normally motivated by fear. When fear is not an obstacle which obscures one's attention to the unfolding of possibilities, one may *respond* to the challenge rather than to *react*. With one's own fear recognized and in perspective, one might ask, "What *is* the other party's fear? And how might I *respond* to *that*?"

Answering to Your Name

Alice:

For the realized sage, the relative, material world does not disappear—even in nondual awareness—any more than it does for an unrealized person. Her *relative* perspective remains unimpeded; but, unlike for others, the relative perspective is not the only perspective accessible to her.

She sees the relative as always within the formless, infinite, eternal and omnipresent Absolute. But: she also sees the everywhere-present Absolute as permeating and saturating all that is relative. It is the Unlimited that "connects" all that is limited, to constitute wholeness.

In other words, those things which are considered to be relative are still always recognized as limited, finite forms: a sage does not step out in front of a moving bus. Nor does she, in terms of activities, cease to eat or to bathe. The material world does not disappear from sight into a cloud of mist, upon awakening. Do not assume that your Spanish or piano teacher does not deserve to be paid, as a consequence of your nondual awakening.

That is the apparent meaning of the quotation concerning "the teaching of nonduality" and "the worldly life." Don't confuse nonduality with duality.

DIFFERENT STROKES, DIFFERENT FOLKS

You've raised a pertinent question, in this age.

There was a time when I studied Krishnamurti almost exclusively; and a (subsequent) time when I studied Ramana Maharshi almost exclusively: these two more than others. I still today refer to these two most often.

Obviously, it is my sense that both were teachers of nonduality. In general, I would say that of the two, Ramana's tendency was to go more quickly and directly to the point of these ancient teachings.

Partly because of that, Ramana's discourse is inclined to be more paradoxical, or opaque, to the neophyte. Krishnamurti's discourse is more accessible to the person who may not as yet recognize that she is what is called a "seeker."

In my own experience, Krishnamurti's discourse was the hallway, Ramana's was the living room. Had I confined myself solely to the Krishnamurti material, it is my conviction that I would not have come to the thorough conclusion of my (dualistic) confusion by that alone. The Krishnamurti material is (now) to me what mathematics is to algebra: there are some questions which can't be resolved without an X in the equation.

Put another way, Ramana speaks directly to what I have found to be the bottom line in my (dozens of) discussions with one-time seekers: the absence of the self-image as a reality. While Krishnamurti comes to this point primarily by inference, Ramana starts with this as a given and extrapolates from there.

So, plainly, the gist of what I'm saying is that Krishnamurti's teachings—in light of the material which is available today (e.g. first edition of *Talks With Sri Ramana Maharshi*: 1955)—is for many, in the general public, a valuable eye-opener but can commonly leave the self-image intact.

Different teachers (of the same subject) put their emphasis on different things. Their life styles—for example, compare Krishnamurti to Ramana—can even be very different. Vive la différence!

You can suppose, then, that I consider it commendable that you are augmenting your offerings of materials with some of the contemporary Advaita discourses. After all, nonduality is inclusionary, not exclusionary.

DYING TO THE TRANSIENT

It could be said that when their spiritual contribution had been expressed, Buddha, Jesus, Ramana and Krishnamurti chose to die.

According to the story, Buddha knowingly ate a meal which (apparently unknown to the others) contained poisonous mushrooms; he is said to have insisted on not sharing the entrée—thus sparing the life of his host and his attendants. This was at an elderly age, and after a lifetime of teaching, but

219

evidently a conscious choice. His action could even be considered as *indicative* of the teaching.

The death of Jesus too, according to the legend, was the culmination of the teaching; and this death, also appears to have been engaged with deliberation.

Ramana Maharshi did not opt to sacrifice his cancerous arm, in order to continue his instructive life.

And Krishnamurti evidently chose to ignore the symptoms of terminal cancer until his final moments, having remarked at the conclusion of his last scheduled talk, "It is finished."

Coming to terms with the "ground" of our being is not a "part" of the teachings, it is a fundament of the teachings.

Mind, Thought, Action: One Source

The core of the nondual teachings, of course, is that there is no such separate entity as the "self" which stands apart from the infinite actuality which is the source of beingness.

An aspect of the realization of this truth is that one confronts the question of "If there is no self, what operates in what is perceived as 'my mind'?"

In the same sense that there is no *material* entity, or form, which is independent of the single, unbroken movement of That, there is likewise nothing *immaterial* that is independent of this same ground of being.

In other words, where it is recognized that there is no such individual configuration as "my" self, it is also recognized that there can be no such configuration as "my mind."

The jnani is aware that there is a concept of "a mind" and there is also, in awareness, a concept that this mind produces "thoughts": but where the conception of the self is absent, the conception of "my mind" is unsupported; and where the conception of the mind is viewed as false, the conception that this mind produces "my thoughts" is also viewed as false.

Who, or what, is this which has conceived the form of the "self"? Whatever is the producer of the sense of self must also be the producer of that sensed self's perceived thoughts; and likewise what we personalize as "my actions," which are a consequence of what is presumed to be "my thoughts."

So, for the jnani there is simply the awareness of the organism and its activities, without personalizing, or identifying with, the assumed process which animates or motivates the organism's activities.

This is finally what is meant by, "You are not the doer."

Ramana: "The mind is only a projection from the Self...one should not even care for the result of the actions.... One remains a witness to them without any attachment.... They are not your own.... Do not think that you are the doer."

ABSOLUTE AWARENESS

There's a Zen master who says: "The sun and the sky: are they the same or different?" If you answer "same," he says "wrong." If you answer "different," he says "wrong."

"Same" is an idea about some things; "different" too is a concept, merely an opposite.

You are pleased when your infant says "mommy," and says "daddy." We would be pleased if we were able to train a chimpanzee to be able to distinguish between "same" and "different" because it would show that the chimp was able to form separative concepts.

The nondual teachers are telling us to transcend all such polarizing concepts such as "same" or "different," all opposing notions such as "good" and "bad."

Where the mind ceases to embrace limiting concepts, reality no longer is compartmentalized, fragmented. Lacking restrictive demarcations, reality reaches to infinity—as does our awareness of it. Reality is, in its unlimited form "empty" or void, a nothingness.

This is the awareness of an "empty mind" (or, no-mind) free of limiting concepts: Absolute awareness.

Not Becoming

The most basic teaching of nonduality, it could be summarized, is the transcendence of dualistic conceptions (such as good or bad, right and wrong).

The fundamental dualistic conception which is deconstructed in the initial phase of Self-realization, particularly, is that of I and not-I, self as apart from other—even to the extent that the *Infinite* could be perceived as other.

A duality which is more subtle, and which needs to be pointedly contemplated, is that of *what is* as contrasted to *what could be* (or, more tenacious, what *should be*).

Whatever the condition is which is actual, it is presently a *fact*. You cannot change a fact: you can only deny it; wish it were otherwise; or react in relation to it. Such a response is grounded in an idea, a concept, of what *could* (or *should*) be *instead*.

It is our *idea* of what could be, as opposed to what is, which becomes then an *ideal*: a standard—which is not actual, not present in reality—to which we aspire to change, or realign, the truth of fact.

Where this ideal-ization plays out most prominently, in our psyche, is in our disposition toward *becoming*, rather than *being*. To desire to become something other than what we actually are, in the moment, is to retain an image of the self which can be enhanced.

Where there is attachment to idealistic standards of what could be (or how I ought to be other than I am) there will not be the choiceless awareness which is the hallmark of the dissolution of dualistic conception. There are not "lapses" of idealized behavior or conditions, where there is the emptiness of choiceless awareness to begin with. For the Self-realized, whatever is present (good, bad or otherwise) is Being itself; one can then only acknowledge, "That *too* is It!"

Or, as has been said, "The 'what is' is what it is!" The dualistic distinction is absent, of "This is it" versus "This is not it."

The consequence of choiceless awareness is a quiet mind. And there being no attachment to an *ideal* of what a quiet mind *ought* to be, there is an absence of agitation in whatever state the mind is observed to *be*.

The net result is to be content with 'what is,' rather than in conflict. It is a matter of effortlessly being present with what is present. Therefore, it doesn't matter *what* is present. Even *dis*content could be present, and one can be content with that. That too is it.

This uncontrived equanimity is the peace and freedom of which the nondual sages have spoken. It is the transcendence of "suffering."

MEDITATION ON ACHES AND PAINS

Dharma Sister:

If you have affection for me, you will naturally be concerned for my health. But if you worry about the developments, that won't help you and it won't help me. This is a matter where we really need to keep our attention focused on the bigger (or biggest) picture. This has to do with the difficulties that our likes and dislikes (shoulds and should nots, better and worse) can create; hopes and desires for things to be other than they are. The greater the hope, the greater the denial, and disappointment and suffering. Anxiety is the consequence of anticipating the future, rather than taking one day at a time. It is ill health that puts us to the greatest test of allowing the moment, liked or not. Anxiety doesn't improve it.

When you've said Goodbye to me, *then* say "Hello" to me.

Today's aches and pains may be followed by an accidental death tomorrow. Let me be ready day by day for death or disaster. This gives depth to life.

NO CONFUSION = CLARITY

Now that you've begun applying your own understanding, you are comprehending on more of a first-hand basis.

"The I-thought is the root of all problems. From the I-thought comes the 'me' and the 'you'"—separation, and consequent conflict. Those two sentences are the essence of the nondual message. "No I," as you say, no "other" than I; no separation of "me" from *anything* else.

"There is no subject and object": this is obvious when the *dualistic* perspective falls away. Where there is *only* One, "subject" and "object" *must* refer to the same, singular One. This is the nondual recognition.

Bear in mind, though, that once the nondual recognition is present (for you), it does not mean that the *dualistic* perspective ceases to be *accessible*: one can (and will), as one previously has, utilize this *relative* viewpoint, where *necessary*. We continue to live, and operate, in a world where most everyone else will relate to us only in the me/you context. While we haven't lost *awareness* of this context, we recognize that the me/you (subject/object) are merely a relational *convenience*, which has no real meaning from the standpoint of the *ultimate* context.

So, material forms—objects—are still objects. And the view that one is, in any way, *separate* from these "not-I" forms renders one a subject ("subject" viewing "object"). But we recognize that *beyond* this *appearance*, all that *is*, is *That*—subject *and* object, in this case.

Enlightenment is to be continually aware of the nondual actuality—even in the midst of dualistic perception. The consequence of this attentiveness is that *names* and *forms* lose their significance: one no longer even *thinks* in terms of "subject" and "object," or other types of separative (this versus that) comparisons; good/bad, past/future, man/God, etc.

The "personal" me, as you say, is a product of recalling the past, and imagining a future. When ideas of "my past" and "my future" fall away, there is recognized only that body-mind organism (not even "mine," since the me is a fiction) which is present in awareness. That which *witnesses* this body/mind has been unchanged throughout all "past," and will remain unchanged throughout any "future."

You can attest, from your own experience, that "In deep sleep, there is no me; no me at all." In fact, in deep sleep, an even more subtle distinction disappears: there is neither a "body-mind organism" (in awareness) nor a "witness" of it. *All* distinctions are absent. *This* condition, the sages say, is our *essence*, our "true nature" or identity.

This "unaware" *presence*, the sages say, is deathless (being, in fact, Unborn). The way you put it is that "consciousness goes back to awareness." Then you add, "Awareness and consciousness are the same." I would say that if you understand the second proposition, you will see that consciousness cannot "go back" to what it has already been "the same" as.

Where we encounter confusion is in thinking in terms of the *names* of all the various *forms*. See that *every* name refers to only One actuality: then none of the "named forms" can create confusion. Where *all* is *That*, what can be confused with what?

Where there is *no* confusion, there is "clarity." Enlightenment is simply *clarity*.

An Immense Void

Thanks for sending the published excerpts of Eben Alexander's book. A neurosurgeon (and son of a neurosurgeon) who taught at

Harvard Medical School, he was raised as "a faithful Christian," he says. And, during a seven-day coma, he had a near-death experience in which he found himself in what he calls Heaven.

He does not say that anyone "there" asked him "What is your religion?", or even "Do you believe in God?" More significantly, no concern was expressed such as, "What good have you done?" *or* "What evil have you done?" Rather, he was instructed, prior to being "sent back": "There is nothing you can do wrong."

How many of your psychiatry patients could have benefited from divine assurance that not a single thing we do is "wrong"?

And whether or not there is anything *beyond* this world and universe, in the near-death experience *this* world and universe is simply a forgotten dream. Even what he found himself entering was "an immense void."

It's interesting, too, the questions that he says occurred to him: "Who am I? Why am I here?" Do these questions not also prompt us, in this lifetime, to investigate the "truth" of this dream-reality?

He likened his experience to what he's heard of "mystical states." And similar to some who've experienced such states, he says: "I intend to spend the rest of my life investigating the true nature of consciousness...the fact that we are more, much more, than our physical brains..."

Dr. Alexander has a fertile field ahead of him, for example when he says: "Modern physics tells us that the universe is a unity—that it is undivided. Though we seem to live in a world of separation and difference, physics tells us that beneath the surface, every object and event in the universe is completely woven up with every other object and event. There is no true separation.

"Before my experience, these ideas were abstractions. Today they are realities."

Indivisible Actuality

From the standpoint of your quandary, either the dualistic viewpoint answers it, or else the nondual viewpoint answers it.

If the dualistic viewpoint is the truth of our actuality, then we need to accept all the dualistic propositions: e.g., there is good and bad; there are good people and bad people; there are good actions and bad actions; there are good consequences and bad consequences. Life then, as we know it, is an interplay of all these various combinational opposites. We then need to continually worry about the ongoing good and bad things these bad and good people are doing. We are one of such people, so we need to fret about what (good or bad) "I" am doing.

The discovery in Self-realization is that there is, in actuality, no such thing as a separate independent "I"; where there is no I, there is not something which is "other than I." An example would be, as per your quandary, "God" as other than I. Therefore, since there is no I or other than I—no "two" things—we could say that there is simply one undifferentiated actuality; just Beingness. Itself being undifferentiated, it has no definable qualities; as Actuality, not anything is excluded from, or apart from, it. It is the *mind* of man which says that *this* is a "part" of it, and *that* is another—"different"—part of it. In other words, there is no oppositional duality in an Actuality of which there is nothing *other* than. In this indivisible Actuality, there is not *this* part—"me"—and *that* part, "you."

There being no "individuals," in this context, there are not good people and bad people; therefore, there are neither good or bad actions or consequences. Nothing therefore to concern yourself about; in fact, no "individual" who needs to be concerned. To the Self-realized, this turns out to be a great relief: no individuals that we need to be anxious about, either *here* or *there*.

To those who are not Self-realized, this makes no sense; in fact, from the dualistic standpoint, this is "bad." Such a person concludes that the dualistic viewpoint is the real answer to the good-versus-evil quandary. The consequence is that they continue to be troubled by an Actuality which they can never be free of.

I-TRAP AHEAD!

For the first time in the two or three years that we've been corresponding, I perceive that John Watt is in big trouble.

"It was a completely spontaneous thing that began as I was at the sink, brushing my teeth. I went and laid down, and began to trace the personal 'I' back—and let it merge with the ALL of the IS. It led to some real peace of mind, or silence."

The crumbling of a huge boulder begins with an insignificant hairline crack.

When we *actually look* for the substantiation of our individuality, what do we find except for thoughts *about* the composition of (our) individual identity?

What is the *origin* (of this medium of self-substantiation) of thought *itself*? Did the medium (or its process) of thought originate with the appearance of the organism identifiable (by some) as #300267? If no particular *individual* can be ascertained to be the *source* of the phenomenon of thought, what is the source that accounts for the thoughts which substantiate individual identity?

What is the source of the *organism* that is subject to the *process* of the medium of thought—the lightning rod for the self-defining construct? Considering that the organism did not appear independent of the world of matter and energy, what is the source of the solar system which spawns the appearance of this organism?

Whatever is the origination of this universe, and its cohesive cosmic system, is inevitably the requisite source of the organism *and* the totality of phenomenon perceivable by the organism. It must be the *source* of any medium or process by which the organism adduces its individuated identity.

So if the organism is not itself the source of the process by which individual identity is predicated, and is not even itself independent of the source of matter and energy in which it appears, what is there *of* it that can possibly be individually *substantiated*?

The source of the organism and the source of the thoughts of the organism are the same source: and that source is not the organism nor the thoughts of that organism. There is no organism nor thoughts of the organism that is *apart* from the source. So what is the only conclusion of "identity" that it is possible to contemplate?

When one does actually take the trouble "to trace the personal 'I' back," what is revealed about *self-identity*? "Who" is it that is identifying "whom"? What is it that is merging with (all of) what? In fact, when the sameness is perceived (what/what)—while brushing the teeth (or, as one Zen monk, while pissing on his shoe)—is there even, in actuality, "merging"?

There is *only* the ALL of the IS. That is *why* there can be peace of mind. And *why* there is silence. Silence is the tongue of nothingness.

Don't spend any more time "spontaneously" lying down, or JW is going to exit like a thought that evaporates!

NIRVANA MADE EASY

You've put your trembling finger on what enlightenment is all about. Buddha's condition was said to have been that of nirvana. Even as per a Western dictionary, the definition of nirvana is "extinction"; the Sanskrit literally means to "blow out," as one extinguishes a candle. The blowing out, in this case is (as the dictionary puts it) "the flame of life...achieved by the extinction of *individual* existence...and absorption into the infinite."

So, we're not only talking about a form of death, but of that death as a consequent opening (or outlet) to the Void, or Emptiness or Nothingness—to the infinite that is absent of form or distinction of any type.

We tend to think of a void as a vacuum; but even in a vacuum, physicists tell us, subatomic particles appear—yes, out of a "void"—and disappear again.

The ultimate, infinite and eternal Void is the omnipresent, absolute ("not relative...without limitation") condition out of which all forms arise and to which all return, without diminution or surplus in either movement ("conservation of energy," as physicists call it).

It is as a manifestation of this formless void wherewith your physical organism originally arose (from cosmic, interstellar constituents), as well as its I-consciousness. Both will, being dependent upon the Absolute, return in time to the generating source.

But this is not a disordered universe; the cosmos is operating in a synergistic interaction of creation and destruction. There is no less "intelligence", or "purpose", in the one development than in the other. In other words, your *death* must be at least as "important", or "meaningful", as your life.

Hence, Rumi says:

> I died as mineral and became a plant,
>
> I died as plant and rose to animal,
>
> I died as animal, and I was man.
>
> Why should I fear? When was I less by dying?

We can assume that Rumi didn't think of himself as apart from the Absolute (or Void) as a mineral, or as a plant, or as a creaturely animal; nor will he presumably perceive any separation when the man and its I-consciousness is extinguished in "absorption into the infinite."

"Extinction" didn't concern "you" before I-consciousness was the present condition, and it won't concern you afterward either. It doesn't even concern you in nightly deep sleep; if you were to die in deep sleep, would "you" know it?

It is possible to blow out that fear of self-extinction during one's conscious, awakened lifetime, Buddha assures us. Ask yourself, where does a flame "go" when it's extinguished?

No Beginning = No Person

Your query: Are there "past lives?"

From the standpoint of a dualistic psyche which makes the divisible distinction of past, present and future, one might

232

suppose such a phenomenon. It broaches the same speculative category as the inquiry, "Is there rebirth?" "Past lives" was not a topic in Ramana's time, although rebirth, or re-incarnation, was.

Another name for ultimate reality is the Unborn. What is unborn does not, in the first place, die. That unborn ever-presence is your true nature: that which you really are does not live or die. And, being ever-present every where, It does not come *from* any place nor transfer *to* some other place or time.

Reincarnation is the proposition that an ego ("I") associated with one body is transferred to another body, as Ramana puts it. Self-realization is the evaporation of the ego. Thus, he says, "The Self-realized cannot be 'reborn'."

"'Life' is Existence—which is the Self [or Unborn]. *That* 'life' is eternal." Even the *thought* of rebirth "is transcended by Self-realization."

This is the same point which Buddha is reported to have emphasized in the venerated Diamond Sutra. The sutra is basically a dialogue between him and a disciple, Subhuti.

Those who consider him to be a "being" that has a "life," Buddha says, "do not understand the meaning of my words."

"Subhuti, those who are called [Buddhas] do not *go* anywhere, nor do they come *from* anywhere."

He refers to his "birth-less nature," and says that those who—like him—"gain perfect clarity...do not create the perception of a *being*, a *life*. Neither can someone who creates the perception of 'a life,' or even the perception of a soul, be called a bodhisattva.... 'No beginning,' Subhuti, is the highest truth....Subhuti, this dharma teaching cannot be heard by those who mistakenly perceive a 'self.'"

No "being," no "life"—no "past life."

MIND'S INTERFERENCE

I agree with your succinct critique of Krishnamurti; and thanks for your well-written monograph.

You say that you regard meditation as a practice, in that "it requires clock time when one is not preoccupied with other things. (Some people may be able to meditate all the time, but I doubt it.)"

Indeed, it's my understanding that when the enlightened masters speak of meditation they are describing a condition which has nothing to do with any sort of designated activity (associated with clock time), but rather a persistent presence of attention, an unbroken "witnessing" which is the consequence of nondual realization.

Your view of meditation is that "it does require that distractions be avoided." What the sages are speaking about is a present awareness which is one's continuing "frame of mind" from the time you wake up in the morning until you fall into sleep at night. Therefore, any and all perceived "distractions" are within (or, a part of) this on-going meditation. Not anything need be excluded, or even presumed a "preoccupation" to be "avoided." *This* meditation *includes* all that is sensed, felt and perceived during the period when we are consciously aware of temporal phenomena.

Even "times when we need to plan for the future," using your example, are not outside of the purview of this undistracted meditation.

In fact, because of its presence as detached awareness, it is not even thought of as "meditation"; the term Absolute awareness could be used for it.

Niguma, the 11th Century (female) Master points out, "thoughts are no different from ultimate reality." And, as the teachers declare, our thoughts—fixated *or* distracted—are end products of the Source, being presented *through* us.

Ramana:

> "Why do you worry 'I didn't [or 'I did'] meditate'?...If the idea 'I did' or 'I didn't' is given up, all actions will end up as *meditation*.... This, indeed, is the state called Sahaja Samadhi."

(Or, Sahaja Samadhi could be called Absolute awareness.)

> "What does it matter if the mind is active [even distracted]? It is so only [as] the Self [or Source or Absolute]! Be *aware* of the Self even during mental activities."

In the idea that the clock-time meditation is somehow preferable to, or better than, "distracted" awareness, "you are destroying that sense of oneness—and creating duality." You are attempting to alter the 'what is', your distracted condition. Adya:

> "To perceive everything as one is not an altered state of consciousness. It's an unaltered state of consciousness; it's the natural state of consciousness. By comparison, everything else is an altered state."

The thought that *this* moment or state (undistracted) is better than *that* (distracted), is the work of a judg*mental*, controlling mind; the desire for "positive" change, by a conceptual process that establishes preferential standards and ideal goals. Adya, again:

> Enlightenment is the natural state of consciousness, the innocent state of consciousness, that state which is uncontaminated by the movement of thought, uncontaminated by control or manipulation of mind. This is really what enlightenment is all about. We cannot come upon this truth of our nature through manipulation. We cannot move beyond what I call the false identity, the egoic identity, by trying to change. We can only start to allow consciousness to wake up from its identification with thought and feeling, with body and mind and personality, by allowing ourselves to rest in the natural state from the very beginning.

Excerpts from Peter Fenner, on noninterference:

> The nondual approach opens up the possibility of liberating 'disturbing' thoughts and feelings by doing nothing!...Dzogchen masters dissolve disturbances and enter unconditioned awareness by letting things be as they are....

> In the nondual approach, we don't judge some experiences to be sublime and others profane....Basically, we don't intervene or meddle in our experience in any way at all; we leave what is, just as it is....When we connect with the source of our being, we're intrinsically free; we feel spacious and liberated, no matter what our external circumstances or internal condition may be....

> The ability to let things be, without judgment or reflection, is a central component of the nondual approach.... When one's awareness ceases to be conditioned by compulsively, or intentionally, engaging and disengaging with different sensations,

then thoughts and feelings float through one's awareness like clouds in the sky.... As the great Dzogchen yogi, Longchenpa, wrote, 'Do not condition your mind by trying to suppress your experience, apply an antidote, or mechanically transform it, but let your mind fall naturally into whatever [condition you find it]. This is the incontrovertible essence of what is ultimately meaningful.'

Horse Sense

Near where I live, there is a small pasture with a black horse in it, and I've had a chance to take a look at him nearly every day I've lived here. I don't know this animal's name—for some reason, I say "Hi, Sport" when he's near the fence when I'm passing by.

There are times when I reflect on his state of awareness; or that of other animals. His concern about whatever is occurring appears to be limited to what is within sight, hearing, smell, touch, and perhaps taste.

He likely remembers things from the past, both positive and negative, and makes associations with things that are important in the present. He probably notices changes, such as even changes in the body as it ages. But I don't suppose he concerns himself about what conditions might be like later in the week.

If Sport's pasture was larger, he'd avail himself of it; but if it was smaller, he'd accommodate to that.

I have watched him now for eleven years. For the first few years, his mother was with him. When she disappeared, I had heard that she had been "put down." I suspect that he has not dwelled on her absence.

He exhibits no signs of loneliness (human passers-by frequently pat his nose when he's near the fence) though he's never known of a mate.

His days are routinely the same, yet he shows no signs of displeasure or malcontent. He is exposed equally to sun, rain, wind, frost and pesky flies. The latter he seeks to avoid; and he sometimes takes shelter from the weather, in a covered stall.

I sometimes think about Sport's state of awareness, his sense of what appears to be unperturbed acceptance of whatever the present conditions are. Even when for awhile he had a pronounced limp, that seemed to be the only change one could notice in him.

Thoughts about Sport arise particularly when my own state of awareness causes me to consider his unperturbed acceptance of the present condition, or when speculations project beyond the end of the week or outside of the pasture where I have any liberty to trod.

Mind at Peace

"I wanted to share with you my recent observations regarding feelings and emotions. It seems that in order to persist, states of mind require my continuous interest in them; maybe even require that I identify with them. I have been experimenting with allowing them to be, with no effort to engage or escape them. I noticed a space opens up and allows for the realization that feelings are objects—they say nothing about the awareness they appear in. Then I discovered I can be at peace even while being aware of intense sensations. Now equanimity is becoming more experience than concept."

Thanks, Julie, for your letter. Yes, a feeling or emotion of some sort is noticed in awareness; a descriptive name is assigned; and the tendency is to either value it and cling to it as positive, or devalue it and resist it as negative.

The option we discover, from the standpoint of transcending dualistic (or relative) polarities, is that it is possible to simply witness what arises on the screen of consciousness; be objectively present with whatever is present; and notice that every such state or condition—whether pleasant or unpleasant—is transitory.

This is basically the landscape of an "empty mind," a mind emptied of the scale that weighs "better" and "worse." Can there be real equanimity where there is attachment to preferences?

I think you'll find that, as this equanimity becomes more prevalent, the "intense sensations" that triggered concerned reactions will be less likely to arise acutely in awareness.

Among other verses of the Hsin Hsin Ming (given in its entirety in *One Essence*):

When the mind is at peace,

The phenomenal world does not disturb it.

When the phenomenal world causes no disturbance,

It is as if there is no "world."

When the mind is at peace,

It is as if there is no "mind."

When "agitation" ceases, the mind is quiet.

When the mind becomes quiet, agitation ceases.

STANDSTILL

A ball, in momentum, follows its assigned direction. When momentum is no longer a causation, it comes to rest. In stillness, it now has the freedom to move in any direction... or not to move at all.

To come to a halt is not merely to slow down. Psychic stillness is not simply a pause between expectations, a casual rest to gather energy to resume pursuit.

Utter stillness is death for the sense of self, it is the demise of the future of promise; it is to sprawl point-blank on the moment. What it might portend, one must admit one does not know.

In that empty space lies the possibility of creation which is not merely a continuation.

THE REAL ISN'T IDEAL

"I don't think my view of the Bible, especially the New Testament, has ever changed as fast as it did during this last month. It's all beginning to seem idealistic to me....

"There is *no* God that has anything to do with what we 'experience'. It just is 'what it is.' And the IS not only has nothing to do with it; the IS doesn't even *know about it*....

"I've already seen enough of this 'stuff'. None of it matters, except *what works* for you. And I've been entertaining a lot of *stuff* that has *not worked for me*....

"The problem with all of that 'stuff' is that if it isn't working for you, and you have adopted it, then you will just keep *blaming* yourself for what you have no control over....

"I do what I need to do, though it is not always easy to determine what that is. The 'anger' is almost a constant, and to believe that I *shouldn't* be, is completely idealistic and the harbinger of guilt."

You have been pondering these matters for the years that we have corresponded. It's good to see that finally you are beginning to recognize the idealizing which has been so much of a fixture in your relationship to the world. Not only has it not worked for you, it does not work for anyone.

To maintain the presumption that "what is" *should* not be as it is, or *could* be other than what it is, is nothing more than a contentious idea: such is the meaning of "idealization."

How many of those people that you come in contact with are resisting "what is" by clinging to the idea that "it should not be"?

How many collectives of people—i.e., countries/governments—are basing their activities/policies on ideals that have no basis in reality (security through aggression or control, for example)?

That you are beginning to notice and question your own idealism ("he shouldn't be doing what he's, in fact, doing") is the proper place to focus this practical insight.

Whenever you establish standards of behavior for yourself—and others—there is going to be disappointment; and, as you noted, either guilt, blame or anger will generally ensue.

As Byron Katie says, "Whenever I argue with *what is*, I lose." No ideals or standards: nothing to lose.

MEETING THE MIND

If we were to say (as some have) that there is one, universal "mind," then that mind would have to include—or, rather, *be*—your mind.

It would also have to be "my" mind.

My mind is constantly changing (we'll propose, by way of illustration) from positive to negative, and back to positive again.

And "your" mind also does this, similar to the way that day changes to night and then back to day again.

Sometimes my mind is, say, positive, while your mind is, the same moment, negative—similar to daytime on one side of the world, with nighttime on the other side of the world.

But this is all the simultaneous workings of the one, universal mind, the mind that by its very omniscience must be—at the same time—both "mine" and "yours."

My mind is, let us suppose, "pro-Israeli"; your mind, we'll suppose, is "anti-Israeli." Does this suggest that the one, universal mind is in any manner in conflict with itself? Is the universe in any way in conflict with itself when it is day on one side of the earth, at the same time that it is night on the other side?

Even if there were a perceived conflict, this "conflict" might resolve itself within the universal mind: "I" might change my mind, at any given moment, and be of one mind with you in your negativism; or you might suddenly have a change of mind into my positivism.

Given this understanding of the nature of the one, universal mind, can I continue to take seriously—to be attached to—my "personal" thoughts, or your "individual" opinions? Under the circumstances, if I *were* to take such phenomenon seriously, that *too* would merely be the working, or manifestation, of the universal mind.

That I take "my" mind seriously, or that I take "your" mind seriously, is no more (or less) important than that I take the "universal" mind seriously.

But in understanding the nature of the universal mind, there is the prospect for a "meeting of the minds."

DIVING OFF THE DEEP END

About the time your letter arrived, my friend Vince finalized his decision and quit his job at the post office. His promptings and motivations are essentially the same as I understand yours to be. My encouragement goes out to you both, in the direction you are heading. It has been my own direction for about the past 22 years. Vince and I went for a walk yesterday, and we talked about the uncertainties he's feeling (both materially and spiritually). He's at an important juncture where he's viewing the hollowness of "normal" life. Therefore, he's also questioning all the activities he's been engaged in for his forty-odd years. He started out as a business major in college, switched to poetry, took up yoga for relaxation, discovered meditation, and was given a book by Krishnamurti twenty years ago. His primary influence recently has been Joko Beck.

But, nevertheless, he had never really come to a standstill. Now he has a sense that unless he comes to terms with the true nature of our corporeal existence, all the motions he's going through (and has gone through) are misguided. He's beginning to look at "*why* am I doing *what* I'm doing?" What is the relationship (of his every daily activity) to concern for what he imagines lies in the "future"; or protection or extenuation of what he deems to be his "self image"; or attempts at control in one's life which are reactions based merely on fear. These questions concerning security, identity, control (of either the "arising" or the "subsiding"), and fearful reactivity as the basis of one's behavior—these questions, which are all interconnected, are now ready to arise in awareness at a time when he has provided the space to accommodate their responses. Crisis interfaces with opportunity, as the Chinese pictogram depicts it.

Sometimes, the title of one of Krishnamurti's books comes to mind: *A Wholly Different Way of Living*. What is, in our society today, the *wholly different* way of living?

I can relate, too, to your "strong urge to be free of all possessions." Consider well that our possessions consist of more than material property: our most basic possessions—to which we are even more *closely* attached—are our ideas, opinions, beliefs, biases, suppositions, theories and preconceptions. When these have gone, who is remaining? It *could* be the guy working in the post office: but he might not be working there for the same reason (reasoning) as the other guy. It might be, in a sense, "someone" or something else that is at work there. He could even, while working at the post office, be engaged in a wholly different way of living. But the recognition of that which is wholly different needs to come first—before *any* worthwhile living.

I don't know whether you noticed, but the topic of "right livelihood" was on the mind of sixty percent of those present at that small gathering. Can any matter of "livelihood" be resolved until we have come to some resolution on the nature of life—existence—itself?

So, I feel that you are likely putting your priorities in their proper order. Out of stillness—the ending of previous motion—new movements can arise, movement which may now head in an entirely different direction. Most people do not ever permit themselves the condition of stillness, and are perpetually in motion. They often think of their lives, thus, as being "momentous," but they typically do not know what it is to truly experience life "in the moment." But some of us take a risk (or risks) to discover what That is.

Koan for the Day

Sekita said: "I believe that we must be careful to keep Buddha-mind undefiled by conceptual thinking."

Sogaku said: "When an ox walked across Muon's sand garden, he covered it with fresh sand."

Not a "Normal Life"

The spiritual life, it has been said, is simply this: One's thoughts, one's words, and one's actions are consistent.

However, if one's thoughts are centered on one's self, if one's words are persistently self-serving, and if one's actions are predominantly selfish, this would not generally be characterized as a spiritual life.

It is because we yearn for liberation from the narrow confines of self-centered isolation that we typically examine the implications of an alternative perspective, a "spiritual" life as contrasted to a "materialistic" life. We could say that in a materialistic life, one's thought, words and actions are dedicated to personal gain, or the enhancement of the individual; the spiritual dedication is oriented differently—toward something which transcends individuality, and thus could be defined as unself-ish.

We could possibly extend the above, then, to say that "in the spiritual life, one's thought, words and actions consistently are not self-centered." That this is a reasonable formulation can be illustrated (probably most would agree) in that the life of the historical Buddha was consistently not self-centered; as was the life of the historical Jesus; and the life of Ramana Maharshi, and Krishnamurti, and Mother Teresa. The life of each of these examples has been dedicated toward that which transcends individuality and the selfish perspective underlying personal gain.

If we were to say that thoughts, words and actions of each of these living examples suggest consistence, then we would have to say that they lived their "philosophy." Put another way, there was no separation between their spiritual understanding and their worldly, or their material, life.

Any thoughts, or ideas, or theories which we hold about spirituality are worthless if we are not living them—acting "out" of them—in our daily life.

If, for some reason, the spiritual ideas (or "teachings") which we hold are not practical in this day and age, then let us admit that fact and abandon these false principles: let us live the teachings that are viable today—even if it is only one of the teachings, or none of the teachings. Let us not profess that we are concerned with "the unity of all things," while we dedicate our time and energy to basically personal pursuits.

To have "spiritual thoughts" which are not consistently carried out in action is okay: but that is not a spiritual life, so let us not deceive ourselves. And, granted, our understanding of the teachings will change from day-to-day, as will our subsequent actions; but living our understanding is at the base of the spiritual life. It is a unification of our spiritual (meditation) and material (action) life.

In Another's Words

Karl Renz is a German teacher of nonduality. His books are translated into English, so that may account for your occasions of lack of transparency.

A book of Ramana's teachings is titled *Be As You Are*; Karl's emphasis is that whatever is occurring with "you," right now, is actually the Absolute (he uses the word Self) doing what it does—through each of seven billion bodies in the world. Doing whatever it is that "you" do, you are simply That (Absolute) in its endless, eternal unfolding (or development). So the part you play is to simply—since you won't do otherwise anyway—be as you are.

He stresses: "Even though you're full of desire to 'improve' or 'change', really see that there is not now—nor will there ever be—a way out of what you are." Forget the "I should..."; "I can..."; "I will..."!

Physicists tell us that the universe evolved from a "singularity" that was unimaginably compact in its magnitude and the density of its potential power. Only as this force erupted, did space and evolving movement in space (which we measure as time) come into existence. In other words, prior to time, space or "things," there was a presence of undifferentiated being. "We" are the product, the result or consequence, of this Being—in fact, every *thing* is.

So, Karl says: "Your true nature [essence, or source] is eternal— prior even to the appearance of time, space, and all arising in it." He adds: "Always come back to the following point: Be [aware that "you" are] *prior* to that which exists in time." Or, even in space. The original Being, of what developed to become you, was not bounded by time, space or material matter (such as flesh); as your original Being, there was only timeless, unqualified existence. (In fact, there was not even anyone to *say* that there was existence.) There was, as your originating condition, simply what in Buddhism they call the Void, or emptiness.

Out of this void or emptiness, all of the forms—the "things"— in the universe arose. So, the totality of the universe represents "nothingness" having taken various forms, or aspects, in the time and space that evolved. While human consciousness differentiates these various forms as "named things," they are merely the presence of Being in manifold appearances. And, Karl says, "This totality [of Being in form] is all there is."

This totality (Absolute; or, as some call it, Self) is the true nature of the seven billion pairs of eyes that look out on the universe. And it is the true nature of everything that those eyes encounter in the universe. "The Self perceives; and *what* it perceives is *only* the Self—because the Self is all there is."

When it becomes clear to you that *your* "beingness" and the "beingness" that you *perceive* has never been dismembered, from the very beginning, you recognize the Totality. In other words, the (small) self has never been other than an appearance of eternal Being, or omni-present Self. "When this manifestation [you] is seen to be only the Self, there is absolute *annihilation* of the sense of separation, of existing as a 'separate' self."

In the same way that you are not apart from the Self, the Self is not apart from any other thing. It—beingness—has no remote *form* of its own; *its* only form is found in the infinite number of appearances that it devolves into. "Just see that what exists in 'no-form' *also* exists *in* form." Both the Self and the self are the same, whether "formless" or "formed."

Among the human forms and actions they take, there are some who perform in one way, and others who perform in the opposite way (or any variation in between). This is the unfolding of the Self, its beingness, in all of its endlessly unrestricted potential. "That which you are exists in any and *every* circumstance."

Out of this multitude of diverse developments, comes our sense, or feeling, of being an "individual," a distinctive actor. "All this takes place as part of the Self's unfolding."

If we do not recognize that we are the Self and that all that we do is the Self's activity, then we will feel, or suppose, a "distance" from the Self—and we will hope to close a "gap" which has never actually existed. The self will seek the Self—being already the Self that is sought. "You don't need the fulfillment of any kind of seeking in order to be what you already are." So, be as you *are*, because *however* you are, it is the Self being what it presently is.

Comprehending this seeming enigma or paradox is what is meant by "awakening" to your true nature; so-called enlightenment.

"Awakening...it's just an 'aha' [I get it!], seeing that what you are is what you always were and always will be."

To Harvest

Re: your telephone comments:

I talk to a number of people, some of whom are not receiving the fruits of living a life of Absolute awareness.

But you are, and you're noticing the changes.

The difference is that you have immersed yourself in the territory that has been discovered, and you are spending your time present and attentive in that open environment.

This evidently is because you have preferred to eschew the distractions, and to focus on what unfolds for those who are willingly present for it.

There's a saying in Buddhism: "The five hundred patriarchs have not deceived me."

A Cloudy View

Is there something you're missing, in the quotation you are citing from Hui Neng, the Sixth Chinese Patriarch? "When *all* views—both 'right' and 'erroneous'—are *discarded*, then the essence of wisdom manifests *itself*." This has led you to conclude that, therefore, we need "to put ourselves" in a particular ("simple") state. This *devised* state you seem to equate as "the natural state."

Were one to discard all views, *right* or *erroneous*, would not the view that there is some view which is required to be "discarded" *also* be discarded? Might not the essence of wisdom automatically manifest, without any assistance outside of *itself*, when not anything is needed to be done? What could be *more natural*, than simply being aware of *whatever* "state" is present, without the thought that there needs to be some effort to change or "improve" it.

As you say, "When we complicate things...we wander far from the natural state." Yet, you emphasize that there is some motivational desire which we need to follow "that is really all that is necessary. So keep it simple."

What is more simple and less complicated than making no effort to engineer a particular state—an *un natural* state? Isn't such an idea a held *view*, whether right or erroneous?

A Cloudy View—Cleared

Dear Robert,

Thank you for your comments. Although your comments extend to only one handwritten page, they give me a lot to ponder! Looking at your first two sentences:

> Is there something you're missing in this quotation you are citing from Hui Neng, the Sixth Chinese Patriarch? "When all views—both 'right' and 'erroneous'—are discarded, then the essence of wisdom manifests itself."

When all views are discarded, this could be called a state of viewlessness, or emptiness, or voidness (the most natural state).

If a state of viewlessness prevails, there is no problem! This is a state that cannot be "engineered," as you put it. When one really and truly lets go of all of one's beliefs, opinions, and views, one is in a state of viewlessness.

All views are consumed in viewlessness. Then what's left? It can't be put into words. But it's not nothing.

"Ignorance is Bliss"

There are many myths concerning enlightenment. Among these is the notion that enlightenment is a "state" of constant ecstatic (if not orgasmic) bliss.

Bliss is a word that the jnanis use, but by that term they mean the sense of freedom and *equanimity* that comes with having transcended *attachment* to "states," and the *expectations* that pertain to them. Put another way, bliss is the aspect of Self-realization which leaves one "care free" as a consequence of the *recognition* that "ultimately, nothing really matters."

Ramana: "[Bliss] is realizing the Self as the limitless...it is the highest self-surrender.... Bliss consists in not forgetting your [Absolute] being.... *Be* the Self, and *that* is bliss."

What is *not* bliss, he says, is "thinking that the world is real"; therefore a concern that some "states" are more significant than others. "[The Self-realized] looks on everything with *unconcern* and remains blissful."

Because of our deep conditioning to think in terms of moving toward the "positive" and avoiding the "negative" (clearly, a dualistic proposition), the newly-awakened sometimes begins to note that "negative" mental states may continue to arise, along with (expected) "positive" states.

The "natural," free and awakened mind—as Dzochen teachers stress—is the passive, objective "witnessing" presence which places no significance on any particular, momentary "state of mind." After all, the fundamental teaching about phenomenal, worldly forms is that "All things change." Why concern yourself with what is inherently impermanent, fleeting—such as whether one's mental state is currently presenting a "positive" or "negative" reflection, signifying "happiness" or "unhappiness," bliss or absence of bliss, "awareness" or lack of awareness.

The Self, that you are, is *all*-inclusive, "limitless": when we expect (are attached to, or haven't transcended) only the presence of "positive" conditions in our waking presence, we are setting ourselves up for the conflict that dualistic polarities invariably present ("better" versus "worse"). Where it is truly comprehended that there is "no division," the polarities are indiscriminately viewed as the "same": "Sun-faced Buddha, moon-faced Buddha." The overall relaxation that results from this "choicelessness" is what is meant by bliss.

If you understand what is said here, you view *whatever* is *present* as That, in one of its myriad expressions (positive *or* negative)— "complete realization" *or* "incomplete realization." And, if you notice that you're *not* viewing whatever-is-present with equanimity or dispassion, that *too*—*that* state—is It.

"I am left with nothing—*special*," to add one word to your phrase. Do not expect *this* That to be any more special than *that* That.

The Teaching "Mystery"

As with anything alleged to be "mysterious," various myths have grown around the unveiling which is known as enlightenment. A "teacher," you will note, spends much time exploring the appearance of these myths.

So, from the standpoint of the seeker, as you say of yourself, the process of awakening has much to do with "making corrections." These corrections are generally in the direction of "subtractions"—the dropping away of the erroneous (mis) conceptions, or myths.

What it finally comes down to is complete "emptiness": there is really not anything that we need to "know." In our primal condition (as Ramana points out) of deep, dreamless sleep, there is for each of us nothing but pure, unadulterated *presence*: you do not even "know" that "you" are present.

For those who are on the "right path"—as you say—an open mind is essential: we are actually in the process of transitioning from the known (I-centeredness) to the Unknown (no-thingness). There is not anything secret about this formless presence; it is what we *are*, in our primal, essential condition.

How "mysterious" is this "teaching"? It has been available, even in writing, for some 3,500 years; and is available in every chain bookstore (not to mention the Internet) this very day. What "school" does one need to "join" to learn the "secret"?!

Even beyond that, many of the Self-realized sages did not even so much as study the scriptures. What they *did* do was drain the mind of their limited *concepts about* things. The *in*conceivable truth then "reveals itself," as you put it. The self inadvertently recognizes its Self. Emptiness sees only emptiness.

Yes, the sensible process at this point is to merely contemplate "daily," as you said, the profundity of this Truth and its ramifications. "All that is, is That doing what it does": what does that imply when we appropriate it to the *incidentals* of our momentary, relative experience?

So the call is to "attend," to focus awareness on the manifestation of this cosmic Truth that's before our very eyes! Pure light, through a magnified lens, can ignite a conflagration.

As many distractions as you have, you have fewer than most people in this world. Others have come to Self-realization within the same situation you're in. That, I'd say, is good news.

NONINTERFERENCE

When I first began meditating, at Big River Farm, my earliest thought was: "Here I am, sitting here for forty minutes, doing nothing. And the world is getting along just fine without me!" This came as a shock.

Sometimes, when I'm involved in an interaction or situation, I think to myself: "What if I had died yesterday, and I wasn't here right now? This current circumstance would play out in its own way, without me. Why do I need to interfere in this occurrence?"

I also sometimes reflect on this ominous reality: nine nations currently have an aggregate of literally thousands of nuclear missiles awaiting launch. A single accidental firing could precipitate an uncontrolled reaction that would result in the extinction of the human species. There is not any day that might not possibly be the day that the bell tolls for mortal man. I do not ever take it for granted that it will not be today, or tomorrow. This recognition informs my behavior in immediate ways.

There are plenty of good reasons to operate on the premise, "Do it now." But there are also plenty of good reasons to ponder regularly, "Why do anything at all?" Or, at the very least, "What do I do (or say, or think) that makes any real difference?"

I have come to notice, for example, that probably eighty percent of the things I think of to say, I do not say. And the majority of the situations I consider interfering with, I do not intervene in. I find myself increasingly listening, watching, waiting and relaxing.

It's amazing how the world gets along without my *intrusion*!

You Are...Here

Thanks, Bill, for your email. As you say:

"This clarity is always available, and the true nature of being." So, the "failure of the mind to work" on this "problem," is a good sign that the falsity of the "problem" has been seen through (i.e., "clarity"). If the Absolute isn't present right here, right now, where in the hell could it *be*?!

"Even the deepest gorges of the topmost mountains can't hide this Ox's [Absolute] nose, which reaches right to heaven....

"A nightingale warbles on a twig, the sun shines on undulating willows; there stand the Ox—where could he hide?!"
                                    – Oxherding pictures #2 and #3

The search ends *here*.

Risking Truth

The whole truth is not for the faint of heart. Though it is as common as the blade of grass, it is the uncommon truth: who is it that notices the blade of grass? A rabbi was asked: "How is it that, in the days of the ancients, the almighty could be encountered even in a stone—but not today?" The rabbi responded, "Because today no one is willing to stoop that low."

Simple truth is not common to the mind of man. Simple truth is acted upon directly, the way that one moves out of the path of a falling rock; one does not hesitate to leave behind one's position, and all else that is unimportant.

A "possibility" is not truth; truth is actuality. An idea is a possibility. One may ponder an idea, but to act is *act*uality. Truth is truth to who realizes it, who *lives* its reality. Our life is not a means to finding truth; life is the expression of truth, *as* it is perceived.

Where that truth may lead is revealed *by* our life, not in advance of it. The truth is that life is filled with risk, and to live truth is to live constantly at risk.

SEEING THE LIGHT

Even some Christians are evidently beginning to get a sense of what the physicists are saying. But dualistic patterns of thought continue to confuse them.

A woman on a downtown street handed me a leaflet:

Sure, your body is made up of water and various organic and inorganic molecules. Water is made up of molecules, too—H_2O, as you know. Our bodies are made up of molecules, which in turn are made up of smaller particles called atoms, which in turn are made up of yet smaller subatomic particles, including protons, neutrons, electrons, quarks, and so on.

As it turns out, scientists have discovered that these smaller subatomic particles are basically made up of nothing more than light-energy combined with...nothing! Atoms are 99.999 percent empty space! Energy, in fact, is just "acting" like solid physical matter by being in many places at one time, with great speed and the help of some other factors too difficult to explain here. But suffice it to say, your body, at its most fundamental level, is made up of pure light energy.

As Einstein told us, energy in the universe can never be destroyed, only transformed.

So if your body is made up of molecules, atoms and subatomic particles—which are actually whirling bits of light, mixed with nothing—that makes you and your body a pretty remarkable thing! On a fundamental level, the energy (which your body has) is something that can never be destroyed, only transformed to a new or different level. That's a scientific fact!

On a second page, an attempt was made to establish (according to the Bible) that God is, likewise, pure light energy (Psalms 104: 1 and 2; "God... who wraps himself in light as with a garment...")

If you are light and God is light, where is there a discontinuity between you and God?

The tract further refers the reader to the quotation at John 14: 8-10. At the Last Supper, Jesus answers various questions. Disciple Philip still does not comprehend Jesus' reference to the identity of his source of being, the Father of all that is. Jesus says, in effect, that he and the source of being are the same: "Anyone who has seen me, has seen the Father. How can you say, 'Show us the Father'? Don't you believe that I am in the Father and that the Father is in me? The words I say to you are not just my own. Rather, it is the Father, living in me, who is doing his work."

If you are in something, and something is in you, is there any distinction between what is "inside" and what is "outside"? Only if you and God are not separate could it be that God is living in you, doing his work!

Yet, a Christian tract will say, "...our relationship with Him is broken and we are *separated* from the one who created us. This is why Jesus Christ gave His life."

At John 14:20 (still replying to Philip), Jesus says, "...realize that I am in my *Father*, and you are in *me*, and I am in *you*." So was Jesus' inseparability from God an exclusive attainment, or is all one? Are any of us "separated" from *anything*?

Any separation we presume is merely the consequence of our dualistic thought patterns. Jesus staked his life on the conviction that such patterns are subject to change.

SILENCING THE MIND

The ending of the movement of thought is a natural outcome when there is no longer any desire for ending it. The concern of the thinker for his thought is a dualistic, subject/object pursuit. Where the idea of a self as "doer" has been transcended, any effort over time to negate the natural process of thought will not arise. Dissatisfaction with the condition which is present will cease to occur for the mind which is empty of willfulness.

Krishnamurti addressed the question (in his final talks at Saanen in 1985), "How can I end my thinking?"

"I would be an ass to ask such a question but I am asking it. How am I to stop my thinking? Is that possible?...is it possible to stop thinking?...

"May I point out, may the speaker point out, that that is a wrong question. *Who* is it that stops thinking? It is still thought, isn't it? When I say, 'If I could only stop thinking then I would have no fear', who is it that *wishes* to stop thought? It is still thought, isn't it, because it wants something *else*?

"So, what will you do? Any movement of thought to be other than what it is, is still *thinking*. 'I am greedy, but I must not be greedy'—it is still thinking."

Robert Linsen, in *Living Zen*, points out that one's mind can become silent only when one ceases to attempt to discipline it, through the intuitive transcendence of the "I" (am the Doer) thought. In other words, the abandonment of effort for transformation allows the mind to accommodate silence.

> "...this silence of the mind, and inner transparence, cannot be the outcome of an act of discipline. The absence of fabrication and objectivization by the mind cannot be the effect of the will of the 'I-process', but arises from an informal and transcendent understanding, of an intuitive nature...So, as Krishnamurti suggested, the full comprehension of this process brings about a silence of the mind. From then on, the Intemporal is fully realized."

Krishnamurti (in *Commentaries on Living*):

> "When the mind makes an effort to transform itself, it merely builds another pattern, different perhaps, but still a pattern. Every effort of the mind to free itself is the continuance of thought; it may be a 'higher' level, but it is still within its own circle, the circle of thought, of time...

> "Any movement of any kind on the part of the mind only gives strength to the continuance of thought, with its envious, ambitious, acquisitive pursuits. When the mind is totally aware of this fact, as it is totally aware of a poisonous snake, then you will see that the *movement* of thought comes to an end."

IN MY BURROW

A corrugated shed that I pass by on my walks has a burrow at one edge, for something about the size of a possum or raccoon. The inhabitant has a few things, I muse, to be concerned about. While curled up at night, there might be anxiety about the entry of a predator; or flooding during a rain storm; or cold that drops below freezing; or the safety of tiny offspring; or about hunger that disturbs sleep.

This human being need not worry about those things: doors have latches; my apartment is heated and has no leaks; I have no infants to protect; and I do not go to bed hungry.

The experience that the creature and I share is that of the aches and pains that come with having a body. However, it's likely that the animal feels what is occurring in the body without any supposition that things ought to be somehow other than the way they are. It is most likely that the animal's attention is on what the day or night presents, without stewing over what might be the consequence, of any of its concerns, "the day after tomorrow" or some point down the road. I'm reminded, in this context, of a statement attributed to Jesus: "Sufficient unto the day is the evil [hardship] thereof."

The animal, presumably, is not dwelling on "Could this pain be arthritis? What if I'm not able to walk? How will I be able to provide for myself? What if there's no cure! Gosh, am I going to die?!" and so on.

All of these drastic experiences will be contended with, by the animal, as and at the time they materialize—just as any of its basic survival considerations are responded to at the time such response is needed.

POONJA'S DILEMMA

H.W.L. Poonja, who died in 1997, searched India for a teacher of enlightenment. He has said that, until he found Ramana Maharshi, all he ever met were "businessmen in robes."

When finally in the presence of Ramana, he described the experience of an altered state of consciousness which frequently occurred to him, and he asked Ramana if this was enlightened consciousness or Self-realization.

Ramana said, "Is that present now?"

"No, not at the moment," Poonja replied.

"Then that is not what you're looking for," Ramana told him.

One of the most common refrains that an Advaita teacher hears is, "I once had a taste of the experience of Oneness, but it evaporated and I haven't been able to bring it back."

Whatever it is that you expect to experience, if it is not present right now, then that is not the "realized" condition that you're looking for.

Every spiritual and religious tradition, since the written word, has described the Absolute actuality (or Self) as omnipresent.

Not only that, but this which is found "at every point in space or time," must be found not only *without*, but *within* as well. There could not even actually be an *interface* between "within" and "without"—simply one unbroken actuality.

This being the case, the Self which you are looking for would have to be the composition of all that you see—and you, as the seer.

So, for the enlightened, Absolute awareness is not a special condition, state or unrepeated experience. It is one's continual realization that not anything could ever, under any circumstance, be separate from omnipresent Being.

Abandon the expectation that you will encounter the Self at some time or place in the future, or "experience" such an "event" again. You do not "approach" That which you already are. Self-realization is merely recognizing that not anything has ever been apart from That which is without limitation in its ubiquitous presence.

REST IN *NATURAL* MIND

The question, of course, is not whether "decisions are being made"—you can verify from your own experience that they appear to be so. The question is, what is the nature of the organism that is aware of this (or any other) experience, occurrence or event.

When it is clear what the "Source" is of both the experiencer and the experience (hint: no disconnection), to "That one" is there any such (isolated) event occurring, such as "decision-making"?

You then query: "What is the impact of how one views this matter?"

If you presume that there is an individual, a self, which "makes decisions," those decisions are probably going to be decided in terms of self-interest. Where there are two, or more, selves deciding in favor of their own interests, isn't conflict likely to ensue?

As to the query, what is the difference between "abiding in the natural mind" (or Buddha mind, or Buddha nature) and not abiding therein: the point Mingyur Rinpoche is making is that a piece of gold obscured by mind is no less a piece of gold than one that is polished and shiny. His youthful "mistake" was in assuming that by polishing the mind, it became more valuable—

"more" Buddha mind (or natural mind). "Any difference between the [two] is superficial."

The importance of recognizing this "sameness" is that it takes the pressure off of thinking that you have to achieve a goal [e.g., "no thought"] or experience some sort of special state [e.g. "loving kindness"].

> "[Instead] we just watch what happens [one's present state—whatever it is] *without interfering.* We're just interested observers...with no investment in how [it] turns out....Simply 'resting' in this way is the experience of natural mind....

> "I [previously] thought that natural mind had to be something... *better than* what I was already experiencing .... I believed that thoughts of anger, fear and so on...were bad or...at the very least inconsistent...[but] all these different thoughts are simply coming and going *within* [that which] remains fundamentally unperturbed by *whatever* occurs within it....

> "...don't try to *stop* whatever is going on in your mind, but merely observe it..."

COMPASSION?

I wake up in the morning, and put my feet on the floor knowing that not anything which happens today really matters, from the cosmic standpoint. So, how shall I spend my day?

Because of this viewpoint, mine is an untroubled life. I am also aware that an untroubled life is not what most of the people I meet are experiencing. Knowing that such anguish is unnecessary, I feel drawn to sharing the viewpoint which has brought contentment to my own life.

I do not do this because I suppose that it really matters. Not anything that I do or don't do will have any significance, at some

264

inevitable moment in the life of the universe when the earth is again uninhabitable.

Nor do I suppose that anything which I choose to do is actually effected by me as an isolated, independent "individual." Free will is not the *original* source of the activities which have been generated upon the earth. Whatever attempt I might make to affect the course of human history, that course will not be dictated by any single person.

And even from the perspective of my individuated consciousness, not anything done or left undone will matter to me, at a definitely appointed time to come. When I close my eyes for the last time, the entire universe will disappear—and all its beings and every one of their entire doings will cease to have reality.

So, my actions are actions without concern for outcome. There is not anything which I have to get; there is not anything which I need to give. It's like a tree which presents the fruits of the day, without personal concern for whether the fruits are harvested or not. This is one of the elements whereby my life is untroubled.

Thus, if I speak to you about contentment, it is not because it's important for you to hear it, or even to act upon what you hear. It's just that this is what this person finds himself doing today.

To say that a person of the spirit acts in "compassion" is already to say too much.

POWER POINTS

Thanks for your response to the Adya material I sent. You are now recognizing that the "natural state," spoken of in the spiritual literature, frees one from the contrived, manipulated and controlled effects conjured by "psychic powers."

"What Adya says about the *contrived* state vs. the *natural* state makes a lot of sense—and causes me to re-visit past 'experience.' 'When the mind is involved in control and manifestation, it can lead to various states of "consciousness" (an unnatural state): you might *learn*...how to...come into psychic powers...but such efforts "leads to a dead end."'

"Now I understand Poonja: 'I used to have (psychic powers) but I gave them up.' Those 'psychic powers' have caused me a lot of grief, especially The Voice. What was the purpose of a guilt-provoking question: 'What can you do to become a better *person*?' There were other problems with The Voice, but it now seems clear that those psychic powers were being 'sought' to *control* and/or *manipulate* the physical (illusory) realm. Dr. Hora says (presumably in the 'natural' state) 'There is no such thing as a person.' So where is the good, bad, better, or best?"

And where there "is no person," where is the repository of extraordinary "powers"? If Ramana were asked, "Are such powers real," he'd typically respond: "As real as *you* are."

About a dozen times in *Talks With Ramana* alone, he was asked questions such as, Does a self-realized teacher have, or need, siddhis (supernatural powers)? His responses were unequivocal.

"Such 'powers' manifest only when there is the ego. The Self is beyond the ego, and is realized when the ego is eliminated...The *one* [powers] requires effort to achieve, and the *other* [Self-realization] does not....Where is the use of occult powers for a Self-realized being?...

"The only permanent thing is Reality; that is, the Self....All the rest is mere phenomena—in It, of It and by It....[Powers] are only transient....All these 'wonders' are *contained* in the one changeless Self....The force of [one's] Self-realization is far more powerful than the use of all other powers....

"People anxious for siddhis are not content with their idea of Self-realization, and so want siddhis associated with it. They are likely to neglect supreme happiness, to settle for siddhis, [while] a Self-realized person will not waste even a thought on them. Let them get that, and then seek siddhis if they so desire! There is no realization in the one who displays them....Self-realization alone is the aim to be gained....

"Occult powers will not bring happiness to anyone, but will make him all the more miserable....Why aim for that which is not essential, but apt to prove a hindrance to realization?"

Playing Games with Life

We have video games, board games and bingo games; game shows and amusement-park games; football games and basketball tournaments; bridge games, poker games and the gaming industry; the dating game and divorce court; hide-the-button and spin-the-bottle games; king-of-the-hill and Russian roulette games; the fortune-and-fame game; power games; cowboys versus Indians and cops/robbers games; the game of "chicken"; cloak and dagger and puppet government games; the fight game; war games; matches, bouts, battles, skirmishes, tests, trials, contests, races and challenges...

All in an attempt to assert that some individuals are more deserving than other individuals. All over the world, we choose up teams which can then compete against each other. Trivial pursuits. We keenly know what competition is, while having little sense of what cooperation is.

Recognizing Absolute Awareness

I would say that the ultimate realization (or phase, of realization) is that the "I" does not exist as a separate entity.

Considering that the I does not exist, "my mind," "my thoughts" are merely another manifestation of the Absolute: *as* is the apparent I.

So, if one does not take one's own existence to be real, how could one take one's "mind" or "thoughts" to be real?

If the I is not real and the mind and thoughts are not real, why would one concern oneself at all about any of those unreal "concepts"? Therefore, it is not worthwhile for one to focus on what "I" am (or am not) to do about—pro or con—"my mind" and "my thoughts."

When this perception is present, mentation about "me" and "my mind" or "thoughts" ceases. There is merely awareness, observation, of "what is."

If "what is" *appears* to be a perceived presence of a "me" and/or "thoughts," it is impartially observed as just another (impermanent) manifestation of the Absolute.

In other words, no distracting energy is put into concerning oneself about the presentation of (what are *among* all the *other*) fleeting "events" in awareness.

After all, in deep sleep neither "I" nor "my mind" or "my thoughts" are present, so clearly these are impermanent and thus not ultimately real. One does not concern oneself about *anything* in deep sleep, so why ought one to concern oneself about these "concepts" in the waking state?

All that one needs to recognize is that there is no "I" to which these concerns can relate.

Then one relaxes into merely being present for whatever appears—for anything that appears—in awareness.

This is Absolute awareness.

"The true 'I' is the Self."

"When you inquire to see what it is, you find there is really no such thing as 'mind.'"

"When the mind has thus vanished, you realize eternal Peace."

"The Absolute consciousness alone is our real nature."

—Ramana

NOT GETTING WITH THE PROGRAM

I was interested to hear what you had to say about your long experience with Alcoholics Anonymous and the Twelve Step Program. As you noted, it's not surprising that one would "graduate" such programs only to become a follower of a guru. Both such involvements have their focus on discipline, through which—given indefinite time—one is expected to become a better person.

You came to recognize that there is not some ideal condition at some future point in time which is a desired goal to be worked toward, but instead the importance of accepting your present condition without ideas of what "should be" or "could be."

You also recognized that essentially there is no "person" to improve, or comparatively make better.

And you also realized that it was more of value to "go it alone" than to be dependent upon any modality, doctrine, theory or practice.

You ended your commitment to the guru for the same reasons you ended your participation in the "recovery" programs, and I am glad to hear that you have turned the page to a previously unknown inner peace, and ended your dependencies. Across the board.

I-DENTITY

There is no problem with the I-thought arising in consciousness (or any other thought, for that matter). It can seem to be a problem only if you do not perceive who (or what) that "I" really is.

The I which is observed and the I which observes it are not separate entities. Every (person's) observed I is unique. The I which observes it is common to every "I"; it is *not* unique. This I which perceives is not bounded, though it sees through each particular set of eyes.

The I-thought which appears in consciousness can be viewed, when it appears, as a "problem." But to the ever-present I which is aware of the I-thought, there is no preference for what appears on the screen of consciousness: the I-thought; not-I thought; no thought; any thought. *Whatever* appears, to this I of awareness (or awareness of I), it observes it without critiquing it.

The observed "I" is merely an appearance in consciousness, superimposed on the omnipresent awareness. Ramana would call the former *self*, the later *Self*; one an appearance limited to a temporary form; the other aspect, an unbounded, universal presence—the *essence* ("essential to") of the former.

When you've come to recognize who ultimately "I" am, then your sense of "identity" will cease to be fixated on the *appearance* of I and will simply rest unconcerned in the awareness of all that appears. Ramana would say, you abide as the Self. As the Self, *all* thoughts are "your" thoughts: no problem with maverick thoughts.

No Grace Period

You ask, "Isn't it somewhere said that the attainment of enlightenment is purely a matter of grace?"

"Grace" is not a word often used by non-Christian spiritual teachers. However, it is sometimes used to refer to what might be called the "gift"—really the impetus—of the arising, within one, of the seeking of the sought. As Ramana has put it, "that you are *possessed* of the quest of the Self is a manifestation of the divine grace....The deep inner movement (towards Self-realization) *is* grace....

"Introversion is due to grace; perseverance is grace..."

What some seekers are inclined to say is, "Someday, if the conditions are right, enlightenment may be bestowed upon me by grace."

The presumption underlying this attitude is that Absolute clarity will make its appearance in awareness at some indefinite point in the future. The Absolute is present here, now. There is not anything which you need to wait to be bestowed upon you. It could be said that it is by grace that you have been inspired to know the Self. But what would know that the Self is known *is* the Self—so no transit of time is involved.

Knowing that grace is not some gift to await in the future is the grace that is now present for you.

I: First Person Singular?

From the standpoint of our habituated dualistic conditioning, the self-reference "I" designates the separate entity which we presume ourself to be. And, of course, it is this I which functions more or less effectively in the relative, material world.

The point of the nondual teachings is to determine the *true* nature of the conscious being which we think of as I.

So, in terms of Self-realization, it is not essential that the conception of "I," as identified with the organism, disappear from the psyche irremediably. The question is: is there an unequivocal comprehension of "who" (or "what") this I actually re-presents?

Prior to awakening, our I is limited to an image of a personal self. When the nondual actuality of our existence is clearly perceived, this sense of "being an I" dissolves into an awareness of *be-ing* which transcends identification of the person.

The I which you have identified with the organism can continue to function, to meet its bodily needs, in the relative work-day world. But the thoughts, feelings, words and actions of this material form are now witnessed in awareness from a thoroughly different perspective. *This* I is the I AM, or simply present awareness, in which the I-am-this or I-am-so-and-so makes its ever-changing appearance. Ramana used the term I-I to refer to that being which goes beyond the limited *person*ified I.

Once the I-I is realized as present, in other words, the activities and experiences of the relative I are seen for what they are: of no ultimate consequence.

Migrating Meditators

Your comment: it appears that the teachings of nonduality are receiving the enthusiastic response that Buddhism aroused a generation ago.

My observation is that the interest in Advaita is fueled, in part, by a disaffection with Buddhism by some adherents.

Consider that there are many who were drawn to the enlightenment teachings of Buddhism in the Nineteen-eighties, for example, who have worn out their meditation cushion and thirty years later wonder when practice will make perfect. A sizable proportion of these veterans are now composing the audience for teachers like Adyashanti, whom they know himself spent twelve years on the zafu before (like Buddha) abandoning discipline.

A fifty-page biannual meditation-oriented magazine dedicated its latest issue to the subject of "enlightenment."* (You might suppose this would be the *persistent* topic.) An editorial suggests the theme: enlightenment just might be a possibility, for those who "commit to more diligent practice."

If what you're doing is not effective, redouble your effort!

There are five letters reprinted in the magazine: here are statements from four of the respondents, in order.

- [Responding to a previous article† "on the possibilities of complete liberation" in which it is said, "I wish we could see more success stories."] These comments are startling, in that we have a large community of dedicated teachers and ardent students—with few graduates. By graduates, I mean those who have entered the stream of *awak-*

---

* The cover is a picture of a woman walking off of a cliff.
† The article's author, "a teacher of Buddhist meditation and philosophy."

*ening....*And if no one is achieving liberation, or the numbers are so tiny, then those *showing* the path must be missing something.

- My own observation, over *32 years* of practice, is that not many people experience any sort of nirvana....*other* paths seem to provide the realization of the unity of all things...So, why does our Theravada practice have so few students opening to the Absolute?

- Perhaps all the requisite teachings are to be found along *all* the paths, if we only know when and where to look, and what to make of them when we encounter them.

- Perhaps we're just looking for liberation in all the wrong places.

A second difficulty, Buddhism is finding, is a consequence of its inability to disassociate itself from elements of superstition, especially in the Tibetan tradition.

Interestingly, this is noted in the same issue of the magazine quoted above. The commentator had been a monk in the Tibetan sect. He has in mind such things as karma, reincarnation, psychic powers, celestial realms, et cetera, and says: "I think we have to stand aside from this type of Buddhist *belief*....we need to disentangle the elements of Indian religion that have found their way into the Buddhist canon....For instance, we can put aside the doctrine of rebirth...it's simply the worldview of the Buddha's *time*."

Notably, in this same issue of the magazine, "one of the very few Asian-born Buddhist woman teachers in the United States" is a practitioner in a lineage whose masters profess "paranormal or psychic powers" which include "clairvoyance, astral traveling, mind-reading, and bi- or tri-location," as well as "knowledge of the past lives of oneself and others...(and) even passing through walls."

Who would want enlightenment, given those attractions?

Ego Riddance

When the divisiveness of dualistic thinking has been seen through, not anything can ever really be a problem again—not for long.

For those who are looking into the spiritual perspective but haven't quite yet entirely relinquished their reflexive, dualistic thought patterns, there will still remain a number of "problems."

Among these: How am I to be free of the tyranny of divisive thought? And/or: How am I to be free of the selfish machinations of the ego? And on and on.

To whom the fundamental realization is that there is no individuated "I," in actuality, where can there be such problems?

There is no individuated I, because there is only (if you prefer the term) God (or Self, Tao, Brahman, Absolute, Consciousness, ad infinitum). God (et al), by definition, is not apart from anything: not anything exists "outside" of that which, by definition, is infinite: *all*-encompassing. No part of "you" (or anything else) is *not* That.

Upon what has the creation of your brain depended? If you assume that "your" thoughts are a product of your brain, from what source has this phenomenon emanated? Who is ultimately "responsible" for these thoughts?

It is these thoughts that give us a sense of being an "individual." It is the individual who discovers, and reifies, the "existence" of God. That is why you are here: to come to love the "spirit" that animates all things—including yourself.

It is our thoughts of being an individual "self" that is the fundament of our ego. The word "ego" is the Latin equivalent of "I." How can the ego be a "problem," when it is recognized that it is not (nor ever has been) "yours"—but God's? And how could "you" rid yourself of ego; and why? Ego is merely a consequence, an aspect, of the process of thinking of yourself as an individual. Who is responsible for the process of human thought? Are you?

When you let go of the idea that *anything* is "yours," what becomes of "Wyatt's ego"? When you let go of the idea that there can ever be anything *apart* from God, what becomes of "you"?

The ego is not a problem. Your body, your brain, your thoughts, ego, emotions, actions, all are God's "creation" and "doing." If not, forget "omnipotent" and "omniscient" as definitive of the First Principle. From the standpoint of God, there can be no such thing as a "problem"; if there were, it would have to have been Self-created.

Even "your" thoughts about "your" self-ish ego are not a problem. If God has generated all that is (as defined), has any of God's doings been done imperfectly? (If so, who's to make the corrections?)

If you consider your ego to be a problem: a miracle is possible this very moment! A letter is held in your hands, suggesting to you that you take it seriously and recognize *this instant* your true nature. There is no "you," in any separative sense. Therefore, there is no "personal" ego. There are no "independent" thoughts. There is but One Thing. Dissolve, immediately, into it and that is God's love—loving itself...and "itself" *is all things*. Lover, loved and loving.

Nothing Is Missing

You ponder "that something may be missing...needed for enlightenment...even though everything *else*...may already be present.

"The missing ingredient may be the fact that I just don't *realize* it..."

It's not that something is missing. It's that something is *not* missing. The missing ingredient needs to be *you*.

Your 30-sentence analogy, using dreaming as its example, contained "I" 18 times, "me" six times, "my" five times. Were "I," "me," "my" (or "mine") not present, there would be no dilemma.

The idea that there exists in reality a separate entity (*any* separate entity), such as "I," is to miss the point to which the nondual sages are alluding. As you, in your dream, suggest to a companion dream character, "you don't even exist." That is what the sages are proposing to *you*.

Ramana's favorite expiation is to establish three "states" (even though they are not separate from each other) of our consciousness: when we are awake (alert to the "external" world); when we are dreaming (cognitive of, and identified with, the non-external fantasizing of the psyche); and that of deep sleep.

In deep sleep, consciousness continues; but without any reference to the "external world" or the "internal world": no identification with either extrapolation, as (otherwise) when awake or dreaming...consciousness with no self-identification (I, me, my) involved.

This "pure" aware presence is what Ramana (and others) refers to as our "true nature"; before anything whatsoever is added to it: No *self-identification* has been imposed on it. "You" are *missing* from it.

In this condition, there are no separate entities, because in this condition the separative thought process is non-existent. Here, there can be no "dreams" (object) nor "dreamer" (subject).

Here, there is not "enlightenment," nor any "person" to be enlightened. There is nothing missing, because there is "nothing from the start" to which anything could be added or subtracted.

You've commented, "There is a state of mind—a way of being— that is *alogical*, that is outside the bounds to which logic can apply; and thus, neither logical *or* illogical."

Yes. But it would probably be more appropriate to say that it is the *absence* of "a state of mind." It is the "empty mind" that carries over, into the waking state, the "formless" consciousness that (in actuality) nothing truly exists as a separate entity: no you, no enlightenment, no problem; nothing to analyze, nor analyzer.

"YOU" ARE "THE BODY"

You ask, "So, the body is not real?"

The body is real as an appearance. All of so-called reality is what appears to us to be "so." But the nature of appearances is that they lead to deception. Appearances are, first of all, subject to change; even unnoticeably. And what appears to be so, may be discovered to be so in relative degrees; or, even, not at all. What is "real" is a relative distinction; what does not *appear* to us to be real, we automatically conclude *is* "unreal."

So, it's not that the body is not real; it's that *appearances* can be unreal; and the body *appears* to be real. The point being made here is that a mirage is a real thing—as an appearance. Your rail-thin figure in the fun-house mirror is a real image, but it's only an appearance. In other words, the appearance is not all there is to the actuality, except to a deceptive degree.

To get closer to the point, what can be said of the body, that appears to be real, can be said of the "self" that is presumed to inhabit the body.

If, despite appearances, there is no "self" in reality, what is "inhabiting" this body?

What is it that concerns itself with such distinctions as "real," opposed to "unreal"? What becomes of that discerning intellect when the unanimated body is finally just so-many pounds of inert flesh?

As Ramana would say, the body is a real as *you* are. At some point, the "you" will disappear, and the "reality" of the body—in fact, all bodies—will disappear along with it.

What remains, then, must be *really* real. What, in that case, will concern itself with whatever has appeared in our analytic consciousness?

"SELF"-SERVING

As you say, it *is* "time to take a look at my 'belief system', and see just what has (and has not) served me."

Hopefully, you're coming to a place of reflection, rather than re-action. One thing that I think you will find has not helped you is the dwelling on the past. When it is discovered that there is no I, in actuality, what becomes of the day-dream that we call the past?

"I guess it's a *good* thing I no longer have my journals," you comment. And, "How could I have had so much experience that means nothing?...Apparently, the life I once knew has long been over: it seems like I'm the only one who doesn't know that."

We "die"—fortunately—each night, in deep sleep, and are re-born each morning. We have a choice (fortunately) to resurrect the dead self by focusing once again on the "who" we believe ourselves to be—*or*, to let that image rest in peace.

In your reflections, consider whether that image of your "self," and its continual maintenance, has—or has not—"served" you propitiously.

SEXUAL EXPRESSION

Thanks for your monograph.

Regarding your letter:

I can say this from experience, the sex drive is wired in. Even though the mind can deny it, the body won't.

Having a sexual relationship of some duration enriches the life experience, in my opinion, in the complete absence of which there would be a sensual poverty.

One of the saddest facets of mankind's existence is the interference in natural sexual expression which the religions of the world have effected.

Shunyata: Emptiness

Thanks for the quote from Traleg Kyabgon.

As to your comment, "it's not true that things are nonexistent": note Traleg's quote of Buddha, that alleges "the *whole* of *reality* lacking in inherent existence."

All "things" are relative things: *any* "thing" that we name "exists" only in relation to all other things (which we would say it's "not"). "Hot" is only hot because of what we describe as "cold," therefore all "things" are "dependently existing." Take away the definition of cold, and "hot" does not "exist."

Is there anything which is *not* dependently existing? Yes, the ground in which the "dependently-arising" things exist (the Absolute, Void, etc.).

But does that *ground* "exist"? No, because—being the only eternal infinity—there is no (other) thing to which it can be compared.

So, we refer to the ground as nonexistent; we refer to what is manifested from this void as "existing." (appear-ances)

And while we are aware of the (nonexistence of) the Absolute, we cannot deny the existent, relative phenomena: "hot water" will "burn you." As Traleg says, "rejecting the inherent 'existence' of things does not mean rejecting 'things' as such." So, it is not realistic, he says, to hold to the viewpoint that "existence" has no relevance. Critics of Buddhism like to claim that it is nihilistic, mentioning the Void, "no God," etc. They do not take into account that the Buddhist view is polarized neither to presumption of existence (such as that for God) nor of nonexistence (because *relative* "reality" is not denied). Traleg: "The wise cling to neither existence nor nonexistence." As a consequence, they do not maintain dogmatic, doctrinaire "moral precepts or principles" (which, again, the critics like to seize on). And there's good reason why they don't:

"He who knows the *whole* of reality to be lacking in inherent existence will never become attached to it." –Buddha

Traleg adds: "through understanding emptiness...there is no longer that *duality* existing...between the self and the world—because...*both* have the *same nature*: which is emptiness" ("the lack of *inherent* 'existence'").

Mu

An example of grasping the *Absolute* aspect first, prior to cognition of the *relative* aspect:

Buddhist teachers like to give this koan. A monk asked the Chinese Zen-master Joshu, "Does a dog have Buddha-nature?"

Joshu replied "Mu!"

If one thinks only in terms of the relative standpoint, the word *mu* means "no" or "not," or "nothing."

If one's awareness is centered on the Absolute aspect, *mu* is an expression whose "not-ness" implies the Void or emptiness or infinity of Buddha-nature (or the omnipresent Absolute) itself.

So, an uninsightful monk would interpret Joshu's answer to negate that a dog is infused with Buddha-nature.

An insightful monk would receive Joshu's answer as a reminder that there is nothing which can be apart from Buddha-nature.

Giving Up the Ghost

Much of the time I spend with people is devoted to discussing what I call "idealizing."

Your situation, in general, is not unusual. You find that—despite about six years of psychotherapy and nearly fifty years of meditation "off and on"—you continue to be critical of yourself concerning "matters large and small in my life." You find that your efforts at self-improvement, in reaction, are insufficient and thus add to the "suffering"—just more grist for the mill of self-critique. One can thus be more disparaging of oneself than even a disapproving coworker.

"I'm trying to observe the *conflict* this causes with me, but it doesn't ease the struggle within me," you say. While becoming aware of this (typical) tendency may be the first step (if you are an alcoholic, the first step is to acknowledge that this is so), obviously the introspection can go further.

In speaking of your attempts to "improve" (your quotes), you follow this word parenthetically with "not accept?" It must be clear to you that at the root of this quandary is the issue of "someone accepting themselves as they are, along with all of their perceived faults," as you put it.

Personally, I don't think in terms of "accept"; those conditions which we have come to notice—you mention such things as anger, anxiety—are, in our perception, a reality. You don't change what is already considered to be a reality; you can only deny, reject, it.

The nondual teachings urge us to transcend all dualistic polarities, "to go beyond the limits of" definitional concepts. You speak of "how things really *are*"; we fix this *existent* condition, as we recognize it, as one end of a polarity—to which we manufacture, or suppose, another polarized conception of how things instead *could* be, or (further yet along the spectrum of contradistinction) *should* be.

While the first condition is the fact, *what is*, the consideration of *what isn't* is nothing more real than a construct in imagination, an idea. We posit *ideal* circumstances ("I should be more like Eckhart Tolle").

So, what goes beyond observing is *realization*. Rather than focusing your attention on your presumed shortcomings, attentively notice the characteristics of the self-*image* that has become established. This image has no more reality than does a ghost. As long as you suppose it has any substance, it will continue to haunt you.

Guru Relationship

From the relative standpoint, the standpoint of the seeker, there is a spiritual teacher who knows (or is aware of) something which the seeker wishes to know.

From the standpoint of an enlightened teacher, there is *this* "person" (or organism) in communication (or "communion," stressing union) with an-other person. Viewing his own person as That, he regards the other person as That, *indivisibly*. From his standpoint, That is merely conversing (or interacting) with That. Under those circumstances, he does not think in terms of "relationship." Relationship is the viewpoint of the *seeker*: the "disciple/guru" presumption.

From the teacher's standpoint, That (as he) is aware of its true nature, while That (as she) professes not to be aware of its true nature. Aspects, or manifestations, of That (Absolute actuality) are interacting, as a jetstream of water may interact in a sea of water. The outcome of the interaction does not matter: whatever the outcome (if any), it is That doing what it does.

What it is doing, in one entity, is asking a question. What it is doing, in the other entity, is suggesting a resolution of the question.

The seeker is proposing that there is an "I" apart from the "guru." The guru is reiterating that the "I" and the "other," in ultimate reality, are the same, omnipresent essence.

When it is recognized (if it is) that you and I are an unbroken whole—along with all other things—it is clear that, from the Absolute perspective, there are *no* relationships that exist.

The disciple *already* embodies this no-relationship condition. There is not, therefore, a condition which the guru embodies which the disciple does not. This is all that the guru can profess to "transmit," and the disciple admit to "realize."

The disciple/guru never really *had* a relationship, and consequently mutually acknowledge that they never will—in fact that they never really existed as separate *realities*.

Koan for Today

Togo said: "Master Chenzai, you sent me to Master Hodei to seek the teaching. He told me I was wasting my time!" Togo snorted and glared: "I could teach him kindness!"

Chenzai said: "Flies can't eat horses."

Nothingness is Wholeness

It is readily apparent that where there is division, there is conflict; and so we speak of the condition in which there is no conflict as "wholeness," absence of fragmentation.

But a *concept* of wholeness can be a stumbling block for the mind which would perceive That.

We all know what a segmented, fragmented orange looks like. And we all know what a whole orange looks like. We are also cognizant that things which are "whole" may vary in size—compared, for example, to the whole earth. As a consequence, it is exceedingly difficult for you to contemplate a wholeness (or "nothingness") which is not in some way enclosed within the imagination. No matter *how large* this wholeness is conceived to be, it will ultimately dissipate into a form which is basically spherical, or circular—limited.

And that, of course, is not surprising, when we consider that this conception of wholeness is radiating from you at its center.

This brings us to a point which is critical.

For the moment, refrain—attentively—from a global or spherical conception of wholeness or of emptiness. Think, instead, in terms of a flat plane which spreads in every direction—*not* from any particular central point, such as where you "are," and therefore not like a pizza pan. Consider that this flat plane not only spreads out in every direction but that there is never any end to its spread—no matter *where* you might take up a centralized position to observe this. Any possible place where you can imagine it ending, if you were to sit at that edge in observation, you would recognize that this is no different than any other spot: in actuality, this plane maintains its spread in every endless direction.

Now then, consider that this phenomenon is occurring on *any* and *every* possible plane, not just on the single flat plane with which you started.

Put another way, there is utterly no possibility of locating or establishing an absolute *central* point anywhere in this wholeness, or in emptiness or "nothingness."

Reread the previous sentence. Note that, given the nature of language, it is unavoidable to use the word "in"—even though it is crystal *clear* that there can be no such locations as "in" (or "out") or "within," in (see that!) the wholeness which has been described.

As soon as *any* point *anywhere* is selected or isolated, it is a basis or starting point in the process of comparison or measurement—and, *simultaneously*, this wholeness *loses* its quality of being incomparable or immeasurable. If that which is without a center were to be given a center, it is no longer that which is without a center. You can continue to *contend* that it has no center, and imagine that *you* are not the center, but whatever it is that you're referring to is not truth.

And so, if I say that That, wholeness, is at any and every point in space or time, this may help you to stretch your mind—but not far *enough*, because it is deceptive. To say that it is *ever* at *any* point is central to limiting it.

PRIDE IN DIFFERENCE

One might count oneself among the majority and feel pride that one is, say, heterosexual. Or, one might find oneself among the unconventional minority and be proud that one is homosexual. And, similarly, a person who is not neurotically fixed on a particular sexual preference, over any other, may be proud to be bisexual. The pride, in all cases, is associated with one's self-image and its continuous maintenance as identity.

Given the circumstances, as in the example above, one may respond, in a particular situation, as a heterosexual; in another situation as a homosexual; and in yet another situation, without deference to either sexual polarity. Where one has no particular image of oneself, extending beyond the moment, there is no investment in perpetuating an attachment to any specific identity.

There are some people who are proud of their capacity for dishonest behavior; there are some people who are proud of their proclivity for honest behavior. There are situations in which either tendency might be justified, even on a moral basis. The person who holds pride in his capacity for honesty has no more *reason*, as a particularly defendable reaction, than has a person with a capacity for dishonesty.

"I HAVEN'T A CLUE"...?

Go anywhere in the universe that you can imagine, at any time, and you are *present*. And you are *aware* of being present.

Because the mind is aware *of* that awareness, the mind is not *itself* awareness. Because the mind is aware *of* being present, the mind itself is not presence.

Sages have reported a condition in which the activities of the cognitive mind are completely silent. There is merely present awareness; or, as it's often termed, "pure awareness." The "subject" is not aware *of*, but *as*. As awareness, the subject *is* awareness— not an "I" who is aware *of* some thing (not even of oneself).

So, it is evident that the "I," which can be suspended in pure awareness, is not *real* (in the way that present awareness is real). Nor is the cognitive mind, which can be vacated, real (in the sense of a permanent actuality).

That which is present (or "pure") awareness can't be known by a "you" which is unreal.

The fact that "you" are not aware of your pure awareness is a clue.

All that "you" *can* know is that you are not any*thing* that you think you are, if you think that it is real.

So the no-thing that remains for you to be, is what you are.

Present awareness is no thing.

You will not experience what you are. The experienc*er*—present awareness—is what you are.

Present awareness will not experience present awareness as experienced by an experiencer ("you").

"You" need only be aware, conscious, of what you are not. You are not any thing.

Even if you were to identify your "self" as present (or pure) awareness, present awareness is universal, unbroken, unindividuated. Being that, there is no "you" that is That.

The mind that is aware of "you" or That (as separate) is not real.

Even "presence" and "awareness" are mere labeled attempts by the mind to be aware *of* that which the unreal has no real comprehension of.

The fact that your mind cannot recognize (your) pure awareness is that indicative clue.

No "Special" Feeling?

You say that you have no *feeling* of (as the mystical literature sometimes states) being "everything everywhere in the universe."

If indeed your *true* condition is that you embody *everything*, anywhere in the universe, there no longer remains a separation or distinction between "things" (more accurately, there never was.) So, what becomes of "you" as an entity which harbors sensations or feelings?

Are you supposing that (to reify the mystic pronouncement) you would sense or feel your self as every planetary "thing" and contiguous "space," in the cosmos? If it is *possible* that the self does not have any verifiable reality, is it possible that the cosmos has no verifiable reality? Could it be that the universe exists in your mind, in the same way that the self exists only in the mind? In Buddhism, they say: "Mind is universe" and "mind is self." Why is *this* said?

When your own reality is nothing more than consciousness, how far do you extend and what do you embody—when every "thing" and all spatial separations are *in* "you," contained within consciousness?

Even if we say we know the cosmos is real because someone set foot on the moon, that event too is only established in human consciousness. Or, we could assert that the cosmos is apparent not only in "my" consciousness but the consciousness of "others." Could it be that those "others" are "known" only in consciousness?

Could it be that there is but one, undivided consciousness—not "mine" and "yours"?

Even if we assume that the cosmos exists apart from consciousness, not anyone anywhere has been able to determine definitely *what* the "cosmos" or "universe" *is*.

So, when you pursue the feeling of what could be meant by "you are everything everywhere in the universe," is there a universe that lives in your imagination—which you are supposing that a separate you will fill? Would the pervading of an imagined universe not be an imagined pervasiveness?

Conversely, if consciousness really is all that is, and you are conscious, then you already are pervasively embodying everything everywhere. What *particular* feeling would there be, then? And what entity would "contain" it?

For a more complete and definitive feeling of being absolutely everything that is everywhere, perhaps that is the condition of death, when the organism no longer functions as an anchor for the personalization of consciousness (in which consciousness is made known to itself in particular).

Why is there the need to feel anything other than whatever feeling naturally appears in consciousness? Is there a "person" with a need for a special feeling?

EMPTINESS AND AWARENESS

What is called the "natural mind" has two simultaneous aspects: emptiness (or clarity; allowing clear, true perception) and awareness (the focused presence of undistracted and imperturbable attention).

The emptiness is a consequence of enlightened realization; it is what is referred to as "absolute awareness." In this realization, it has been recognized that the ultimate actuality is void of characteristics or attributes; as Hui Neng put it, "There is nothing, from the start."

This mindful presence of emptiness is the condition which is regarded as awareness. It is a continual clear perception of the actuality that all that is sensed, and known, ultimately has no independent existence or permanent reality. All that is experienced is witnessed in consciousness as meaningless, from the standpoint of the emptiness of unadulterated, unembellished being.

Abiding, effortlessly, in this empty awareness is what is known as the "natural mind," one which is unencumbered by the overlay of mental impressions.

The emptiness of one's consciousness of it's content—all the acquired mental impressions—is what Krishnamurti maintained permits one the state of attentiveness which he termed "choiceless awareness," and which has generally been referred to as merely "witnessing." The underlying condition of the emptiness of the natural mind is what allows the continual nonobjective, uncritical state called witnessing. This underlying natural emptiness of the mind is its *pre*conditioned, unblemished, abiding temperament, an unformed presence from which our concepts of form tend to arise.

Says Traleg Kyobgen Rinpoche, "The nature of mind is indistinguishable from ultimate reality, which is emptiness...said to be completely undifferentiated and spacious, and is the source from which all our experiences arise. It...unlike our thoughts and emotions, does not exist as an entity."

And Dzogchen Ponlop Rinpoche says, "Yet the mind is not just space; it is full of awareness, full of wakefulness, which is always in union with emptiness. This aspect of awareness is mind's luminosity [clarity] quality."

Sogyal Rinpoche: "The nature of mind is the very root itself of understanding [discernment, wisdom]. In Tibetan, we call it rigpa; a primordial, pure, pristine, awareness that is at once intelligent, cognizant, radiant, and always awake...always present."

Chang Chen-Chi: "Once the essence of mind is recognized, the yogi will be able to absorb himself in it at any time or place, without difficulty....No effort need be made, and no object or idea need be worked on."

As Ponlop Rinpoche says, "There is nothing we need to get rid of, because faults do not exist in the nature of mind."

The nature of mind, the "natural mind," denotes the illuminated presence of what is known as empty, or undifferentiating, awareness.

Perfecting the Ego

At least, you are growing wiser with time. You write:

> "I can hardly perceive anyone here as being awake, including yours truly. Otherwise I wouldn't continue to be 'annoyed' by those who are 'asleep', when they do things unconsciously."

When you *are* awake, you will cease holding your behavior up to standards of perfection. You *do* get annoyed. This may never change. And you say:

"Yet, the question remains; why am I here?

"I do not like the metaphysical/metaphorical reasoning of The Course, which seems to come about in the statement: 'You would not be here in a body if you were not in opposition to God.' I've always concluded that this is a guilt-provoking statement."

It is similarly a guilt-provoking proposition to conclude "I tend to get annoyed—but I *shouldn't* do that." What you are calling, in the following paragraph, "the operation of the ego"—

"While the 'behavior' has not changed, the way I viewed it has. After a while of observing the annoying, mindless, and often compulsive, addictive behavior, I became 'aware' that what I was *really* observing was the operation of my own ego. That is the 'reactionary' device, which tells me *the* 'solution' is *outside* myself. However, if that is the case, there may be no resolution for the problem."

—is this presumption that you are a superior person who should never get annoyed at the "annoying, mindless" behavior of the people you come in contact with. Inconsiderate people are likely to be around for a long time: and you *have* noticed that *they* have not changed. But the way that you view behavior—yours *and* others'—*can* change. Otherwise, if their behavior continues unchanged—and your *reaction* to it—"there may be no resolution" for your discontent.

So, your expectations that things *ought* to be other than they *are* can be a "problem." You have said:

"All I can say is that I was wrong about my 'perceptions' and the *projections* that resulted from them."

You have even, wisely, stated this:

"Are they offenses? Only if someone 'separate' is there to take offense."

So, when the self, that you think you are (what you call the ego) melts away, you might notice that the "offended" had been giving rise to the "offender".

Likewise, you might notice that you had been viewing your self as an offender for having committed the sin of being annoyed: an offense to your critical ego. Egoically, you don't think *you're* perfect—but you think you're capable of it. And since you are, even an awakened person ought to be!

FACING THE MUSIC

It would be accurate to say that, for the spiritually awakened person, there will be some bodily changes noticed, yes.

But then, it is equally true that for the non-awakened person, there will regularly be bodily changes noticed.

Physical changes come with the territory; no one is exempt from aging. In fact, enlightened sages are not exempt from even such things as terminal cancer.

Probably the difference between the jnani and the ajnani is that the former does not expect any situation or development to be other than it actually is.

We are all "terminal"; physical death therefore is a *natural* consequence. Why resist what is naturally to occur?

It is via this objectivity that the sage does not focus on (or "identify with") what is occurring with the body whether positive (even "bliss") or negative (physical discomfort).

With this non-attachment to "outcome," there actually occurs a deep physical relaxation. And this relaxation can be noticed at both high tide and low tide.

On a more personal level, I have found that disciplined daily exercise and a *high-quality* (not $ cheap) daily vitamin-mineral supplement are among the major aids to sleeping well. And a placid mind is a big help too.

Passing Memories

When the attention on our self-centered pre-occupation *dis*integrates, changes will be observed in the realm of the psyche.

Among these are what you are likely noticing. Memories spontaneously occur like vagrant ghosts. They idly drift past, on the screen of consciousness, like icebergs on a current. They generally replay moments when our attention was especially present and in the "Record" mode. It seems like watching a movie in which a stand-in plays your part.

The purpose of these memories, which are like segments from a story-board, appears to have been to place the persona in a context of time and space—with continuity. The chain of memories perpetuated the "you"—from the present, back to your earliest memory as an "individual" child.

As the consciousness clears of compulsive, reflexive egoic feedback, these uninvited depictions can be regarded like "screen savers," and witnessed with the objectivity due such.

Though some of the displays may be more or less dramatic than others, it's a fact that the screen itself assumes no interest in what is imposed on it. Undiscriminating awareness is that screen.

EXPECTATION FOR WHAT'S NOT

Using the Krishnamurti quote you gave, as a means for "exploring the whole 'thinking' question":

> "Thought must be completely still... there cannot be a movement of thought..."

What do you imagine is the meaning of this, in actual experiential terms?

Thought: is there more than one variety of thought? The dictionary cites three examples; "reflection; meditation; cogitation." And it adds: reasoning, conceiving, imagining, considering, concentrating. What, specifically, did Krishnamurti have in mind when he said "thought"?

If we read far enough, most every teacher who speaks about "ending thought" clarifies that what needs to cease its movement is *conceptualizing*.

Can conceptualizing cease? Well, what *is* a concept? To have a concept is to imagine or form an idea or image of something which is not a present actuality. For instance, any idea or projection of what will happen in the future can only be a concept.

Or to consider the condition of the abiding absence of mentation, when that is no one's actual state or experience, is a concept.

Since a concept is based upon something which has no reality in one's experience, surely this form of idealized imagining can be dispensed with. How much time ought we to spend in suppositions about conditions which are not presently manifest? The teachers seem to be saying that one's attention can be directed to the reality of being, rather than the desire of becoming. Better to be an authentic John Doe than a would-be Krishnamurti.

John Doe doesn't even have any way of knowing precisely what Krishnamurti's subjective experience entirely was, anyway.

In any case, cogitating about the presumed state of no-thought is not the way to bring discursive thought to an end.

Unanticipated Development

You ask about celibacy (personally, in relation to me). The dictionary defines this as "refraining from sexual intercourse" (and implies that it pertains to the unmarried). As a research psychotherapist, perhaps you have a more specific definition: one can have something of a sex life, apart from coitus, of course.

Of those you mention, only Ramana (so far as we can know) was actually *abstinent* during his lifetime (masturbation at some point?: we can't know). Nisargadatta was married. Krishnamurti is alleged to have had at least an affair. Meister Eckart (though a friar) we cannot know about—especially during the age in which he lived. Buddha had been married. And Gandhi: not everyone would classify him as "a teacher of nonduality".

In my own case, first there was celibacy, following my second (and last) marriage. (More than 25 years ago.) Then there has been abstinence. Not anything moralistic about this (or even idealistic), and not even intentional in a programmatic way: more a byproduct of Self-realization.

How so? Firstly, when the subject-object mindset ends, others are no longer seen as a sexual (or any other) object.

Secondly, as a consequence of desirelessness in terms of pursuit of pleasurable (or other) experiences, passivity tends to discourage potential sex partners; thus "celibacy."

From the end of my second marriage on, I never ruled out sexual intimacy or even re-marriage. Yet at 76, and after more than twenty years of nondual realization, I have only in the past year been having a "romantic" (she'd laugh at this word: she permits me to hug her, but not kiss her) platonic relationship. (Haven't deeply kissed anyone since my second marriage.)

I've had a reasonably wide range of sexual experiences, and still find the female form particularly attractive and can still feel arousal; the sexual instinct is hard-wired in, I've observed. And during the celibate period, I still enjoyed self-gratification. But interest has waned of its own accord, and celibacy eventually became abstinence. I don't even have sexual dreams any more, though some occasionally involving affection.

Finally: The sexual energy that has progressively waned has found its expression (without any intention on my part) in something which I had never understood the meaning of before: shakti. Only someone who understands what this is, could relate to what I'm saying.

There's much too little said about sexuality in spiritual writings: I'm glad you asked.

WISING UP

You write in your monograph: "What is the message? To have a spiritual awakening? Acquisitiveness, ambition and being goal-directed are certain to cause conflict and divisiveness."

And your letter indicates that you are beginning to see the effects of goal-oriented ambition, in attempting to be a corrective to each of your string of cellmates.

The belief that you need to improve each of these other persons, and the ideals that you've been basing these attempts on, "have been tried and tested here—and probably going back more than twenty years now."

That seems to be changing: "It's absolutely about the way I am 'seeing' things *now*.... It's been *my own thought* that has questioned how I've been treated, and more importantly, how I *really* desire to treat others." Right! Do you like it when others point out *your* imperfections?

> "You begin to see the ignorant behavior of others, who are constantly 'blaming', and trying to fix anything and everything, as long as it is outside of themselves."

And when you are blaming your cellmates for their ignorant behavior, and trying to fix them (and the prison system and society), isn't this "outside" of the would-be fixer?

Here is probably the wisest thing I've heard you say yet:

> "If I forget all of my thoughts about 'helping' him (do what he really doesn't want to do), I can gain much 'rest', and a lot of time for 'the deep'.

> "I've been way *too serious*, and for quite sometime now I've been changing the way I interact with all of the characters here. It doesn't matter *how* they react to me—because I'm no longer interested in 'giving' them anything."

Believe me, when you've really got something worth giving, you don't have to lay it on people—they'll ask you for it. It will be abundantly apparent in your behavior and attitude, your presence.

Well, maybe at last you've understood something:

"As long as you *want* anything from this world (or its inhabitants), you cannot know patience. I contemplated this idea for two days—and couldn't explain what I understood, if I wanted to."

Having a desire to change the world or other people (or even your "self") is still a desire: Buddha spent his life talking about the suffering which is a consequence of *any* desire.

You end your letter with a Krishnamurti quote: "It takes great intelligence to be alone."

To be alone is basically to not need anything from anybody—and that includes the need that they change in order to be the way you think they ought to be (even for their own supposed good).

By changing the way you "interact with all the characters—no longer interested in 'giving' them anything," you will surely have more "time for 'the deep'"—and be less "certain to cause conflict and divisiveness."

Do "You" Exist?

If there were no conscious person alive in the universe, there would not be anything which is considered to be "existent." On the other hand, there would *neither* be anything which would be considered to be "non-existent."

In other words, the ideas (or concepts) of both existence and non-existence are dependent upon a consciousness which considers (and gives names to) such propositions.

So, this is what the sages mean when they remark that there is neither anything which exists or doesn't exist: "nothing exists" (outside of the realm of consciousness).

Among the things which "exists"—*in consciousness*—is "me": the idea that there is a separate entity, in the universe, which has been labeled "my body"; and that, "in" this body is a selective realm called "my consciousness"; and that this consciousness is apprised of a separate entity which is regarded as "me."

Where there is not something which regards itself as conscious, the body and mind and person do not exist as reality. In deep sleep, there is not the notion of a "me" which concludes that "I exist" (or, even, that "I do not exist"). This also will evidently be the condition which persists when the physical organism ceases to function (so-called death).

Both "existence" and "non-existence"—both merely ideas in what we call consciousness—come and go, with life and death. So, these are unreal, in the ultimate sense: what is eternally actual does not come and go.

What is eternally actual, therefore, is nothing: not any "thing" (since all things are the creation of consciousness). You cannot even say that the eternally actual is "real," since both "real" and "unreal" are ideas (like "existence" and "non-existence").

So, what you have written is correct: it is only through consciousness that we conclude that "my body" exists, and that therefore a separate "I" exists as a physical form.

Thus, as you've put it, "only through [the supposition of] the body does the 'I' come." If that is the case, when the body ceases to exist, the I ceases to exist; it is impermanent, unlike the eternal actuality, and so has no lasting or ultimate reality.

Meanwhile, *what* does (what we call) your consciousness "exist in"?: the presence which is eternally actual. This presence has no notion of being existent or non-existent, of being "some thing" or "no thing." This is the presence which pertains when "your body" is in dreamless slumber. So, this eternal actuality, this presence, claims no "body," no "self," and no "mind" to foment perplexing questions. Where it is recognized that ultimately there is *nothing*, there are no problems.

DEMYSTIFICATION

Despite the impression you may have gotten from your reading of spiritual material, Self-realization is not rocket science.

I have just had a dialogue with two sisters, both of whom have been seekers for years. I met with the younger; at the end of an hour, awakened clarity was present for her. She asked if she could phone her sister. (Both were staying at a bed-and-breakfast inn, on their visit from San Diego.) Upon hearing of her younger sister's news, the older sister came to join us.

I asked the younger sister to explain to her sibling the essence of the awareness which had now become clearly her own. She was able to do so in such a direct way that her sister too realized the message of the nondual teachings.

That "you" and what is being sought are not two different things is not a difficult matter to comprehend, to *awaken* to.

ANOTHER KOAN FOR THE DAY

Usho said: "Master Sekita says that without his practice, he would not have become enlightened."

Tasho said: "When Assai grew feeble at age 80, he walked fifty miles to ask his sister his name."

Letter From Home

I've read and re-read the twelve sentences in your letter. Every sentence is a reflection of Self-realization. You wouldn't have been capable of saying what you've said if the clarity of realization was not present.

The key is, as you've said, "living *in* and *as*" the mystery: "everything is *one* reality." The "peace of *not* knowing" is what is meant by emptiness: "the equanimity of benevolent indifference."

The personality that is "slowly dissolving" can lead to—as Krishnamurti titled a book—*a wholly different way of living*, in and as that which transcends relative appearances.

Pre/Post Mortem

Yours is the Sixty-Four Dollar Question, Lou: "In death, is there still an awareness of life?" Let us see what can be intuited.

Are we perhaps getting a daily—actually, nightly—clue as to post-consciousness? To use your words, "being *presence* without awareness of any *thing*, because every thing disappears." Where "self" and "body" drop away in deep sleep, can we anticipate death to be anything less?

Our fundamental state of awareness is an aspect of the Ultimate Reality, but this all-inclusive Reality would not be aware of any thing which is not "itself." Being all things, it is not any thing in particular, so it is not subjective regarding whatever could be objectified.

So, if this Ultimate Reality is *your* ultimate reality, you would not be aware of life (as objectifiable, or an appearance) because you *are* life. And if you were aware of life, you could be aware of death. In a reality where there is no conceivable thing, there would presumably be no defined states as "existing" or "not existing." I suppose we could say, what is it about nothingness that you don't understand?

Regarding the fear of death (which you identified as "the fear of nothing"), mere Presence is present as "self" now. When (limited) self falls away from (unlimited) Presence, is there no longer the actuality which we think of as Presence? That is the actuality into which the self initially appeared. Where could it go when the self disappears? (There's a bumper sticker to the effect, "We are not bodies having a spiritual experience. We are spirit having a bodily experience.")

So *post hoc*, you will in a sense be "more" than Lou; but in an equal sense, you'll be entirely nothing. In neither sense, of course, will you be Lou. (Which you are not even, in deep sleep, now.)

My newly-published book, *One Essence*, can assist you in attuning to this Absolute ("without limitation") perspective. Meanwhile consider that, every night, you are receiving a reminder of your Ultimate Reality. And that Reality knows nothing of fear, "death" as apart from "life," or "Lou" who conceives of either. Could this be a hint as to how we are to live our life?

A woman asked Ramana, "Is it possible to know the condition of an individual after death?"

Ramana:

> "It is possible....You are eternal....Until this truth is realized, there will always be [anxiety] due to false values arising from wrong knowledge and wrong identity."

Thinking of this earthly drama as "God's play" could be an acceptable metaphor, as long as a couple of elements are clear; God is in no way standing apart from the play, but unfolding *as* it moment-by-moment; therefore it is not a pre-planned play (as if a product of a limited, human-like mind), but is perfectly spontaneous, un-precedent-ed, un-pre-meditat-ed. (Even more miraculous, given that circumstance!) It is you, doing what you're doing right now—*whatever* "you decide" to do; *and* whatever occurs as a consequence of what you do. (Or vice-versa, regarding so-called others.) A form-less development.

So, as you say, each "individual" can be considered an actor, producer and audience. And, as you say, each actor "is the same" (Formless), "yet different" (manifest form). This is the paradox which dualistic perceivers ("me," as opposed to "God") are not comprehending.

Also, as you put it, to know "all" (absolute awareness) is to know no-thing. ("God," being "omniscient," "knows all" effortlessly— without a *separate* mind—by *being* all.)

As you also put it, all that we "do" is, in actuality, doing nothing. As Hui-Neng declared, "If there is nothing from the *start*, where can the 'dust' [the presumed consequence of actions] alight?" If all that is done is the Absolute "doing what It does," no special or *partic*ular thing has ever really happened. (Thus David Godman's three volumes on Poonja—"Papaji"—*Nothing Ever Happened*.) This, too, has to do with "omnipotence": if God/Absolute is the presence in all that occurs, it is not a divine *effort* to be *omnipotent*.

Your last line grasps the point:

"Realizing all,

there's no knowing

or doer."

The Absolute awareness can know nothing other than its Self, can do nothing other than what It is doing: and that is where each "unique" form—"you"—comes in. (That is the one/all realization.)

Your added "Gotcha" makes it clear to "me" that it's clear to "you"; or, that Absolute awareness is present in realization of its Self.

GASSHO

Han-shan hurried to the master. Once in his presence, the master asked, "What is the nature of your realization?"

Han-shan: "I have shed body and mind."

The master: "Shed shedding."

Han-shan bowed. "Your teaching is nothing special."

INTIMACY WITH THAT

It's no small question that you've asked. My (second) wife and I separated some twenty years ago. In the final days before our separation (then divorce) is the last time that I was intimate with anyone. And it's not that I planned that it would be that way.

Instead, I remained open to the possibility of another (romantic) relationship. But due to what developed to be a passive nature, none has ever materialized.

As you know, after that marital separation, I spent three (fruitful) years seeking Self-realization. The masters assure us that such Self-realization is life-changing. And it is, in more ways than one.

One of the factors is a transcendence of the pleasure/displeasure dichotomy, as well as that of security/insecurity (social, or familial, in this case). I no longer felt that a "marital" relationship was of a high value, in my newly-revised scale of concerns. In any case, with my lack of interest in financial security, what kind of "responsible" mate could I have been?

The overriding factor, as a consequence of the shift in values, has been the continual impulse to place myself at the service of others—in the only way in which I can any longer truly be of service, and that is in assisting in the transmission of the dharma.

Notice, for example, that in the lives of the great sages, two threads are prominent: no preoccupation with romantic life; and 24/7 availability to be of assistance to those who perceive that they are lacking peace and tranquility.

This is not to say that one *can't* have a domestic relationship and yet be a spiritual presence. But it is to say that this is one of the *possibilities* that seems to prominently manifest in what unfolds for the awakened. One simply follows the light wherever it leads, and it leads each person differently.

You say, "I want a life that I can be content in, and more or less flow with it naturally." I submit that in such a life the emphasis on like/dislike and want/don't want, or need/don't need, will be basically transcended.

I have generally surrendered to what unfolds, and I have no regrets for what has unfolded so far. My life is relatively Spartan and without frills (such as interpersonal attachments), and I wouldn't trade it for my life at any point in the past. ("Keep it simple, stupid.")

This is the price of contentment, and you might find is the consequence of wholeheartedly living the teachings.

And, of course, this is not a change (as in "life-changing) that everyone is willing to accommodate. "That's what makes chocolate and vanilla."

MESSAGE RECEIVED

Hi Robert:

I've been re-reading your response to my letter.

It is clear from my letter that I am coming from a dualistic point of view.

At the end of the letter, you ask me what ought to be done, about my interpretation of what's occurring. What needs to be done is for me to stop living in a world that is make believe. I can see, as long as I continue to bounce back and forth between the relative and the absolute, that I will have no peace.

Looking over the letter, I was surprised how caught up I was in all this stuff that was obviously judgmental, and totally made up in my mind. Pure imagination!

So again, at the end of the letter you say. "So what do you think ought to be done about that? And you underline THAT.

Nothing needs to be done about THAT, THAT is perfect! And *that* is what I am.

End of story.

I want this to be the end of *my* story. And I know the wanting of the story to end is just another story and that's ok too, because that's just That, thinking that.

I know what I am.

This space that I am has always been here. It doesn't matter what comes and goes in it. It never does. And it is Ok with everything. What I need now is vigilance. Vigilance to the truth.

When the whispers of the small self try to cause me to doubt, I will welcome them here, no longer afraid.

I now see clearly, all is That and welcome. There is nothing to resist. And nothing to get.

Your words are very clear, Robert. Thank you.

When we met, you said Krishnamurti said just seeing the false as false was enough.

It's funny, but I was reading Nisargadatta recently and came across a talk where he said exactly the same thing.

All is well! I hope we get a chance to talk again soon.

Sending a heart felt thanks, Jim

A CAPITAL LETTER

Jim:

A capital letter—the kind of that makes my day. This represents clear seeing! In terms of vigilance, you can't lose That which never was not already present: you can only deny what has been seen.

But I understand what you mean; you'll be giving attention to what is now unfolding. Keep a copy of your statement and re-read it from time to time. Also, *One Essence* could be particularly meaningful to you at this time—now that you'll thoroughly understand it.

If at any time you need to talk further, that's what I'm here for.

Cordially –RW

!@*#&

My brother was four years older, so I picked up a varied lexicon of cuss words from him, as a child. And cussing, when there is a frustration or disappointment in the moment, is a deep-seated habit that I suspect is likely not ever to change. And I have no need for it to change.

For one thing, this habitual response (whether enunciated, or not) has been a reminder—when there is an incident that provokes a damning expletive—to notice the (also habitual) tendency to suppose that a situation *ought* to be *other* than what it actually *is*.

So, sometimes, when I bruise my foot or cut my finger or whatever, my attention is sharply called to my temperament (by my reactive cursing) and I'm reminded to reflect: "Are you presuming that *what is* 'should not be'?!"

I would venture that "arguing with reality" is *the* major behavior that is at the root of human distress. The dissatisfaction, with whatever reality is present, not only is projected externally but internally as well. The impulse to insist on change in others, change in the world, and change in our "self" is the same sweeping judgmental movement.

People sometimes find it difficult to comprehend that the nondual teachings (unlike all else they've been exposed to) are not about focusing attention on any thing getting "better." It's about recognizing that "better" or "worse" have no ultimate, cosmic meaning, and therefore make no lasting difference.

How many teachings, out there, tell you—assure you—that you are perfect just as you are? And, that what's *in* this moment must be what it's *supposed* to be, because that's what it *is*.

For me, the watchword is "*being* present with what is *present*." And even if, in a particular moment, I'm *not* being agreeably present (such as when swearing), that *too* is what is present; and I don't concern myself with the need to make the *what is* "better."

Drowning with No Lifeline

Thank you for your long letter.

It is worthwhile to note that no two experiences of Self-realization are exactly alike. It is also important to note (particularly if extraordinary sensations were a part of it) that the pivotal moment is now simply a memory in the past. Some people make the mistake of attempting (or hoping for) a reliving of what is indubitably a unique occurrence. What is important, instead, is the moment-by-moment *living* of Self-realization, once the wonder of discovery has passed.

As you say, in your fourteenth and concluding paragraph, "I understand that all this is meaningless discussion": for you, realization is clearly present, and all the rest is merely preamble. In your words, this perspective is no longer a matter of "intellectual understanding." Essentially, the things which you describe would be recognizable by anyone who's undergone this transition. Reduced to a paragraph:

"[Before], every activity or thought process was separate. Now it is felt that there is no discontinuation. Continuity in the awareness is not lost, even if thoughts or activities happen. Individuality has gone. The differentiation between 'you' and 'other' simply vanishes. Thoughts do come, you still interact with others, but you know that you are interacting only with yourself! There are feelings like anger, joy, happiness, worries, etc., but they don't prolong. There is only the sense of being, existence. 'Efforts' are not possible for any further so-called seeking. The very basic and simple meaning of *Nondual* renders every concept or definition meaningless."

You also state, "The feeling of *Being* takes over." You asked if there will be a "deepening." I prefer the word "unfolding." The shift in perspective, as you noticed, is instantaneous, an authorless insight beyond the time frame of "becoming." But once the realization is present, the unfolding (or "deepening") of its being is what "takes over" for the rest of one's life. You might say that drowning in Being is the deepening. Anything shallower can be said to be "meaningless discussion."

SPIRITED DIALOGUE

Ron Bonilla was a seeker of the Absolute from the days of his youth. Of Hispanic heritage, burning questions were first raised for him while a parishioner in the Catholic Church, and he subsequently roamed across the Christian spectrum, even to the Eastern Orthodox Church. I don't recall meeting anyone who's had more experience with the various forms of Christianity. It was *disillusionment*, mainly, that led Ron to look beyond, for that which can't be contained within a chapel.

By the time we had talked, he had acquainted himself with the teachings of nonduality to the extent that all he needed was confirmation that indeed he had realized the Self.

As many do, who've ended their search, he's felt the urge to share his awakened perception with those who still are experiencing the agony of perceived separation from ultimate Reality. As a consequence, Ron has set up a blog site, *Nonduality State Park*, wherein he's begun writing brief, occasional monographs on personal insights relating to Advaita.

Prior to meeting Ron, I'd heard from a Catholic priest in California who'd just finished reading my book, *Living Nonduality*. He too came for a visit, and told me that he had discovered the Eastern (and Western) Advaita literature, over the course of the past several years. It so affected his homilies, as a priest, that he basically was asked to resign—which he has recently done.

He still has a circle of parishioners who look to him for guidance and spiritual inspiration. So, he has begun to write a "letter" which he xeroxes and sends to them from his (now) rural abode. Sending one to me, he asked for my comment. I felt that it didn't venture far enough away from Christian doctrine to clarify his intention to express his current perception. My suggestion was that he expose his readers to the teachings of Meister Eckhart— Catholicism's most profound mystic—and that he point out to them the essence of the message that Eckhart delivered in his sermons (which resulted in his being called before the Inquisition).

So, when Ron Bonilla asked me to suggest what he might consider a worthwhile theme, my response was: "Doesn't it say in the Bible, 'The harvest is ready, but the workers are few'? With your extensive experience with Christianity, there are many 'disaffected Christians' (Ron's phrase) who could find of value what you can tell them."

We have all grown up in a Christian culture; many of us have a personal background in it (I, for one). The Eastern teachings, such as Advaita, have been basically hidden from view of churchgoers. They are confused about the "individual's" relation to "God." We know their concerns. And we can address those concerns. There are those who are ready, even prepared, to hear what we can share with them.

RAMANA WAS RIGHT

Thanks for your "good news" report: "IT/I [finally] *looked*, and saw—Nothing!!!" Consequently, "I also saw my entire life's history ripped out of a history book, right down to the first page. (Mom + Dad had it right: "You're going to amount to nothing.")"

"This is a 'gift,'" you say, "to the 'me', who doubted it ever would happen!"

This brings to mind a Buddhist expression (made by a Zen master upon awakening)—"The Buddha and the five hundred patriarchs have not deceived me!"—and a couple of statements by Ramana: "Is it possible for everyone to know—beyond all doubt, and by direct and immediate experience—that what he knows is really the natural and primal state? Most certainly. For everyone it is undoubtedly possible...become nothing. Only a person who is nobody can abide in the (Absolute)."

And you can now appreciate why Krishnamurti said: "Do you know what I want to be? Nothing. Absolutely nothing!"

315

"The 'new Norm,'" you report, "seems to function without the usual confusion; and all that he did was done with efficiency (a very welcome change)."

With his dis*appearance* into nothingness, the "old Norm" can no longer be the doer of what is done. "You" have finally gotten out of your own way (Alan Watts titled his autobiography, *In My Own Way*), and have stopped *trying* to be something that you're *not*—your *image* of what it is "like" to be an enlightened person.

Ramana again:

"Every individual is 'seeing' a separate world [i.e., enlightenment as a condition *apart* from your *present* condition]. But a realized being does not see anything other than himself [just as he is, *here* and *now*]. This is the state of truth."

Now you understand what I mean when I say, "It's not a matter of addition; it's a matter of subtraction": not making the self more "like" some ideal, but abandoning the *conception* of self as a concrete form or entity.

This "gift" has been a consequence of your sincerity and determined persistence, in spite of discouragement.

And, as you indicate, Self-realization is self-confirming. When you can look at what the teachers have said and recognize "I understand completely what is being said," you confirm the transmission ("mind to mind," the Buddhists call it).

Yes, of course, I will continue to be here for you—by letter, phone or in person—as developments unfold which you may want to discuss.

Thanks for your letter and it's contents. It's reports like this that "make my day."

Transcendence of Being

Ty was sitting quietly, doing nothing. Completely at ease, his gaze rested on the linoleum that lay between his feet. Having "nothing on his mind," his senses were absorbed.

Without warning, the air around him seemed charged with a rush of energy; a distant but audibly-rising "whoosh" crackled the atmosphere, as if it were about to explode. A sudden jolt shattered his body and liberated his spirit, leaving in its residue an utter absence of sense of self.

Mrs. Fenwich brushed the crumpled plasma off of her flyswatter, over the edge of the trash can, and replaced it on its hook beneath the sink. With a Kleenex, she wiped Ty's memory off of the floor.

The Blood of the Relative

Evidently, you are quickly getting the message of nonduality. Taking your observations in a slightly different order:

"Like looking at a goldfish bowl, until the looker disappears."

Well said. Observe the "movements of the mind" just as objectively as you would (amusingly) observe the movements of the goldfish. All movements of the mind are phenomena, in time. All phenomena (and all that is *a movement in time*) is temporary (L.: tempus, time), impermanent: *comes* (has a beginning) and *goes* (has an ending). Your true nature, the sages aver, is timeless—not a mere passing phenomenon. You are That, the Absolute. All phenomena (all that is relative, limited) appear within the Absolute, the unlimited: You. You are that universal consciousness which passively witnesses all of which it is aware, at any location or moment, the mind display included. Recognizing your Absolute nature, "the looker" disappears.

"No seer nor seen."

"Seer" and "seen" are relative (dualistic) distinctions; the artificial isolation of two "elements" of the one, indivisible actuality. Both seer and anything that is seen are merely manifestations of the bountiful Absolute; seer and seen are more of the impermanent phenomena—the same as thought is. (In fact, it is thought which designates the arbitrary labels "seer" and "seen": it is all self-created—or Self-created—mind stuff.) Seer and seen are in their fundamental essence, then, the One actuality—as are all *things*. See*ing*, consequently, is that (or That) too: no more substantial ("real") than seer or seen. So, it can ultimately be stated, "no seer or seen or seeing." Not anything remains *but* the Absolute: "That (or Self) is *all* that *is*. Seer owes its existence (reality) to That; seen, too; and seeing, as well. All named things are simply That in one of its myriad disguises (manifestations).

"Consciousness appears in three states: awake, dreaming and deep sleep."

As with seer, seen and seeing, all three so-called "states" are relative (dualistic) terms, which attempt to distinguish limited conditions (that are only temporary phenomena) amidst the permanent and unlimited actuality (That, as we call it). "Turiya" (beyond) is mistakenly said to be "the fourth state"; it is instead *meant* to serve as simply another reference to That.

Ramana: "[Turiya] is not apart from anything; it forms the substratum of all happenings; it is the Only truth; it is your very Being....no other than the Self [Absolute]." That which "is not apart from anything" is clearly not a separate "state." *All* states are temporary; relative to one another; and therefore have no more intrinsic reality than their "seer." As you say, the Self *is* all states—and yet even more than this. As you point out, our troubles begin when we "divide the One into two" (or more), and then suppose that these fragments have an independent reality. We are supposing that the pot shards have more reality than the pot which was their source.

Yes, "How can there be movement, when there is only One thing."

Movement (even as change) is obviously relative (hence Einstein's Relativity Theory). "You" are That; "space" is That; so, *what* could be said to be "moving" in *What*? Moving is another "description" of an element of the singular actuality—just like "seeing." All that ever "moves," as the Buddhists say, "is your mind." Movement—like space, time, cause-and-effect—is an idea conjured by the divisive, separative thought process: no more a fundamental reality than is a thought itself. Movement is, even by definition, a temporal phenomenon.

What Harrison evidently was saying is that it is an obstacle ("block") to think in terms of moving "toward higher consciousness." There are no isolated "states" of consciousness; "there is *only* consciousness," as it has been said. Higher and lower are obviously relative terms, ideas. The Absolute as thoroughly is present in anything "lower" as it is in "higher." And only in duality is there a "you" moving toward something that is "not you." You are all that is: so, *what* could "move" toward *What*? It is these dualistic ideas that "seekers" find "obstructing" their recognition of the Absolute—which is *present as* them!

What do all the named things (whether concrete or immaterial) "exist" in: they exist in consciousness, as re-presented by "you." Even the "you"—"your" body, mind, identification— are dependent upon consciousness for "your existence." Pure ("undefiled," unconditioned) consciousness is present in deep sleep, as well as (like Ramana says) being the substratum of the dreaming and waking conditions. All things arise and subside in Consciousness (turiya: "your very Being...the Self")—the ultimate "beyond," the "state" that is all states (and yet even beyond that).

You do not give attentive importance to the zigzags of the goldfish. Cease to focus your attention on the comings and goings of dream figures (the "me" and "not me"); passively witness the products and effects of Consciousness, until it is clear to you that you are the creator of all that is—and then even "the looker" is known to be just another needless distinction.

THE GOD OF UNREALITY

Padamalai is a collection of writings by a disciple of Ramana Maharshi, Muruganar (who died in 1973, at the age of 83). Composed over about five decades, about half of this Indian poet's compositions were chosen for print by David Godman, a later follower of Ramana. Both Muruganar and Godman seem to have comprehended Ramana's message, and parts of this book are Muruganar's transcription (originally in Tamil) of what he understood Ramana to say. Ramana evidently thought highly of Muruganar and approved of his verses.

I'll try to respond to your questions (that the text has raised) in order.

As I've said before, "consciousness" is an ambiguous word. The consciousness which is said to "divide itself" is that which would be called "waking consciousness"; for example, it manifests as the cognition of one's own thoughts. It refers to the mind that is mired in the "relative," or dualistic, perspective.

However, the word "consciousness" is also sometimes used as a synonym (usually with a capital C) for the Absolute. That is why Godman explains, "Where there is 'true knowledge'—jnana [enlightenment]—consciousness does *not* divide itself..." In other words, one's perception is that of *non*duality.

So, to which does "the false appearance" (of the world, or "other" relative entities—such as your body) manifest: to dualistic consciousness, or to the non-divisive Consciousness that is present to the jnani? Obviously, the former.

Muruganar quotes Ramana: "all this external, material universe is unreal.... There is nothing other than [the Self]." All entities, limited and impermanent, are "false appearances" when not viewed to be merely shimmers of the (unlimited and permanent) Absolute. Because the formless Absolute is difficult to envision, cultures often assign a form and a name to it: for example, God. In India, one of these "god" names is Iswara. A characteristic often ascribed to such an entity is "creation."

Our idea of "creation" is just *that*—an *idea* about something. For there to be creation, as such, there would have to be an *intent* to create. A "God" might be said to have an intent; but the formless Absolute has no need of *intentions*, since there can be nothing in opposition to it.

Ramana explains about Iswara's fundamental identity:

> "The process that brings 'the world' into existence [relative con-sciousness] simultaneously brings Iswara into 'being'....But this is only true from the *relative* standpoint of those who have not realized the truth...From the *Absolute* standpoint, the *sage* [in Consciousness] cannot accept any *other* existence than the *im-personal* Self, one and formless....

"The forms and names of God are many and various, and differ with each religion. *Its* essence is the same as ours, the real Self being one, and without form. Hence, forms it *assumes* [such as in consciousness, or imagination—a word relating to "image"] are only [self-] creations or *appearances*. 'Iswara' is imminent in every person and every object [world, body, etc.] throughout the universe. [Therefore, "Iswara" is simply another name for the Absolute.] The *totality* of all *things* and beings constitutes 'God' [or the Absolute; Iswara, Brahman, etc., etc.]"

Godman: "Iswara is, from the standpoint of absolute reality, an *unreal entity* that ultimately has to be transcended [for jnana]."

Ramana:

"Iswara, God, the Creator, the personal God, is the last of the unreal *forms* to go [in order to awaken]. *Only* the Absolute being is *real*. Hence not only the world, not only the ego [self], but also the personal 'God' [e.g., Iswara] are of *unreality*."

If only the Self (Absolute) is real, then all else is unreal—including the self ("me"). For the ajnani (unenlightened), it is the relative consciousness which creates (or, in which arises) all separations, all entities (limited, impermanent), all forms—including the form of "me," or "I." Then this (divided) I looks out on what it envisions as a (divided) "world."

The jnani looks out and sees *only* the Absolute. *And* for the jnani it is not "I" doing the looking—it is the Absolute. His eyes are the Absolute's eyes, and all that can be seen is the Absolute.

Godman: "This Infinite eye sees and knows nothing other than *itself*, and it accomplishes this without the *false division* of 'seer' and 'seen'."

322

Muruganar says: "without eyes [the Absolute itself is entirely formless] You see [through the bodily manifestation]. Who can see you?!"

The Absolute is only—and always—"seeing" itself.

Ramana:

"First [on initial awakening] one sees the Self as objects ["The world is the Self!"]; then one sees the Self as a void ["I am the Self—and the Self is no-thing!"]; only in this last state [complete Self-*realization*] there is no seeing..." There is no "me" as "the seer." There is only "the one who sleeps [body] without sleeping [Absolute]."

"Only that stage is final where there is no 'seeing'... no seer, seeing and *object* [that is "apart" from the Absolute seer] to see. What exists then is *only* the Infinite eye [the eye as merely another aspect of the Absolute]....The real Eye is the Self....

"If you realize you are without form, that you are unlimited, that you *alone* exist...what is there to be seen 'apart'?...if the Self alone exists, it is *both* 'seer' *and* 'seen'—and above [beyond] 'seeing', or being seen....There is nothing *apart* from the Self."

If you *understand* these pages, you understand the fundament of Ramana's enlightenment teachings. Not even a poet can put it in *better* words than he does, even with fifty years of trying.

(But we can thank him for preserving the quotations you have read here.)

WHEREVER I GO, THERE I AM

Friend Cheyenne Bear writes to Robert, from the desert:

Wherever I go, there I am—in all the myriad forms that encompass what has become an infinite, boundary-free life.

There is a gravitation toward blessed anonymity and absorption into the natural world, where remnants of personal identity evaporate in the dry desert air.

Quiet mind teaches the exquisite perfection of the interconnected web of all animate and inanimate life. Every cactus and grain of sand is in divine temporal placement. Opposites perfectly balanced: sun-faced Buddha, moon-faced Buddha.

Letting go of the distinction and interference allows the Way of things to flow in natural harmony. All is well in this prickly, but peace-filled, world.

Thoughts of Death

You can't think too often about death. As Paul Krassner has said, "The central fact of my life is my death."

We're ever only one breath away from non-existence. Pick up a newspaper any day and you'll read about someone who went out their front door and never returned. In the space of a heartbeat, this entire universe—everything that you have ever been aware of—will disappear with the closing of your eyes for the last time.

You cannot remind yourself too many times: This may be the last year which I will see; This may be the last month that I'll be alive; This week could be my last; There may be no tomorrow following today.

Put the present moment—moment by moment—into its overall context. Do not take if for granted that your "future" is anything but a word. Organize your life in such a way that each day is lived, contentedly, as if it might not be further extended.

WHAT OTHER STATE?

What does "nondual" mean to you?

If there is such a thing as a "nondual state," or condition, isn't there then only one all-inclusive state? There "not being two"— the definition of nondual—what alternate state exists *outside* of, or apart from, the nondual state? If, indeed, there were another such state in existence, then the nondual state—by definition— would not *be* in existence.

So, if we grant the above, concerning the nondual state, then any "state" that we declare (subsequent to the affirmation of a nondual state) must be viewed as a form that we have posited as existing *within* the nondual state. In other words, we have allotted that only the nondual state is actual; so any condition which we presume to be otherwise *is* merely the *nondual* state (which we are *supposing* to *not* be the nondual condition) by another name.

Hence, if nonduality is the actuality, any state which we term "dualistic" must be—essentially—the nondual condition, which we are contradictorily *terming* "a dualistic state."

The dualistic state, here, lay within the actuality of nonduality. So (even if we accept it as such), the "dualistic state" is not the actuality, but a (pre) conceived condition or state we have proposed within the *actual*, all-inclusive state.

The enlightenment teachers tell us that the nondual condition is the actuality in which *all* exists and is experienced. Anything which appears to be *other* than the nondual condition is merely a false, a mis-taken, appearance. So, any perceived dualistic condition (however assuredly we propose it as that) is still actually the all-inclusive nondual condition which we have *misconstrued* as something which it is not.

Your statement: "At any given moment, we are either in a nondual state of connectedness or a dualistic state of separateness: one can't be in both simultaneously."

A teacher of nonduality would say that if you are in a "state of separateness," you *are* in "both simultaneously": you are, in *actuality*, in the condition of nonduality while *mistakenly* supposing that you could possibly be in some "other" condition— such as a "state of separateness." There is no such actuality as a state of separateness in the context in which the "nondual state" has been affirmed as having any actuality.

Where the existing condition is "not two," there is no "either" and "or." Where the fundamental condition is "connectedness," there is no "separateness." If (in the context of nonduality being the actuality) you suppose that such a thing as separateness truly exists, you are proposing two distinct conditions, in denial of "*not* two."

"If you wish to abide as the Self [nondual Absolute]," you quote Hittlemen, "you cannot see [affirm] multiplicity and diversity [that is a contradiction]."

You like the statement of Zen master Merzel: "The key point is to cease seeing things in a dualistic way, to free ourselves from dualistic ideas, and ultimately from dualistic consciousness itself." Then why say, "I rest in a state of connectedness with everything, as much as possible"? The "state of connectedness" is what you have termed nondual. If it is your realization that the nondual condition is the all-inclusive actuality, what other state *could* you abide in?

This is why Merzel said what he said. So, what *does* nondual *mean* to you?

"What About Love"

What you are referring to, Mary Ann, as "the Absolute totality" is also known as the Void, or Emptiness, in the sutras. This is to say that it is No-thing-ness. Being no definable thing, it is devoid of definable characteristics; or in itself, as you say, it is "devoid of feeling, and impersonal."

All qualities and characteristics, then, are projections of the consciousness, or mind, which manifests from this nondescript ground of Being. This includes such categorizations as "love" or "hate." To that which simply eternally and infinitely Is, "creation" and "destruction" are distinctions reserved for the mind in which they're conceived.

And yet, there is something about the aliveness in the universe, and its balance and harmony, which—though benevolent is too strong of a word—sages tend to describe as at least benign, if not charitable or perhaps indulgent. Some go so far as to give this cosmic tendency the title Love (as in "God is Love": Ramana). At the very least, most think of the cosmic orderliness as at least a positive element.

The second part of your query has to do with the realization of this Emptiness, or Absolute: "Does love then fit into the equation anywhere?"

If you were to think in terms of what you might describe as loving—or benign or benevolent, even compassionate—behavior, where would you more likely expect to see this expressed: in a self-centered person or in a person whose limited self-identification has evaporated?

When a person has emptied out her conditioned conceptualizations, such as the self-image, there is something else which is operating through the organism. Looking at the lives of the enlightened sages, this appears to have a benign, or charitable, cast to it.

Krishnamurti often spoke about this development.

Love is the total absence of the separate "I," ego, or self.

There is no reason for love. To have a reason for love is to have a motive, which comes from the separate self....

If you have no love, do what you will, go after all the Gods on earth, do all the social activities, try to reform the poor, enter politics, write books, write poems—you are a dead human being. Without love, your problems will increase, multiply endlessly. And with love, do what you will, there is no risk, there is no conflict.

What is Seen

It is good to hear from you that "seeking *and* seeker" have come to an end: the observer and the observed are not now two different things.

Thanks for your comments about what is now seen through the eyes: no longer conceptual objectification, "so nothing is seen; at least, no-thing in particular...a seamless indivisible whole is observed—by 'nobody'...this is not a spacey, disassociated state...attention can be changed...in which case anything can be *conceptually* seen: some 'thing' is seen."

For an awakened person, as you described, relative objects can be viewed and identified as such by their names. But one now, as it were, sees through objects as separate entities, in the sense of recognizing that the commonality of all appearances is as *manifestations* of a ubiquitous, interpenetrating Beingness, or formless Presence. Thus, the observer and the observed are perceived as indistinguishable from each other: no-body is aware of no-thing.

THE DEEPEST ATTACHMENT

The lesson of the spiritual sages, generally, is that it is not material things which are problematic, in our lives, but rather our *attachment* to these physical things. And similarly, it is not ideas—or even our thoughts, per se—that are the source of suffering and conflict, but our attachment to ideas and to the virtuosity of thought. Nor are the *conditions* in our lives necessarily determinate; it is the position that we cling to in regard to these conditions which limits us.

But, while attachment has been addressed in general, too little has been said specifically about attachments to life itself and attachment to physical health. It is one thing to come to terms with the complete death of one's ego; it is another thing to come to terms with the complete cessation of one's physical existence. But to die to attachment is to die to all aspects of life to which it is possible to be attached—including one's attitudes about preferential conditions of health, and even, ultimately, the condition we conceive of as "being alive."

Krishnamurti stressed in his final talks, while ill with cancer, "End your attachment to everything. *Everything!*"

"Presence became Reality!"

I will read your letter at the next group meeting, because there are some in the group who—now Self-realized—are reaching out to others in order to transmit the dharma.

As you indicated, when the questions have ended (or all answered themselves in nondual awareness), the seeking has ended. Presence—all that is present—is what (we now discover) we have actually been looking for. We stop excluding anything from (or adding anything onto) the Totality. It is sufficient as it is—and "as it is" is Presence, in its totality. You cannot possibly be apart from That. And so you can write, "The Presence, that phenomena now appear in, is home!"

As this nondual awareness becomes more customary, we can talk about any of the discoveries, if you feel the need to.

What Motive?

A course or workshop in "esteem-building" may increase one's self confidence, as you say; but what is that increase in confidence *built* on?

It is one thing to learn something of practical value (for example, a foreign language); but where is the substance in a "motivational" seminar?

And motivated toward what: greater acquisitiveness? A more "successful" self-image? The tangible rewards that a self-improved you will now implicitly deserve?

Without any substantial increase in your functional net worth (such as, for example, learning computer skills), will you not merely have an inflated—and unrealistic—view of your "potential" value to society?

Yes, of course this is "faith-based." An anthropomorphized God "helps those who help themselves." (Or, evangelists say, who help evangelists.)

Contributing to society through acquiring a practical skill (in a different type of course, workshop or seminar) is an undertaking of a different sort than is empty self-aggrandizement.

Post-Op

Due to the richness of your comments, there is much that I would respond to.

You expressed this well:

> "This awakening has settled in, and for the most part, everything is as it was previously, with exceptions. Past and future are alien, but available to refer to whenever wanted, much like an encyclopedia is used for reference. It seems that 'time' has slowed, but more gets done with less effort."

Also, too, your statement: "All our lives, we have been... hypnotized by the hypnotized." Conditioned, of course, like our predecessors who were conditioned *before* us. But regarding your analogy, it reminds of Adya's (referential) "awakening from the *trance.*"

It may be, perhaps, that (as you say) "it must be that many are awakening." Given the population explosion, though, I tend to wonder to what real extent there is an increase, percentage-wise.

There is a true sign of a change in perception, and that is a change in *behavior*; I see some of these changes reflected in your reports of developments. When the sense of complete identity with the self-image disappears, it cannot help but have an effect on how the "person" relates to the world that had been perceived.

It is this behavioral aspect which associates sometimes begin to take cognizance of, and which reverberates as a silent inspiration for inquiry into the dharma.

Regarding enlightenment and sexuality, much could be—perhaps needs to be—said. As you noted, Buddha can be supposed to have had a satiating sex life as an indulged prince; and—like many other *sages*—evidently was profoundly conversant with the contentment which is contiguous with thorough non-attachment. This can be reflected in Ramana Maharshi (for example), who—trans-formed around age 16—never felt the need for a sexually dependent relationship throughout his lifetime, evidently.

You remark that Adyashanti says that remnants of our individualistic conditioning will regularly tend to resurface, even after awakening. Yes, since we are so habitually reconfirmed in our dualistic mindset for many decades, these reflexive associations do not generally disappear overnight. But not anything which appears on the screen of consciousness need be a *problem*. It will be seen for what it is (another impermanent manifestation of That) and permitted to pass across the screen of consciousness (like those active screen-savers) without a compulsion for interference. As Suzuki Roshi said: "The true purpose of Zen...is to see things as they are...and to let everything go as it goes."

And, you say, "since awakening, I have been reading others' comments and listening to tapes, etc." This can be useful, in more than one way. It can help to reaffirm post-awakening comprehension; and also to remind you how astonishing it is that this truth is in no way disassociated from us, and yet we managed to disengage with it for so many years.

"I understand now," you concluded, "why I didn't see a TV in your residence." No TV, no computer, no car: I have had these things and I have known the responsibilities of ownership (in either direction). My resources are limited to one endeavor, and what most fully contributes to that. Nothing is more worthwhile, for me.

UNSCENTED SUTRA

A translation of the Lankavatara Sutra speaks of four types of spiritual experience.

There are those, for example, who ritually meditate as a doctrine, and "advance by stages until they reach the cessation where there are no thoughts [thought negation]. This is called the Dhyana (discipline) practiced by the ignorant."

There are the analytical who go "beyond individuality" in that they understand that there is 'only One,' with "no such ideas as *self, other* and *both*"—but who, because they have not relinquished relative definitional concepts (such as self and One) have not penetrated to the truth that there is not even one. "This is the Dhyana devoted to the examination of meaning"—where there really is none.

There is the condition in which the Yogin recognizes that he is That and ends his transformation there, content to sit in blissful contemplation of "the reality of Suchness (where) there is no rising of discrimination"—"the Dhyana with Suchness for its *object.*"

Then there is the one "without a scent of saintliness" to whom nirvana *is* samsara, and who appears as no one special in the marketplace but "devotes himself, for the sake of all beings, to the accomplishment of incomprehensible works—the Dhyana of the Tathagata." ("Withered trees he swiftly brings to bloom." — *Oxherding Pictures.*)

The Tathagata is not only free (even free of "freedom") but fully functional. Huang Po clarifies the issue that while the awakened has an uncluttered mind, this is not to be interpreted as mindless (so far as the relative mind is the subject): "When the senses and thoughts are annihilated, all the passages to universal Mind are blocked, and no entrance then becomes possible. The original Mind is to be recognized *along with* the working of the senses and thoughts [no attachment to annihilation]—only it does not belong to *them*, nor yet is it *independent* of them....Do not try to grasp Reality by rejecting your senses and thoughts! When you are neither *attached* to, nor *detached* from, them, you enjoy your perfect unobstructed freedom; then you have your seat of enlightenment."

Samsara *is* nirvana. (So to the Tathagata, both distinctions are meaningless.)

TRANS-MISSION

"Things have settled yet more. I am able to settle back into 'Laura.' Everything feels different but some things are familiar, like some of my preferences. It just feels like I get—at a gut level now, instead of faith— that this life of separation is a dream, etc."

Regarding what you describe as your inability to express to others the nature of "this shift in perspective": do not expect anyone to comprehend the presence, that you are now aware of, who have not themselves been affected by this unitive realization.

As Ramana has said (as well as others), "Only a jnani (Self-realized) understands a jnani."

That is not to say that you should not try to communicate, to someone who is sincerely interested, what has been revealed. But recognize that there are some limitations in attempting to describe the nondual perception to anyone whose perspective has not transcended duality.

You, as much as anyone (having spent years pondering it), now appreciate the difficulty which nondual teachers have had in transmitting this non-linear awareness to separative psyches.

The Picture of Samadhi

Not enough can be said about what "Samadhi" really is. In the West, this word description is highly misunderstood.

You write: "I always thought Samadhi was reserved for a select few yogis that just sit passively in full lotus pose, eyes rolled to heaven, totally inert and oblivious to the 'marketplace' or worldly happenings around them."

Yes, this aspect *is* in one edge of the picture. This is the "practitioner" who consciously makes an effort to "merge with the One," not fully recognizing that the practitioner *is* the One itself. Having not transcended duality, this is called savikalpa Samadhi.

There is then *another* who has the distinction of being able to merge with the One at will, and who now teaches the practice because this is what "holy" ones do. This is called nirvikalpa Samadhi.

Some *transcend* the state of *incomplete* awareness of their always-already existing presence *as* the One, and recognize that *whatever* they do (or *don't* do) is ultimately without significance. It is to this main part of the picture that the peripheral figures point. This is called sahaja Samadhi (which literally means "steady state"); effortless, full, and lasting realization of One's true nature. Because this yogi has no intention in either sitting or not sitting, usually no one notices him in the picture of Samadhi.

In sahaja, Ramana says,

> [You] are unaffected by what you do or say or think.... [It] is the definitive state of realization, in which one can live a normal, natural [unencumbered] life, fully aware of the Self at all times.

Yes, as you said in your letter, "So, Samadhi [in its *fullest* sense] is just as natural a state as breathing, *or* the fleeting feeling of being out-of-sync with so-called 'enlightened behavior'—and *not* just reserved for those who've 'blissed out'."

Your more specific interpretation is a suitable "Western" description of sahaja Samadhi: "passive awareness of whatever happens to be present, allowing thoughts and/or actions to be as they are, with no conditioned stigma of shoulda, coulda, woulda."

As per Ramana: "If the thoughts 'I did' and 'I didn't' are given up...[this] indeed is the state of sahaja Samadhi."

Unity and Reality: One

In your (long) letter, you say that the Poonja material I sent has been startlingly instructive: "There is an awakening in progress here...I see things differently."

This is affirmed to me by some of your other comments (which I will cite):

"It is important that I question this 'I', and let it be dissolved" ... "If there is only One, why would 'I' need to be in *relationship* to any 'thing'?" ... "There is no 'me' to own a problem" ... "Whether (I am experiencing) sickness or healing is none of my business. 'My' mind (?) has stopped objectifying the condition as *mine*" ... "The Self that I AM chooses not to interact ...at the level of ego ... because at the level of Reality, the I does nothing—only the Self" ... "Things are running smoothly—by its Self" ... "Reality can only be accepted" ... "It's all God. I am That! All this is That! That is all there is!" ... "In this regard, there can be nothing to 'forgive'" ... "I have been blessed mightily."

These are expressions of a comprehension that Poonja would recognize, and you have rightfully put them into your own words.

And the quotations from the Course In Miracles were also pertinent (regarding "your one responsibility"—awakening), but it is noteworthy that you are beginning to see the limitations of any "holy book" and its promises: the "responsibility" is for you to know these truths *first-hand*, and not second-hand as "teachings."

I, too, would repeat, "atonement might be equated with total escape from the past (and total lack of interest in the future)." There being no "me," in ultimate Reality, what becomes of the me's "past"? Will that, too, not be "dissolved"?

Lastly, it's gratifying to see that you are able to recognize the duality (all the "me's" and "God's") in the Unity poem. If one were simply to replace the word God with Omnipresent, it would be apparent that the two "entities" must cancel each other out, leaving only timeless Presence. If indeed it is, as the author claims, "In your hands I place my total self," what could remain for the 18 references to her individual self, in the poem's 19 lines?! As you indicate, the poem speaks more of "separation" than Unity.

THE COMPLETE LIST

About 35 years ago (after reading Watts' *The Way of Zen*, and the *Tao Te Ching*), I made up a "practice" list of 17 pointers: I recently came across the sheet. Example objectives: "Be affirmative, rather than negative." "Cooperate, instead of competing." "Forget *should*, *ought* and *must*." "Don't invest in the past; don't rob the future of its surprises." "*Accept* negativity, as well as positivity."

With deeper understanding of "present awareness," I put all such directives aside. They all have in common the supposition that they are a means to an end; the end being sahaja Samadhi, or so-called enlightenment. (Samadhi, "putting together," means nondual realization; sahaja means natural, or effortless.)

Nondual realization, I came to discover, can be (and has been) summarized in five words: all that is, is That ("That" being the omnipresent actuality, generally called the Absolute). The realization of this fundamental truth—with the same certainty that one realizes, for example, the truth that change is irrepressible—is the substance of enlightenment. This truth clearly says, in terms of the nature of the Absolute, that there are not any two things: *All* that is, is *That*. So, *nondual realization is simply the dissolution of separative perception*, in terms of the actuality of our ultimate existence.

338

The *profound impact* of this non-separative realization is that, from the standpoint of the ultimate truth, all appearances of individual entities are false, illusional appearances. Therefore, the appearance that there is a separate individual which I conceive as "me" is merely a matter of misidentification: all that is, is That. That, being all that is, is both omnipresent—present *everywhere*, at *all* times—and inseparable, in its infinity.

Under these circumstances, I can in no way be apart or separate from the Absolute: Tat Tvam Asi—That thou art.

Being that *naturally*, how am I to get closer to, or to unite, with That? Wouldn't that be silly, to make an effort to find what is already mine without effort? Where am I to look to discover That: all that *is, is That.*

If all that is, is That, and if there is any such thing as perfection, then perfection must be That. *And* "all that is" must be perfect—exactly as it is!

Therefore, what do I need to do, to perfect myself? Draw up a list of 17 ideal objectives? Try harder to become more like someone who is no *more* the Absolute than I *am*? Dedicate the next ten years to a critical practice? Complete some particular act, or not complete some particular act?

If all that is, is That, then "all that is *done* is That, doing what it does." There being, in truth, no me, whatever this *organism* does is That doing what *it* does. So, "who" is going to perfect itself? "Who" is going to get closer to That: all that is, is *That!* Thou *art* That.

Whether or not I *realize* I am That, I am That. Since all that is, is That, how much *more That* can I be, *either way*?

This is the non-separative realization: there is nothing to "get," and no me to get it. The "getter" and the "got" would be the same, inseparable thing: all that is, is That.

With the recognition of the truth of this nondual actuality, I laid my practice list aside. Of what use is the reminder of "acceptance": to *accept* is to acknowledge that things are okay as they are. If I am not "accepting," *that* is the way things are. If I desire to *change* that condition, that too is It.

To *focus* on letting go of past and future concerns is to *further* indulge in separative ideation: past/present/future. From the standpoint of Absolute awareness, the sages remind us, there are no such realities as time, space ("here" versus "there") or cause-and-effect.

The point of these *examples* is that it is the separative, divisive, "dualistic" mind-set which is the hitch, the limitation to "putting together"—samadhi, or enlightenment. When the separative perspective *dissolves*, samadhi is a *natural* and *effortless* outcome—sahaja.

To draw up a practice list, as I did, is—at least—an indication of my desire for enlightenment. But, the sages remind us, desire is a sign of the sense of separation. (Don't *have*/want.)

Recognizing that desire for enlightenment is moving in "the opposite direction" from enlightenment is a step into the "grace zone": as desire and attachment to all things withers, the "me" diminishes in influence. When the "me" is absent—the separate, individual entity—what then remains?

The greatest self-improvement, that could result from my list of 17 ways to approach perfection, is when the "self" ceases to exist. To dwell on my list would, otherwise, be simply to focus continual attention on what is a misidentification from the start.

Sahaja samadhi is to be aware—under all circumstances—who the doer is. For that, the list will end with 1.

"Tat Tvam Asi—That Thou Art," proclaim the Upanishads, the esoteric concluding books of the ancient Indo-Aryan scriptures known as the Vedas. This proclamation lies at the heart of Indian spirituality: that the essence of all beings and all things is indivisible, infinite, unchanging Spirit." – Ann Cushman and Jerry Jones, *From Here to Nirvana*

SHAKTIPAT?

If you feel that you experienced a transmission, as you described it, it would not have been a (conscious) consequence of "the eye contact that we shared."

The arousal of a temporal phenomenon is not anything which I would have intended. Such experiential occurrences (generally termed shaktipat, in the Hindu tradition) will not lastingly endure. So-called altered states have each a beginning and an ending, and are thus impermanent. That which it is my intent to transmit is not impermanent: it is the awareness of the Self *in which* phenomena arise and dissipate.

What "seems like a transmission," to you, is what is termed in Buddhism the mind-to-mind transmission of the Dharma—which is to say, the same as that in the last phrase of the preceding sentence.

LIGHT THE LAMP

Consider this to be encouragement to act on your impulse to transmit the dharma. While I'm sure you will not feel any zealous compulsion to do so, there are a few reasons why it can be of potential benefit to all concerned.

For almost everyone who has realized the freedom accorded by the nondual perspective, it has been through the un-selfish assistance of others, who have preceded us, that we have come fully into the light of this annihilating truth. Once our self-concern has dissipated, we become even more acutely aware of the perceived suffering of those around us. It then seems only natural that we should feel drawn to assuring them that their existential anxiety is unwarranted, based on our own discovery.

While this may be of benefit to others, in varying degrees, it can be worthwhile for you as well. For one thing, the attempt to communicate the substance of this realization will cause you to focus on its elements in a manner which will unveil any residual dualistic conceptions which might otherwise recurrently appear in present awareness. And the on-going process of proffering this communication will consequently keep a sharp edge on your moment-to-moment expression of the Absolute.

One, obviously, is not able to share this mind-to-mind transmission if one does not have its essence oneself. And when one does genuinely have it, it expresses itself effortlessly as a loving presence made manifest. It is the motivating spirit behind what Peace Pilgrim was considering when she said, "Ask not what you can get [when there is no longer a self-center]. Ask what you can give [when all that's held is nothing]."

After all, what is occurring except That (in the guise of the finder) connecting with itself (in the guise of the seeker)— the components being mutually attracted to each other (as appearances of the Doer)?

The Problem of Change

Problems—and their solutions—have a common origin: resistance to change. A solution is a way of making things happen, as contrasted to letting things happen. A solution is an attempt to control the challenge of change which we define as a problem. Change will not lastingly be controlled; each solution is followed by a renewed problem.

When we have no expectations, there are no significant problems in the present. To expect is to await, to anticipate our due. It is to suppose a mechanical or equitable relationship between cause and effect—such as: solutions will lead to a conclusive end to problems.

Expectation is an idea which attempts to draw the Past and the Future into the existing moment. The Past and the Future are themselves ideas.

Change evokes insecurity; and security is the self's backbone. The self is our conduit to continuity, the prospect of which offers hope to lead us out of the pain of our existence. Change is unremitting—a painful problem to the self which seeks, hopes for and anticipates security.

The Natural Fit

Yes! As I see it, you see it clearly. The real "view" is a view of nothingness; a view absent of beliefs, opinions, preferences, differences—dualities (such as "logic" as *opposed* to "illogic"). When one sees with the *eyes*, the eyes do not interpret; it is (divisive) thought which draws conclusions ("final summation; judgment") concerning what the eye has encountered. As Krishnamurti says, when we look at a sunset, what need is there to conclude, "This is (or is not) a more spectacular sunset than yesterday"? He urges us to watch how comparative, separative thoughts follow upon *initially*-unmediated experience. We *have* an immediate experience of our *undifferentiated being*; but moment by moment that experience is *filtered* by the separative thought process—primarily making *comparative* (dualistic) conclusions ("I am experiencing this; I am *not* experiencing *that*.")

As a consequence of this (unnoticed) process, we continually attempt to *modify* present *being* to be this *form* or that form ("I have a monkey mind; I need to still the mind").

But what we're being advised is to *not* attempt either to create or to change any particular condition. Then, we are not operating from an *ideational* framework that maintains that 'what is', instead, *could* be or *should* be other than what it *is*. This, of course, is what the Buddhists mean by having no abiding (residing) place, "nothing on which to [conclusively] stand;" a mind that dwells upon "nothing special," no "gaining ideas" ("Things would be better if I just...").

"The *full awareness* in yourself of a mind," as Hui Hai says, "that dwells upon no-thing is known as 'having a *clear perception* of... your own true nature'": your nature when the eye *encounters*— prior to the mind *discerning*. "A mind that dwells upon no-thing is the Buddha [primordial] mind, enlightenment mind, uncreated [*uncreating*] mind," he continues: "No abiding place... is truly the abiding place of the [enlightened] mind."

"Free of all views," as you put it—not viewing from a *fixed*, fractional position; instead, "*directly* experiencing things as they *are now*...There is no need to change my—impermanent— condition: I'll experience *whatever* I'm experiencing." No effort or mentation ("practice, discipline") is required to *remain* in the natural, *unmediated* condition. As you said, to decide "what to

do" about the what-is, is to "throw one back into the relative"—
duality ("I should do this; or I should do *that*"). Not "trying to
make things fit into a certain (pre meditated) framework," as you
said: left as it is, "everything *fits*" in the Buddha mind.

The Price of Peace

We will sacrifice and take all manner of risk in that conflict we
call war, but not yield anything for peace. In the same way, we
long for inner peace and tranquility, but will not let go of our
contentious desires—or, more, specifically, that hub of desire, the
self.

Freedom is fraught with the risk of conventional error. There are
no guarantees in a universe without limitation. There is no one
to blame, when you assume neither the role of follower or leader.

Let us quit our insistence that our highest goal is the establishment
of global peace and brotherhood, and admit that at the top of
each individual agenda is personal security, material comfort and
privacy—the pursuit of individual "happiness," which means
gratification of egoistic desires.

To a Truth-seeker

It's good to hear that you have begun to introduce your
understanding of the teachings of nonduality to your contacts.
There's no better way to keep a sharp edge on Absolute awareness
than to (as I have) speak about it, write about it or read about it
day after day. Not everyone whom you share this teaching with
will be receptive to it, of course, but there will always (eventually)
be some few who will be grateful for your having been a catalyst
in their awakened life.

The reason why *you* have been able to absorb so much of this material, in a short time, is because you read, *and* contemplate what you've read. This is how, and why, it worked for me, too.

While you continue to remind me how thankful you are, I am thankful to you for giving open-minded attention to the words that I devoted time to writing to you. Not everyone has the capacity (or tendency) to receive, even when something has been freely given. Your concern for the truth has been its own reward. "The truth shall set you free." (John 8:32).

Potent-ial

Humans, collectively, would rather see the world evaporate in a puff of plutonium smoke than to surrender the individual sense of self. Is this not an emergency?

We all stand—spiritually—in the path of a tornado. Our conditioning has immobilized us with hypothermia of the soul; dallying to preserve the security of our ego, we waste that energy whose potential is love.

Time is Comparison

The grasses on the slope, on both sides of the path, are still pleasing to behold, but they are different than they were one month ago. Now they are dry straws, more brittle in the breeze.

Coming here today, and comparing their flat hue to the lustrous green of last month, we would say that they are dead. But on what day would we declare that they had died?

Change, though as subtle, can be more dramatic. A couple of weeks ago, the seed-heads of the grasses were still full and a golden blond. Gaily offset against this background, there grew among them a spindly weed with a violet flower of four dainty petals. Today, the lanky weed towers above the frayed grasses, and, where its petals once were, the calyx has swollen and opened to yield a bright yellow thistle-like flower. The calyx itself has produced spiny spikes all around its surface, and is now a formidable cocklebur. One would not believe that the same stem recently bore the fragile violet flower, save that a few remain among them for testimony.

Man measures change, with such benchmarks as "sunrise" versus "sunset," and we refer to this measure as time. We arbitrarily say that "four weeks ago" there were violet flowers, "today" there are only cockleburs.

Measurement is comparison, and comparison is a willful act of choice. For those who have forsaken the habit of subjective comparison, time loses its relevance.

What is the importance of time to that ground squirrel who has scampered out of the brush and now bends a stalk of grass to lunch randomly among its seeds?

Time is the scaffolding upon which our sense of self rests for support. It is commonly accepted that that which I call my self was born on a particular day and will die on a particular day. And during its supposed existence, this self will be able to identify itself only in comparison—in contrast—to all that with which it interacts. We fail to see that while the cocklebur and the violet flower are *different*, their real *identity* is the same.

WHOLLY

Abandon the self-centered life, which is limited by fear and desire. Open to selfless existence, in which there is no concern for outcome (and, thus, neither fear nor desire).

Sever your attachment to life as the world knows it, the world which seeks comfort and resists insecurity.

Die to the self, so that there is space for the unknown, the timeless and indivisible. Engage a wholly different way of living, a life of *being* rather than becoming. To die to the self is the wholly different way of living.

Let go of desire and of fear. Be not afraid of death nor of life.

A review of Robert Wolfe's *Living Nonduality*

A lot of books on nonduality have a simple approach that repeats the same message in a limited number of ways. This makes sense as the message is just a pointer that if you follow will lead you to a direct experience. The message is NOT the experience itself. If the message got more complicated, then one would worry that the pointing is no longer direct enough. Thus, elegance and depth are sacrificed for directness and simplicity.

It was difficult for me to imagine any other way. In *Living Nonduality*, Robert Wolfe does the unimaginable of keeping the pointers simple, clear, and direct, but somehow adding elegance to the picture by managing to talk about nonduality in so many beautiful and interesting ways. He brings a wider range of concepts, people, and ideas into focus. He talks about Jesus, quantum physics, romantic relationships, political activism, and whatnot, in a series of short essays and dialogues.

He does an amazing service to anybody who wants to communicate nonduality through his clear and meticulous explanations of the absolute versus the relative. This is not only a book for the spiritual seeker, it is a book for the spiritual teacher.

I consider Robert Wolfe, simply on the basis of this fascinating work, one of the greatest living Western masters of nonduality.

A. Saribay, Istanbul
(review on goodreads.com)

Books by Robert Wolfe on Nondual World Traditions
with reader comments

India, Advaita
ALWAYS-ONLY-ONE: A DIALOGUE WITH THE ESSENCE OF
NONDUAL INDIA

"a fresh and concise expression of the Ashtavakra Gita"

Asia, Zen Buddhism / Taoism
ONE ESSENCE: THE NONDUAL CLARITY OF AN ANCIENT
ZEN POEM

"go directly to the heart of the centuries-old message of nondualism"

Middle East, Christianity
THE GOSPEL OF THOMAS: THE ENLIGHTENMENT
TEACHINGS OF JESUS

"my whole perspective on Christianity has changed"

Contemplative Journal from Retreat in California
ELEMENTARY CLOUDWATCHING: 31 MEDITATIONS ON
LIVING WITHOUT TIME

"reading it is also a meditation"

Contemporary Science
SCIENCE OF THE SAGES: SCIENTISTS ENCOUNTERING
NONDUALITY FROM QUANTUM PHYSICS, TO COSMOLOGY,
TO CONSCIOUSNESS

"clears many misperceptions"

Robert Wolfe
www.livingnonduality.org
robert@livingnonduality.org

c/o Karina Library Press
P.O. Box 35
Ojai, California 93024

To leave a review and help others discover this work:
www.livingnonduality.org/reviews

To support the reach of Robert's works:
www.livingnonduality.com/donate

Alphabetical Title Index

35259124R00213

Made in the USA
San Bernardino, CA
19 June 2016